BECOMING A COACH

THE ESSENTIAL ICF GUIDE

**JONATHAN PASSMORE
AND TRACY SINCLAIR**

Becoming a Coach: The Essential ICF Guide

© Jonathan Passmore and Tracy Sinclair

The authors have asserted their rights in accordance with the Copyright, Designs and Patents Act (1988) to be identified as the authors of this work.

Published by:
Pavilion Publishing and Media Ltd
Blue Sky Offices, 25 Cecil Pashley Way
Shoreham by Sea, West Sussex
BN43 5FF

Tel: 01273 434 943
Email: info@pavpub.com
Web: www.pavpub.com

First Published 2020. Reprinted 2021.

All rights reserved. No part of this publication may be reproduced, stored in a retrieval system, or transmitted in any form or by any means, electronic, mechanical, photocopying, recording or otherwise, without prior permission in writing of the publisher and the copyright owners.

A catalogue record for this book is available from the British Library.

ISBN: 978-1-912755-95-0

Pavilion Publishing and Media is a leading publisher of books, training materials and digital content in mental health, social care and allied fields. Pavilion and its imprints offer must-have knowledge and innovative learning solutions underpinned by sound research and professional values.

Authors: Jonathan Passmore and Tracy Sinclair
Editor: Vivienne Button
Production editor: Michael Benge, Pavilion Publishing and Media Ltd
Cover design: Emma Dawe, Pavilion Publishing and Media Ltd
Page layout and typesetting: Phil Morash, Pavilion Publishing and Media Ltd
Printing: CMP

Praise for *Becoming a Coach*

"*Becoming a Coach* is the perfect place to start your coach development journey. The book provides a comprehensive coverage of the issues in coaching and offers an essential guide to the new ICF coach competencies for new and developing coaches."

Marshall Goldsmith
Thinkers50 #1 Executive Coach for 10 years

"In this crowded, confusing profession called coaching, Sinclair and Passmore have written the guidebook that clears the fog for coaches on their path to coaching excellence. *Becoming a Coach* clarifies the distinction of coaching and why it is so effective, provides specific practices for embodying a coaching mindset, and is full of tools that will elevate your coaching impact. No matter where you are on your journey, this book will give you a bright light to follow."

Dr Marcia Reynolds, MCC
ICF Global Board Past Chair
Author of *Coach the Person, Not the Problem: A Guide to Using Reflective Inquiry*

"This is a very comprehensive textbook to understand professional coaching from internationally recognized specialists. It includes a wealth of information and tools a coach requires at every stage of development and practice."

Osama Al-Mosa, MCC
Leadership Development Specialist, CCL
Founding President, ICF Jordan Chapter

"I believe that this is the most up-to-date and practical guide for any coach (ICF or otherwise). It provides real, practical examples and offers in-depth understanding of the 'what', the 'who', the 'how' and the 'why' of coaching backed up with academic rigor. This is an outstanding resource for any coach, no matter how skilled. The clarity and life Sinclair and Passmore bring to the competencies and approaches to coaching really demystify the science and the art of great coaching practice."

Hilary Oliver, PCC
ICF Global Board Chair 2017
Coach, Coach Supervisor, Mentor Coach and Coach Trainer

"Whether you are becoming a coach, or are a seasoned coach supervisor, mentor, trainer, or educator, this book is your vital companion. The authors bring decades of experience and research into one powerful resource. Grounded in evidence-based models, plus tools, activities, reflective exercises and more, this book is a must-read!"

Dr Laura L. Hauser, MCC, MCEC | Training Director, Team Coaching Operating System® | Faculty, Fielding Graduate University coaching programme | Executive Officer, GSAEC.org

"This is one of those rare books that has something for everyone. One of the most comprehensive guides to becoming a powerful coach, which starts from the basics and takes us to the essentials of mastery. This book has embraced the complexity of coaching literature, approaches and tools. It has then structured and presented them in a fashion that brings together the chaos to a usable format. I can safely say that this book would offer a new idea, approach or perspective even to the most experienced of coaches."

Shweta HandaGupta, MCC,
Change Leadership Coach, QuadraBrain® Transformation Solutions

Global ICF Young Leader Award Recipient, 2018

"An impressively grounded, accessible, comprehensive resource for coaches at all levels of experience. The depth of understanding offered provokes insight, shares knowledge and yet leaves the space to be yourself as a coach."

Karen Dean Master Certified Coach; Co-author *Coaching Stories: Flowing and Falling of Being a Coach*, Originator of me:my™coach online framework for coaches to self-monitor and Coaching Supervisor.

"Discover both inspiration and pragmatic guidance for being fit and sustaining authentic presence as a coach. Explore ways to claim your transcendence from models toward your unique coach expression."

Janet M. Harvey, CEO inviteCHANGE, ICF Master Certified Coach and Accredited Coaching Supervisor

Acknowledgments

First, we would like to express our sincere thanks and appreciation to our colleagues from the International Coaching Federation (ICF), who have kindly helped us ensure that this book aligns with the intention and integrity of the ICF Core Competencies. We would especially like to thank Carrie Abner, Vice President, ICF Credentials and Standards; George Rogers, Director of Quality Assurance, Credentialing and Accreditation; and Joel DiGirolamo, Director of Coaching Science, for reviewing various drafts and making sure the guide adheres as closely as possible to the ICF competencies.

However, in producing a book of this type, mistakes do happen. Although we have tried to ensure the book faithfully captures the ideas and research, any errors are ours alone.

We would also like to thank everyone who took the time to review this book and share their endorsements. We are delighted and humbled to have received such positive comments and encouragement.

Finally, we would like to thank our family and friends for their support, encouragement and understanding as we spent many hours immersed in creating this material.

We do hope you enjoy reading *Becoming a Coach: The Essential ICF Guide* and that it becomes a useful source of reference, whatever stage you are at in your development as a coach.

Contents

About the authors 3

Section 1: Setting the Scene 5

    Chapter 1: The Journey Toward Maturity 7

    Chapter 2: What is Coaching? 11

    Chapter 3: Who am I? 19

    Chapter 4: Who are my Clients? 29

Section 2: Developing Core Coaching Competencies 37

    Chapter 5: Introduction to the ICF Core Competency Model 39

    Chapter 6: Foundation Domain, Competency 1.
Demonstrates Ethical Practice 47

    Chapter 7: Foundation Domain, Competency 2.
Embodies a Coaching Mindset 63

    Chapter 8: Co-Creating the Relationship Domain, Competency 3.
Establishes and Maintains Agreements 71

    Chapter 9: Co-Creating the Relationship Domain, Competency 4.
Cultivates Trust and Safety 79

    Chapter 10: Co-Creating the Relationship Domain, Competency 5.
Maintains Presence 85

    Chapter 11: Communicating Effectively Domain, Competency 6.
Listens Actively 93

    Chapter 12: Communicating Effectively Domain, Competency 7.
Evokes Awareness 99

    Chapter 13: Cultivating Learning and Growth Domain, Competency 8.
Facilitates Client Growth 107

Section 3: Approaches to Coaching 115

    Chapter 14: The Universal Eclectic Coaching Approach 117

    Chapter 15: Behavioural Approach and the GROW model 125

    Chapter 16: Humanistic Approach and the Time to Think Model 131

    Chapter 17: Cognitive-Behavioural Approach and ABCDEF Model 141

Chapter 18: Gestalt Approach and Chairwork 147

Chapter 19: Solution-Focused Approach and the OSKAR Model 153

Chapter 20: Systemic Approach and Force Field Model 159

Chapter 21: Psychodynamic Coaching and Transference 169

Chapter 22: Integration 179

Section 4: Coaching Practice 189

Chapter 23: Ethical Practice 191

Chapter 24: Contracting with Clients 201

Chapter 25: Taking and Managing Coaching Notes 209

Chapter 26: Maintaining Presence Through Mindfulness 215

Section 5: Developing Your Practice 221

Chapter 27: Continuing Professional Development 223

Chapter 28: Personal Development Plans 229

Chapter 29: Supervision 235

Chapter 30: Reflective Practice 247

Chapter 31: Mentor Coaching 253

Chapter 32: Coach Knowledge Assessment 263

Chapter 33: Progressing Your Coaching Skills 267

Section 6: Tools and Techniques 279

Chapter 34: Coaching Tools 281

Chapter 35: Resources 313

Chapter 36: Appendices 325

References 339

About the authors

Jonathan Passmore

Jonathan is a chartered psychologist with the British Psychological Society, an ICF-credentialed coach, and a trained supervisor who holds five degrees in business and psychology. He has worked in coaching and personal development for more than 20 years, at global firms including IBM Business Consulting and PWC, and psychological consulting firms such as OPM and Embrion. Most recently he has worked as Director of Henley Centre for Coaching, Henley Business School, where he is also Professor of Coaching. During this time his clients have included board directors, celebrities, government ministers, public sector managers, and start-up entrepreneurs.

Jonathan has published 30 books, including *The Coaches Handbook*, *Top Business Psychology Models*, and *Mindfulness at Work*, in addition to 100 scientific articles and book chapters.

He has been recognised for his coaching practice and research, winning multiple awards from professional coaching bodies and the academic community. He is listed in the Top 30 Global Gurus and Marshall Goldsmith Thinkers50's Top 8 coaches.

Tracy Sinclair

Tracy Sinclair is an executive coach and consultant who works internationally with organisations across all industry sectors. She is an ICF-credentialed coach who runs her own coaching business, which offers professional coaching services and coaching culture consultancy to organisations, as well as providing ICF-accredited coach-specific training, mentoring and supervision services to professional coaches. Tracy is also a Lecturer in Coaching at the Henley Centre for Coaching, Henley Business School. Alongside her corporate work, Tracy founded and leads an initiative called Coaching with Conscience, which exists to have a positive impact on society and our environment through coaching.

Tracy is dedicated to the development of the coaching profession and the coaching community, and as such has volunteered her services to the International Coaching Federation (ICF) for more than 10 years. Tracy was the President of the UK ICF from 2013–2014 and has been an ICF Global Board Director since 2016, serving as Treasurer in 2017, Global Chair in 2018 and Immediate Past Global Chair in 2019. During 2020–2021, she serves as a Director at Large on the International Coaching Federation Global Enterprise Board.

In recognition of her efforts, she was named as one of the Leading Global Coaches winners of the Thinkers50 Marshall Goldsmith Coaching Awards 2019.

Section 1: Setting the Scene

This initial section consists of four chapters, which are intended to set the scene and provide an introduction and context for the rest of this book.

Chapter 1 addresses the topic of coaching maturity and describes some of the steps to becoming a qualified coach by engaging in accredited training and progressing toward a credential from the International Coaching Federation (ICF). We argue that these steps are not just a means to an end and that there is no end to the level of experience and maturity a person can seek and gain over time. In this way, we propose that maturity is an ongoing and lifelong journey of development and growth.

In Chapter 2 we look at the definition of coaching. First, we explain why clarifying the definition of this way of working and communicating is important. We also note that several definitions exist and share with you some examples that highlight foundational themes and similarities – alongside slight nuances and distinctions – in each case. This chapter also looks at some of the differences between coaching, other ways of working, and alternative professional services available to clients. We start with the coaching and mentoring continuum because these two modalities are often confused and intertwined. We explore the differences between these ways of working further in Chapter 31 and also outline the coaching–therapy and coaching–consultancy relationships.

In Chapters 3 and 4 we look respectively at who we are and who our clients are. The enquiry into who we are looks at the concept and benefits of self-awareness and self-reflection (an area that is also explored in Chapter 30). We mention the Myers-Briggs Type Indicator® (MBTI®) model as one of the many lenses we can use to gain insight into ourselves. Furthermore, we emphasize the importance of self-awareness and how it is highlighted within the ICF Core Competency Model. Finally, we offer some suggestions for tools and approaches that coaches can use as reflective practices to enhance their self-awareness as they develop on their own journey toward increased coaching maturity.

The final chapter of this section offers reflections on the coaching mindset we hold with regard to our clients. Once again, the idea of lenses is highlighted, and we share several examples of tools we can use to help shape and develop our coaching mindset so that we engage with our clients from a positive vs. deficit perspective. We note that such tools are not only useful for the coach; they may also provide powerful windows for our clients to 'see' themselves, thus enhancing their own self-awareness as part of the coaching process.

Chapter 1: The Journey Toward Maturity

There is much discussion in professional coaching circles about coach development. The ICF have their own terms for the journey a coach takes in their development from student to Associate Certified Coach (ACC) to Professional Certified Coach (PCC) and finally to Master Certified Coach (MCC). In this book we have focused our thinking around the term 'maturity' as an alternative way of thinking about coach development, recognizing that many high-performing coaches may not yet be an MCC. In this chapter we introduce the idea of maturity. We suggest that coach development is a continuous process, not a destination, and that even for the MCC development continues. We are all on a developmental journey.

Coaching Maturity

In coaching, as with all professions, there are levels of competence or skill. As a new ICF coach, your journey might have started when you first received coaching from a colleague at work or through a professional coach. This might have got you interested in the power of coaching, and its potential to help you discover for yourself the best options for you. Or you might have decided to attend a short coaching skills course, which engaged your curiosity. Whichever way it might have been, you have decided to become a coach. You have formally started on your journey of development.

However, completing a formal training programme – such as Approved Specific Coach Training Hours (ASCTH) or Approved Coach Training Programme (ACTP) – is only part of the journey. To become an ICF-credentialed coach, there are other aspects to complete, including:

- Coaching hours log
- Coach Knowledge Assessment (CKA)
- Mentor Coaching log
- Coaching assessment

You may currently be on that journey now, or you may already be an ICF ACC or a PCC. In fact, you may already be an MCC who is keen to extend your learning. Or you may be someone who has practiced coaching for years but has never got a formal coaching qualification.

Whichever it is, the journey toward maturity does not stop at any of these points. We have used the phrase 'maturity' – as opposed to 'mastery' – as mastery can imply an ending. We become a 'master' as a result of years of training and practice. In contrast, the phrase 'maturity' implies an infinite process, in which development never stops. We can always become more mature, more reflective and more insightful about our practice.

In fact, we believe that the coach who stops learning is the coach who is ready to stop coaching. Coaching requires us to remain curious about our clients and ourselves, to view our clients as having the capacity to learn and change. We must then role-model this belief in our own behaviours, as learners and practitioners who are open and ready to adapt to clients and the dynamic world in which we work.

In this book we offer multiple ways of continuing to develop – from a focus on coaching competencies, coaching models, coaching practice and, ultimately, eclecticism and integration.

Box 1.1: The Journey to Coaching Maturity

Coaching focus	Approach	Focus
Model focus	Control	How do I take the client where I think they need to go?
		How do I apply my model with this client?
Techniques and tools focus	Contain	How do I provide space for clients to think, but ensure they achieve their goal?
		How can I use these tools and techniques?
Philosophy focus	Facilitate	I believe X about the way the world works. Given this, how can I best help my client?
		How does this client – and their issue – fit this world view?
Integrated–eclectic focus	Enable	Are we both relaxed enough to allow the issue and the solution to emerge through a collaborative conversation – one in which neither of us know the answer or the direction of travel before we start?
		What multiplicity of models, frameworks and perspectives will best serve this client and this conversation? Are we recognizing the historical, national, cultural and personality differences of this unique person and this moment in time?

(Adapted from Clutterbuck and Megginson, undated)

Although the table above shows several levels toward coach maturity, we feel there may even be a level beyond what is shown here, which could transcend the illusion of models.

Most coaches go through a series of common experiences, as illustrated in Box 1.1, starting with a focus on models ("How do I apply my model with this client?") through a focus on tools ("How do I apply these tools with this client?") and onward through a philosophical approach, in which the coach assumes people are similar to them, toward an integrated approach. In reaching the integrated position, the coach draws from a multiplicity of perspectives and employs multiple frameworks, models and tools, without becoming obsessed with any of them. The coach also takes into account systemic factors; adapting, flexing and partnering with their client, without vested interest or ego, to help the client move forward.

Here are some of the changes that you might experience on your journey of personal development:

- From a narrow perspective that a single coaching model is best (often the one you were taught on the programme), toward a broader perspective that different people may learn and change in different ways.
- From a need for certainties and a search for the perfect solution to enjoying the journey of coaching, with its uncertainties and ambiguity, and allowing whatever emerges to emerge.
- From a focus on solving the client's current problem toward a focus on helping the client develop greater self-awareness and personal responsibility.
- From a performance orientation and a focus on doing to a presence orientation with a focus on being.
- From preoccupation with either the self or the client to a focus on the relationships between yourself, the client and the client's systems.
- From a focus on the conversation to a focus on the relationship.

Where are you on your own journey? You may like to reflect on these questions. Of course, a series of questions such as these in a book is only a rough guide. What is more important is to start thinking about these elements and explore what your next steps might be in your own developmental journey. We hope this book will prove a useful resource for you when it comes to understanding the ICF competencies, how to apply them in your coaching practice, reflecting on your wider practice as a coach, and recognizing that your development is a journey not a destination.

Conclusion

In this chapter we suggested that all coaches – be they novices, professionals and masters – are on a personal journey of development. We have argued that instead of a focus on a specific stage (e.g., ACC, PCC or MCC), it might be more helpful for all coaches to see development as a journey of continuous improvement and growth.

Chapter 2: What is Coaching?

Coaching Defined

Since coaching started its accelerated journey of development as a separate discipline in the early 1980s (Brock, 2012; Passmore & Theeboom, 2016), definitions of coaching have been part of the debate within coaching practice and research. Almost every book, article and blog has offered its own take on 'What is coaching?'

The search for a formal definition of coaching may be considered an academic pursuit by many practitioners. However, we believe there are at least three reasons why considering 'What is coaching?' is important.

First, a clear definition is essential for coaching practice. A standardized definition makes it clear to clients what they can expect from a coach, and that we are all delivering the same service.

Second, a definition of coaching is vital for research. We need to clearly delineate the domain of coaching to understand the phenomena being studied. As coaching is still an emerging research domain, it is crucial to define the key components that distinguish coaching from other similar helping interventions (e.g., counselling or consulting) and provide a platform from which theoretical contributions can develop.

Third, a consistent definition is vital for coach education and qualifications. A shared understand of what we do enables us to develop a shared body of knowledge and an agreed standard for training, with a scientific-based framework to support its pedagogy.

The ICF holds a similar view and has provided a clear definition of coaching: "Coaching is partnering with clients in a thought-provoking and creative process that inspires them to maximize their personal and professional potential."

Alternative Definitions

In reality there are a host of coaching definitions used by different writers, each reflecting different nuances placed by the writers, researchers and practitioners on different aspects of their work. In Box 2.1 we have included different definitions to compare and contrast with the ICF definition. Only by thinking about how others define coaching can we fully understand the nature and boundaries of our practice.

John Whitmore, widely credited as one of the founding thinkers in coaching, placed a marker in the sand in his seminal book *Coaching for Performance*. For him, coaching was about "unlocking a person's potential to maximize their own performance. It is helping them to learn rather than teaching them – a facilitation approach" (Whitmore, 1992, p. 8).

Whitmore drew heavily on Timothy Gallwey's book *The Inner Game of Tennis*. Gallwey (1986) noted in sport performance that the internal state of a player was a significant factor, further arguing that it was more significant even than the opponent in individual sports like tennis and golf. If the individual could control their self-talk, sizable performance gains could be made. At the core of coaching for John Whitmore was a belief that its purpose was to help individuals develop greater self-awareness and personal responsibility. He believed that this was how performance could be improved: "Performance coaching is based on awareness and responsibility" (Whitmore, 1992, p. 173).

Other founding writers offered alternative definitions. Laura Whitworth was one of the pioneers in the US – along with Thomas Leonard (Brook, 2009) – and developed co-active coaching, which she defined as "…a relationship of possibilities… based on trust, confidentiality…" (Whitworth *et al.*, 1998).

These definitions highlight the nature of the coaching process and its dependency on people, interpersonal interactions and collaboration. This relational aspect distinguishes coaching from other training interventions, in which arguably knowledge exchange is at the heart of the process.

Jonathan Passmore and Annette Fillery-Travis have adopted a process-based definition in an attempt to differentiate coaching from mentoring, counselling and other conversation-based approaches to change, while still linking the concept to John Whitmore's fundamental purpose of coaching (self-awareness and personal responsibility). They define coaching as "a Socratic-based dialogue between a facilitator (coach) and a participant (client), where the majority of interventions used by the facilitator are open questions [that] are aimed at stimulating the self-awareness and personal responsibility of the client" (Passmore & Fillery-Travis, 2011).

Tatiana Bachkirova, a leading UK coaching academic, suggests that coaching is "a human development process that involves structured, focused interaction and the use of appropriate strategies, tools and techniques to promote desirable and sustainable change for the benefit of the coachee..." (Bachkirova *et al*, 2010, p. 1). While, Yi-Ling Lai (2014) states that coaching is a "reflective process between coaches and coachees, which helps or facilitates coachees to experience positive behavioural changes through continuous dialogue and negotiations with coaches to meet coachees' personal or work goals". Again, positive behavioural changes are highlighted as the main purpose of coaching, with the recognition that a structured process is involved. Moreover, 'negotiation' is put forward in Lai's reinterpretation of coaching that reflects the previous definitions – i.e., coaching is a relationship-based learning and development process.

The definitions offer the reader a diversity of perspectives, while retaining the essence of the ICF definition of a collaborative, non-directive process between a coach and client.

Box 2.1: Definitions of Coaching

1. "Coaching is directly concerned with the immediate improvement of performance and development of skills by a form of tutoring or instruction". (Parsloe, 1995)
2. "Unlocking a person's potential to maximize their own performance. It is helping them to learn rather than teaching them." (Whitmore, 2003)
3. "A collaborative, solution-focused, result-orientated and systematic process in which the coach facilitates the enhancement of work performance, life experience, self-directed learning and personal growth of the coachee." (Grant, 1999)
4. "The art of facilitating the performance, learning and development of another." (Downey, 2003)
5. "[Co-active] coaching is a powerful alliance designed to forward and enhance a lifelong process of human learning, effectiveness and fulfilment." (Whitworth et al., 1998)
6. "Psychological skills and methods are employed in a one-on-one relationship to help someone become a more effective manager or leader. These skills are typically applied to a specific present-moment work-related issue… in a way that enable this client to incorporate them into his or her permanent management or leadership repertoire." (Peltier, 2010)
7. "A Socratic-based dialogue between a facilitator (coach) and a participant (client) where the majority of interventions used by the facilitator are open questions [that] are aimed at stimulating the self-awareness and personal responsibility of the participant." (Passmore and Fillery-Travis, 2011)
8. "A reflective process between coaches and coachees [that] helps or facilitates coachees to experience positive behavioural changes through continuous dialogue and negotiations with coaches to meet coachees' personal or work goals." (Lai, 2014)

> 9. "A helping relationship formed between a client who has managerial authority and responsibility in an organization and a consultant who uses a wide variety of behavioural techniques and methods to help the client achieve a mutually identified set of goals to improve his or her professional performance and personal satisfaction and, consequently, to improve the effectiveness of the client's organization within a formally defined coaching agreement." (Kilburg, 1996, p. 142)
> 10. "A human development process that involves structured, focused interaction and the use of appropriate strategies, tools and techniques to promote desirable and sustainable change for the benefit of the coachee." (Bachkirova et al., 2010, p. 1)

Coaching and Mentoring

Coaching and mentoring are often considered to sit on a continuum. Both coaching and mentoring are concerned with personal and professional development, but the amount of input by the coach–mentor increases as one moves along the continuum toward mentoring (Figure 2.1).

In this sense, mentoring may be better regarded as a form of tutelage, in which a more senior or experienced mentor shares their knowledge and insights with a more junior or less experienced mentee about how to improve in a specific job, role, vocation or organization.

Figure 2.1: Coaching–Mentoring Continuum

Coaching → Mentoring

More facilitation — More guidance

Some writers have suggested workplace mentoring involves a relationship between a less experienced individual (*protégé*) and a more experienced person (the mentor), where the purpose is the personal and professional growth of the protégé (Eby *et al.*, 2007,). The mentor may be a peer at work, a supervisor, or someone else within the organization, but it must be someone who is outside of the protégé's chain of command. Others have argued that coaching also differs from mentoring in its use of structured processes – such as the use of coaching models like Goal, Reality, Options, Wrap-up (GROW) – and the use of specific tools and assessments to provide awareness in the client (Joo, 2005).

A further difference is the length of the relationship. Although coaching assignments are more frequently completed in several months, mentoring relationships often continue for a period of several years (Passmore, 2016).

Finally, the main purpose of workplace coaching is meant to be on improving performance or well-being through self-awareness and learning, whereas the purpose of mentoring varies widely from socialization of newcomers to management development (Joo, 2005).

Coaches must be careful not to get drawn into mentoring relationships when they have contracted to deliver coaching. Specifically, coaches should be wary of being drawn into a long-term relationship that creates a sense of dependency in the client, leading to a coaching relationship that continues for years rather than months. There is nothing wrong with such a relationship, but in our view this is more likely to be mentoring rather than coaching.

A second danger for coaches is being drawn into providing advice. Less experienced managers may request this from their coach and less experienced coaches may fall back on past behaviours, sharing their experience or knowledge as 'this is what you should do…' advice to their clients. Again, we would see this as mentoring, not coaching.

These styles of engagement can be immensely useful for senior executives, who value having a trusted advisor available to them, with whom they can talk their issues and problems through regularly – gathering their views and using them as a guide.

Coaching and Therapy

Understanding the difference between therapy or counselling and coaching is important both for coaches and clients. Clients can sometimes end up in coaching when they really need help from a trained therapist for a clinical condition. At the same time, coaches can be drawn into talking about issues outside their area of knowledge and training.

The need for a clearer distinction between counselling/therapy and coaching is emerging as the use of psychological models and tools in coaching interventions has increased (Bachkirova, 2008). Such a differentiation is essential to ensure the coach remains within their area of competence and within the terms of their contract.

The similarities between the counselling/therapy and coaching domains are numerous. Both are concerned with the 'relationship'. They both recognize the need for engagement or 'client's commitment' to the process; they both rely on the 'practitioner's self-awareness' to facilitate change; they both recognize the need to keep the conversation moving forward. In addition, both counselling/therapy and coaching share a number of basic required professional skills such as listening, presence, trust and evoking awareness.

However, we suggest that there are at least three differentiating aspects. First, the initial motivation of clients to undertake counselling/therapy is different from coaching. For example, the individual usually expects to eliminate psychological problems and dysfunctions through counselling/therapy sessions. In this sense, therapy may be considered primarily problem-focused. Coaching clients are seeking something different. The coaching client arrives in anticipation of an improvement in personal and professional development – in this sense, it may be considered solution-focused.

Second, the focus of counselling/therapy may involve any matters relevant to the client's mental well-being, whereas the coaching process is usually restricted to the agreed and contracted goals. The expected outcomes and evaluation methods are usually defined prior to the first session with the involved parties (e.g., clients, supervisors and other stakeholders).

Third, the time horizon for the work is longer. The coach might contract for four, six or possibly 12 sessions, whereas a therapist contracts on a week-by-week basis, with a view that the relationship takes as long as it takes. In many cases a counselling relationship will continue for a year and sometimes for many years.

Coaches need to be wary when working with clients who may be presenting with clinical conditions. Such clients should be referred to their medical doctor or a therapist before starting a relationship. Coaches should also be careful not to get drawn into extending their work into these areas – for example, a workload priority discussion including workplace stress, which extends to anxiety or depression, and the client's use of medication for a clinical condition. Once again, coaches need to be clear during the contracting phase what coaching includes and, when non-coaching themes emerge, for those discussions to be signposted to the appropriate trained professionals. Additional guidance and resource references on this can be found in Chapter 6.

Coaching and Consulting

The final area of confusion can be around consulting. Like mentoring, consulting has an advice or input element. During their engagement with the organization, coaches may be part of a wider organizational change agenda but their focus is on individual change using a facilitative style. In contrast, consulting is more likely to be about providing expert advice to individuals, teams or the board.

One boundary area is team coaching. We view team coaching as a different intervention to individual coaching. Working with a team as a group, even with a facilitative style, is different from working individually with members of the team. We suggest there is more in common between team coaching and Action Learning Sets than there is with one-on-one coaching, in which an intimate, personal and intense relationship is created and the coach is wholly present with the client on a moment-to-moment basis during the session. Such intensity of connection cannot be created within a group. Team and group coaching can be hugely beneficial, but its successful delivery requires an additional skill set beyond the core competencies of a personal coach.

Conclusion

In summary, coaching is a distinctive approach. It is different from mentoring, counselling and consulting in its focus on a one-on-one facilitated relationship that is short term and generally focused on helping clients identify and work toward a goal or new insight.

During the contracting process, coaches need to ensure their clients understand what is coaching and how it can help them. This helps to create a shared understanding of how the coach and client will work together and also helps to manage the client's expectations as to what the coach will and won't do during the coaching assignment.

Chapter 3: Who am I?

In coaching, understanding who we are is as important as understanding what coaching is. The coach plays a central role in the work with the client. We might even say the coach is the tool in the coaching relationship. By understanding themselves, the coach can get out of the way of the work the client needs to do, as well as using self-disclosure and their own stories to help clients on their journey of self-discovery.

In this chapter we will think about ourselves as a central tool in the coaching process and consider ways that coaches can become more self-aware. One way to self-reflect is by using personality questionnaires; another is keeping a personal journal; and the third is by consciously viewing one's coaching practice as a continuous learning journey of self-discovery. We will look at each different approach.

Who am I?

Coaching is a highly personal process. It requires the coach to be authentic. Through this, a relationship of trust can develop, allowing clients to become more open and intimate in their coaching work. At the same time, the coach needs to keep out of the way. The coach's task is to manage the process without significantly shaping, directing or influencing the content.

In our view, the coach is a tool that can help their client to achieve their agreed goal. This goal may be a new insight about themselves or a situation, or a plan of action. To achieve this, the coach needs to have a high degree of self-awareness in order to know when to intervene and when to step back, or also to provide a reflection, a reframing, a new metaphor, or insight. For example, coaches may use silence, thereby allowing the client to reflect and process the conversation, creating the space for personal insights to emerge.

Self-Awareness and Self-Reflection

The terms "self-awareness" and "self-reflection" are often used interchangeably, as if they mean the same thing. We, however, see a difference between them. For us, self-reflection is a process that the coach can engage in, which will help them become more self-aware. In contrast, self-awareness is the outcome of this process. It enables the coach to become more sensitive to their feelings, behaviours and thoughts, then to place these within the context of their personal history and personality, and in response to their environment and their client.

Individuals with a high capacity for self-awareness are more likely to:

- be willing to take a candid look at themselves
- identify strengths and areas for improvement
- be able to experience a full range of emotions
- identify and heal their deepest emotions
- stop doing things that don't work
- think, feel and behave consciously
- behave more proactively
- be willing to learn, grow and change
- be open to new experiences
- be more comfortable with their own vulnerabilities.

Lens

There are many ways we can become more self-aware and understand ourselves better. Coaching is one of these ways, as is gathering feedback from others and observing our own behaviours, thoughts and emotions. However, simply observing, getting feedback and having coaching does not generate the self-awareness. We need to think about the data we are gathering and make sense of it for ourselves. In other words, we need to reflect on this feedback.

The Personality Type Lens

Psychometric questionnaires can be a useful tool to help us look at ourselves. There are scores of different personality questionnaires that we can use (Passmore, 2012). Some of these questionnaires are based on type models of personality, which draw on the ideas of Carl Jung. The most popular examples are MBTI, TDI, Insights, DISC and 16Personalities.

Jung (1923) proposes that each person has behavioural preferences and that by understanding these preferences we can adjust our behaviour toward others, thereby reducing conflict and improving our relationships. As coaches, we can use the questionnaires with our clients (given appropriate training) and also with ourselves in order to deepen our understanding of our own preferences and how these might affect our approach to coaching.

In Table 3.1 we have summarized the four orientations, based on the four key questions that the model asks us to consider. This is followed by Table 3.2, which explores the preferences in relation to coach behaviour.

The theory behind the 16Personalities, MBTI and the other Jungian questionnaires states that we all have preferred ways of relating to the world. For example, we may have a preference for using either our right hand or our left hand when we write, whichever feels easier or more comfortable. What it does not assess is how capable we are at writing. If right handed, we tend to ignore the possibility of using the left hand. If we do try to use the left hand we might describe the experience as "awkward" or "unnatural".

Like the left hand/right hand dichotomy, 16Personalities and the other Jungian questionnaires shows us that we have two choices in relating to the world around us and we tend to choose one at the expense of the other. There are four areas where we are confronted by this choice. The first area is represented by the choice between Introversion (I) and Extraversion (E). The second area is represented by the choice between Sensing (S) and Intuition (N). The third area is represented by the choice between Thinking (T) and Feeling (F). The fourth area is represented by the choice between Judging (J) and Perceiving (P).

Table 3.1: Four Questions

Question 1: Where do people gain their energy?

Extraversion	Introversion
People who prefer extraversion gain energy from the external world of people and events. They focus their attention on things in the external world. They are invigorated by interacting with people and events.	People who prefer introversion gain energy from the inner world of thoughts and feelings. They prefer to focus attention on their internal world, often because there is so much happening there. They are invigorated by spending time alone with their thoughts and feelings.
■ Sociable ■ Seeks excitement in external world ■ Gregarious, with a wide circle of friends ■ Speak first, think later ■ Breadth of interests ■ Find out what they think by talking ■ Expressive	■ Quiet ■ Deep ■ Think first, speak later ■ Private and contained ■ Prefer one or two close friendships ■ Depth of interests ■ Prefer to express ideas through writing
After a hard day's work, extraverts might typically recover their energies by going out with a group of friends.	After a hard day's work, introverts might typically recover their energies by having a quiet evening in with a close friend.

Question 2: What type of data do people pay attention to?	
Sensing People who prefer sensing take in information through their five senses, trusting what they can see, hear and touch. They prefer information that is tangible, concrete and present-focused. They are observant of the real world around them, prefer detail and practical problem-solving. ■ Practical ■ Present-focused ■ Detail conscious ■ Focused on what is real and tangible ■ Trust experience ■ Like facts ■ Need to have the facts presented one by one	**Intuition** People who prefer intuition take in information by seeing the big picture, focusing on the relationships and the wider, strategic implications of facts. They are attuned to the meanings of facts – the trends, the implications, the patterns behind the facts. They prefer new possibilities and different ways of doing things. ■ Abstract and theoretical ■ Imaginative ■ Future-oriented ■ Trust intuitive insights ■ Strategic ■ Like ideas ■ Need to have the big picture in order to see the relevance of facts
Question 3: How do people make decisions?	
Thinking People who prefer to use thinking when making decisions tend to look at logic, facts and objective analysis. They want to find out the objective truth of a situation. Alternatively, they will look for the best possible outcome according to the ideals of fairness and justice. ■ Analytical ■ Objective ■ Logical problem-solvers ■ Impersonal ■ Fair ■ Principled ■ Task-centered	**Feeling** People who prefer to use feeling when making decisions will use their subjective feelings to guide their judgment. They are attuned to the needs of others, are empathic and weigh the feelings of others in their decision-making. They value compassion, appreciation of others and interpersonal harmony. ■ Sympathetic ■ Compassionate ■ Attuned to the needs of others ■ Responsive to others' feelings ■ Guided by personal values ■ Subjective ■ People-centered

Question 4: How do people orient their lives?	
Judging	**Perception**
People who prefer to use their judging process in the external world like to live in a planned, orderly way. They like to make decisions, reach closure and then put a structured plan into place in order to implement them. Plans, schedules and getting things done are important to them. ■ Scheduled ■ Organized ■ Methodical ■ Decisive ■ Good at implementing decisions ■ Get things done ■ Plan in advance ■ Dislike last-minute changes	People who prefer to use their perceptive process in the external world like to live in a spontaneous, flexible way. They prefer to understand and experience life rather than control it. They prefer to delay decisions until the last minute, staying open to possibilities and options. ■ Spontaneous ■ Flexible ■ Leave things to the last minute ■ Respond to change ■ Casual ■ Prefer to delay decision-making ■ Respond to the moment ■ Avoid rigid plans

(Adapted from Rogers, 2017)

Table 3.2: Coaching Preferences

	Likely strengths	Likely areas for development
Extraversion (E)	■ Helping clients explore a wide range of issues ■ Establishing the coaching partnership ■ Thinking on feet	■ Using silence ■ Helping clients explore issues in depth ■ Reaching the 'Way Forward' stage
Introversion (I)	■ Helping clients explore issues in depth ■ Reflecting on strategies ■ Using silence	■ Helping clients move to action ■ Helping clients explore all relevant issues ■ Establishing the coaching partnership

Sensing (S)	■ Observing details ■ Using the 'Reality' stage ■ Helping clients decide on practical steps in the 'Way Forward'	■ Taking the big picture into account ■ Generating ideas at the 'Options' stage ■ Using intuition
Intuition (N)	■ Seeing the big picture ■ Using intuition ■ Generating ideas at the 'Options' stage	■ Being specific ■ Testing out intuition ■ Helping clients decide on practical steps in the 'Way Forward'
Thinking (T)	■ Being objective ■ Challenging	■ Picking up on clients' feelings ■ Being empathetic ■ Challenging in a supportive way at the right time
Feeling (F)	■ Being warm ■ Being empathic	■ Taking thoughts into account as well as feelings ■ Challenging the clients ■ Being more objective
Judging (J)	■ Being organized ■ Being decisive	■ Helping clients make decisions in a timely way ■ Being flexible
Perceiving (P)	■ Being spontaneous ■ Being flexible	■ Being organized ■ Helping clients make decisions

(Adapted from Passmore *et al.*, 2006)

The Personality Trait Lens

A different way of thinking about personality is to look at personality traits. The most common traits are the Big Five – sometimes also called the OCEAN model. The model is based on five factors: Openness, Conscientiousness, Extraversion, Agreeableness and Neuroticism.

Table 3.3: The Five-Factor Model of Personality	
Big Five Factor	Description
Conscientiousness	Careful, reliable, hardworking, well-organized, punctual, disciplined, ambitious
Extroversion	Sociable, fun-loving, affectionate, friendly, talkative, warm
Agreeableness	Courteous, selfless, sympathetic, trusting, generous, acquiescent, lenient, forgiving, flexible
Openness to Experience	Original, imaginative, creative, broad interests, curious, daring, liberal, independent, prefer variety
Neuroticism (Emotional Stability)	Worrying, emotional, high-strung, temperamental, insecure, self-pitying, vulnerable. (Emotional Stability: Calm, at ease, relaxed, even-tempered, secure, hardy)

(Adapted from McCrae & Costa, 1987)

Although there is little research exploring personality preferences and coaching styles, we can conclude from other areas of research that conscientiousness will help in learning and application. High conscientiousness scores are associated with work success. Perhaps this is not surprising because – to paraphrase a famous golf player – "the harder [you] practice, the luckier [you] get".

A second factor that may influence coaching outcomes is agreeableness. Individuals who are empathetic and selfless are more likely to build better relationships with clients, and we believe this makes for a better coach than those who are selfish or self-serving.

Finally, we can assume that those with high neuroticism scores are less likely to be effective coaches. Being highly emotional, insecure and vulnerable is likely to be negatively correlated with successful coaching outcomes. However, having trained hundreds of coaches throughout the years, we know many who are neurotic but have developed skills to manage their neuroticism when they are with clients, enabling them to focus on their client's needs, not their own.

The Third Lens

A third personality lens to look at ourselves through is the specialist questionnaire. Examples include emotional intelligence questionnaires such as Emotional Quotient Inventory (EQ-i) and Mayer-Salovey-Caruso Emotional Intelligence Test (MSCEIT), resilience questionnaires such as MTQ48, leadership questionnaires such as the Transformational Leadership Questionnaire (TLQ) and the Integrated Leadership Measure (ILM72), and strengths questionnaires such as Values In Action (VIA). (We will explore VIA in Chapter 4: Who are my Clients?)

Each of these questionnaires provides a different perspective on who we are, which offers us the opportunity to think about ourselves, and how our preferences or style of engaging can help or hinder our approach as a leader or as a coach.

As part of your development we would encourage you to complete two or three different questionnaires and spend some time journaling and reflecting on how these might have an impact on you, your approach to coaching, and how you build and maintain relationships with your clients.

Journaling

Having explored a variety of different lenses, it is important to reflect on this feedback and to develop a coaching mindset (we will discuss this mindset in more depth in Chapter 7). The coaching mindset aims to encourage us to be open, curious, flexible and client-centered.

> **Box 3.1: The Coaching Mindset**
>
> The coaching mindset:
> - acknowledges that clients are responsible for their own choices
> - engages in ongoing learning and development as a coach
> - develops an ongoing reflective practice to enhance one's coaching
> - remains aware of and open to the influence of context and culture on self and others
> - uses awareness of self and one's intuition to benefit clients
> - develops and maintains the ability to regulate one's emotions
> - mentally and emotionally prepares for sessions
> - seeks help from outside sources when necessary.

One way of exploring and noting our development is a personal journal. A part of your daily or weekly practice as a new (or as an experienced coach) should be writing a journal to provide a record of your developmental journey.

You could start by writing about the start of your journey. We suggest some useful questions to consider as you start this journey in Box 3.2. This is not an exhaustive list, but instead provides a platform from which to begin your exploration.

Some people like to use a longhand style, writing whole sentences about their experiences in a highly structured and considered way. Others prefer to write using a stream of consciousness; dictation software is often great for this style of writing. Finally, some prefer a more fluid approach that uses mind maps, drawings, and a less structured style. The style is less important than providing a mechanism for you to capture your thinking and a record to look back on each month or each year, which highlights your journey and what you considered to be important at that time.

We appreciate that some people find this process hard. We would urge you to keep in mind that this is your 'secret' journal. It's not for anyone else to read, review or assess. There are no right or wrong answers, and no right or wrong way to write the journal. It's your choice.

Box 3.2: Starting Your Learning Journey

A few questions to consider as your start your learning journey:
- What have you done before in your career?
- What do you know about coaching?
- What experience have you had of coaching, and what happened?
- What attracted you to coaching?
- What do you want to get from learning more about coaching?
- What gifts are you bringing to the journey?
- What areas of learning do you think you will need to really focus on?

Reflective Practice

The purpose of writing is not only to create a record of where we have come from, but more importantly to provide an opportunity for reflection. In the past the focus was on coaching practice: the more hours, the better the coach.

But we know it is not as simple as this. Our experience of driving a car reminds us that simply spending more hours driving does not always equate to continuous improvement. What matters just as much in this equation is a growth mindset (i.e., being open to and having a desire for improvement) and reflecting back on each driving experience with a question – e.g., what can I learn from that experience to become a better driver? The journal is a tool that we can use to encourage the reflective process. It helps us take the time to stop and consider what has been going on and to capture these thoughts. In Chapter 30 we offer you a structured process for reflection, using eight questions to guide your way.

Understanding Ourselves

Whether you complete two or 22 questionnaires, each is only a black and white pen sketch of who you are. The reality is we are infinitely more complex, multilayered and variable than any single questionnaire can explain. The British poet Philip Larkin noted the complexity of the human experience in his phrase "the million-petalled flower of being here" (Larkin, 1973).

Although questionnaires are useful, and we encourage you to use them as one way of exploring more about who you are, we also issue a caution: don't let the questionnaire define or limit you. The questionnaire only produces a report based on what you put in. The evidence suggests that we all change with time as a result of different learning and life experiences. Thus if you complete the same questionnaire after studying for 12 months on a coaching course, your results are likely to be somewhat different to the report you completed on the first day of the course. Furthermore, how you see yourself when at home or how you perceive yourself on a course may well be different to how colleagues perceive you at work or how your friends see you at a social event.

Conclusion

In this chapter we have argued that self-awareness is an important part of coach development. Self-awareness can be developed through active self-reflection, based on insights and evidence gathered from feedback and also tools such as psychometric questionnaires. We looked at three different lenses: type, trait, and what we called the 'third lens'. By using two or three questionnaires coaches can gain new insights when reviewing this data, as well as reflecting more generally on our coaching practice. We suggest one way of doing this is through a personal journal. We also urged caution: the results from any one questionnaire are not the full picture of who we are, because as humans we are multifaceted, complex, and amazing.

Chapter 4: Who are my Clients?

In Chapter 3 we argued that self-awareness was an important aspect for the coach, and we offered some ideas for becoming more self-aware through using different lenses to consider who we are. These included psychometrics as well as self-reflection and journaling. We believe the same principles apply to thinking about our clients. We believe each is a unique person, with their own personal strengths as well as their own biases, prejudices and 'messed-up-ness' of what it is to be human. Yet in spite – or, maybe, because – of this, they are wonderful.

In this chapter we draw again on the concept of the coaching mindset, applying the idea to how we think about and see our clients. Should we see them as people to be fixed or as wonders to behold?

Deficit Psychology Model vs. Positive Psychology Model

For the first 100 years or so, psychology's primary focus was on explaining dysfunction. This deficit or 'disease' model, as it has become known, meant that psychologists were highly active in thinking, researching and writing about human mental illness and dysfunction. This led to classifications such as The Diagnostic and Statistical Manual of Mental Disorders (DSM), a manual that describes hundreds of mental conditions, how to diagnose them, and how to 'fix' them.

What got neglected was the more positive side of human functioning. What do humans do when they are at their best? Of course, there were many examples of individual psychologists like Carl Rogers and Abraham Maslow, and movements like the Human Potential Movement, who were concerned with these aspects during this period, but this was far outweighed by a focus on negative behaviours and functioning.

In the past few decades, greater focus has been placed on these more positive aspects of human behaviour; out of the Human Potential Movement (also known as humanistic psychology) has come positive psychology. This new approach argues that we need equally to consider positive aspects of human functioning, as opposed to solely focusing on the negative, and to study these with similar – specifically, quantitative – methods to dysfunction.

Lenses

A useful starting point for this approach is to consider our mindset. As a coach, are we looking for what's wrong in our clients, or are we helping them to look for what's right? The ICF competency 'Embodies a Coaching Mindset' – although sometimes difficult to observe – encourages us to work with a positive attitude toward our clients and to be open, curious, flexible and client-centered.

Although we are not suggesting we be naïve and ignore unhelpful behaviours or clinical issues, we should start with a focus on the positive and the potential that resides in each and every client. One way of exploring or thinking about this is in terms of strengths. There are a wide range of strengths tools that have been published (see Box 4.1 for examples).

Box 4.1: Examples of Strength Questionnaires

- The Values in Action (VIA) Inventory of Strengths
- Realise2 Strengths Assessment
- Strengthscope
- CliftonStrengths
- High5

We will focus on reviewing the most popular and widely used tool, which is Values In Action (VIA) Inventory of Strengths (Peterson & Seligman, 2004). The tool was initially developed from a research project to identify and map human strengths and has now been completed by hundreds of thousands of interested participants.

The model identified 24 strengths from the research. These are clustered into five groups under the headings Wisdom and Knowledge, Courage, Humanity, Temperance, Justice, and Transcendence (see Table 4.1).

Table 4.1: VIA Inventory of Strengths	
Wisdom and Knowledge	■ Creativity ■ Curiosity ■ Judgment ■ Love of learning ■ Perspective
Courage	■ Bravery ■ Perseverance ■ Honesty ■ Zest
Humanity	■ Love ■ Kindness ■ Social intelligence
Temperance	■ Forgiveness ■ Humility ■ Prudence ■ Self-regulation
Justice	■ Teamwork ■ Fairness ■ Leadership
Transcendence	■ Appreciation of beauty ■ Gratitude ■ Hope ■ Humour ■ Spirituality

The writers argued that an awareness of an individual's strengths can be helpful for people through a virtuous cycle. The first step is developing awareness. This may be gained through the completion of a questionnaire such as VIA or from reflecting on personal experience. With awareness, the individual can become more conscious of choices, selecting to draw on one or more of their perceived strengths. By using these strengths more frequently, the idea is that the individual feels more confident and thus is more likely to achieve a positive outcome, which in turn encourages greater use of the strength (see Figure 4.1).

Figure 4.1: The Virtuous Cycle

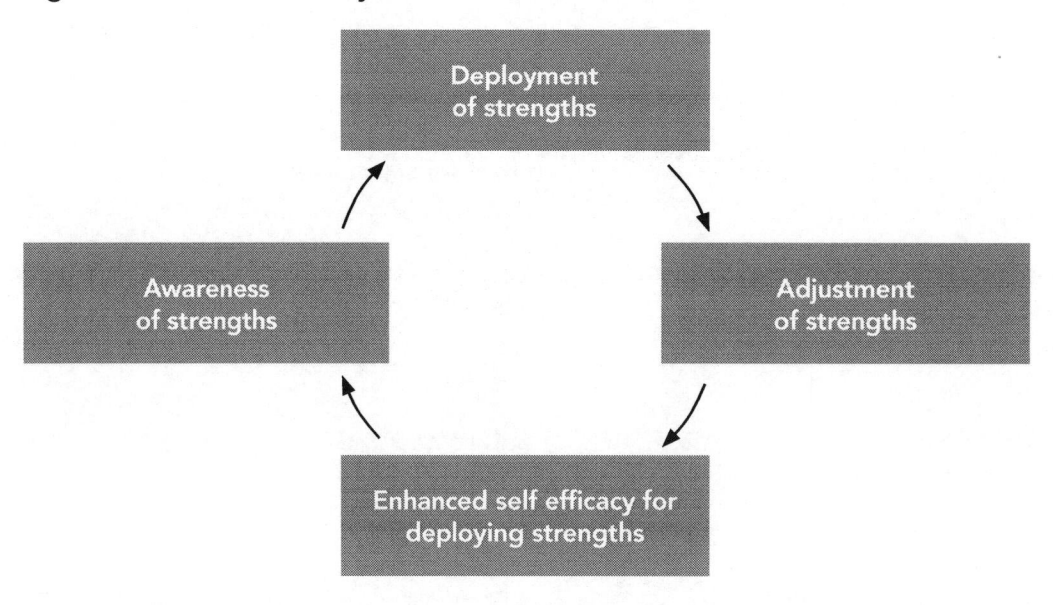

```
         Deployment
         of strengths
         ↗          ↘
Awareness              Adjustment
of strengths           of strengths
         ↖          ↙
      Enhanced self efficacy for
         deploying strengths
```

It's worth saying at this point that, as in Chapter 3, we urge caution with all psychometrics. Although psychometric tests are helpful, we need to be careful they don't define us or limit how we see our clients. Just because a client scores lower in one strength than another – for example, higher for Brave and Creative, but lower for Forgiveness and Love – this does not mean they are unable to forgive or to love others. Recognize that psychometric tools are tin openers, not tape measures; however, we would encourage you to be curious and explore with the client their own perceptions of their scores.

A second element to consider is how race and gender may affect how people see themselves and report this using the questionnaire. One study (Brdar *et al.*, 2011) investigated gender differences in the relationship between character strengths and life satisfaction. Two questionnaires were administered to 818 students (488 women and 330 men): the Values In Action Inventory of Strengths and the Satisfaction With Life Scale. The results revealed that zest, hope, and gratitude had the strongest link to life satisfaction. What was also interesting were the gender differences that emerged across 10 of the character strengths, although there was no difference in life satisfaction scores (Box 4.2).

> **Box 4.2: Strengths by Gender**
>
> **Strengths by Gender**
>
> The five highest-weighted strengths for **women** were:
> - integrity
> - kindness
> - love
> - gratitude
> - fairness
>
> The five highest-weighted strengths for **men** were:
> - integrity
> - hope
> - Humour
> - gratitude
> - curiosity

These results suggest that women and men (at least those in this study) see themselves differently in terms of the strengths they report, which could relate to cultural factors about the strengths different societies value in men and women in the 21st century. A second part of the study also looked at men's and women's views on predictors for life success. These resembled the main results, which again may echo gender roles: women favored love and beauty whereas men favored creativity and perspective (Box 4.3).

> **Box 4.3: Predictors of Life Satisfaction by Gender**
>
> **Predictors of Life Satisfaction**
>
> Significant predictors of life satisfaction are also different.
>
> For women, life satisfaction was predicted by:
> - zest
> - gratitude
> - hope
> - appreciation of beauty
> - love
>
> For men, life satisfaction was predicted by:
> - creativity
> - perspective
> - fairness
> - humour

The findings seem to be partly congruent with gender stereotypes of what we consider to be desirable in women or men, with women scoring higher on kindness and love whereas men score more highly on humour and curiosity.

Non-judgmental, unconditional positive regard

We suggest the coach seeks to cultivate a mindset in which each client is held in unconditional positive regard – that we prize each client. This can be hard, as we often bring our own biases and prejudices into the work we do. So how can we do this?

Of course, each experienced coach has their own approach. One strategy that we have found works well is to look for 'me toos'. What can we find in what the client says, or does that make us think or feel 'me too'? Maybe they like a certain type of music or sports team, wear a certain style of clothes, or have a certain type of accent. These can all be things that turn us off, but by searching for and finding one 'me too' we can start to build a bridge for the coaching relationship.

The second aspect is working to be non-judgmental. This requires us to avoid judging our client as good or bad, and accept the client for who they are. Our role is to help the client to make sense of and to evaluate (evoking awareness), and – if they wish – to plan and implement change in their thinking, feelings or behaviour (facilitating client growth). But how can we do this?

Each experienced coach will have their own approach and you will need to find your own way, but here is one that we have found useful. When listening we aim to stay in the present moment, for if we start reflecting back during a session there is an increased danger of evaluation. By staying present we can be with the client, actively listening, engaging and encouraging the client to explore for themselves. In this way we can work with issues that in other situations might cause distress, such as anger, frustration or sadness. Our time for reflection is when we note such feelings after the session in our journal and to take these emotional responses to supervision.

As you engage in your coaching training it is worth spending time with your supervisor, mentor coach, and your trainer to reflect on the question: what would be the 'worst' thing a client could say to you? Here are some examples from our work as trainers (Box 4.4). Of course, someone else's 'worst' might be your 'best', or at least not cause you any anxiety or emotional response. We each have our own personal perspectives. Thinking through what yours are will help you to better understand the diversity of the world, and how people may think, feel or behave toward you.

You may like to give some thought to what your 'worst' four or five examples might be and write down in your own personal learning journal.

Box 4.4: Examples of the 'Worst' Things a Client Could Say

"I am having an affair with [insert the name of someone you respect or love here]"

"I think you are a terrible coach and I am going to report you to the ICF for [insert what you feel is the weakest aspect of your coaching practice here]"

"I need to tell you I have just been released from prison as I have served a sentence for [insert the crime that creates the strongest disgust reaction in you here]"

"I like to [insert a behaviour you find difficult here] at weekends, and am thinking about how I…"

"I really hate [insert the faith, gender, or ethnic group of your choice here]; and I do my best to avoid employing any in my company"

As we will see later, the ideas of non-judgmental, unconditional positive regard are drawn from the work of Carl Rogers and his "necessary and sufficient conditions"

(Rogers, 1957). We will explore these conditions as part of the humanistic person-centered approach to coaching in Chapter 16.

Conclusion

In this chapter we have considered how the coach must develop and retain a focus toward their clients. This focus can be developed through the coaching mindset of positivity and non-judgmental, unconditional positive regard. By avoiding stereotypes and seeing each client as a prize to be held, the coach can start to manage the relationship in service of their client, avoiding the dangers of their own expertise and presuming "It's another case of…".

Section 2: Developing Core Coaching Competencies

This section looks at the ICF's approach to coaching and coaching competence. We begin Chapter 5 with a brief history of the ICF and how its core competency model came about, and look at the competency review process that led to the approval of the most recent body of work in September 2019. We also share a high-level overview of the model, along with an outline of how it sits within the ICF requirements for a credential application at three distinct levels. The subsequent chapters in this section take each competency in turn and offer a more in-depth exploration of what is meant by each one and how they are demonstrated in coaching practice.

It is important to note that the competencies should not be applied in any specific order. Although some aspects lend themselves to being demonstrated during the early part of a coaching conversation and others toward the end, the reality is that the competencies should present as an intertwined flow in a natural conversational style. However, for the purposes of this book, each competency will be addressed in the order they are noted in the overall model.

The ICF Core Competency Model is described under four 'domains' and we begin with the Foundation Domain, looking at Competency 1: Demonstrates Ethical Practice, in Chapter 6, and Competency 2: Embodies a Coaching Mindset in Chapter 7. Professional and ethical conduct along with a commitment to developing and embracing a particular coaching mindset are considered foundational to any good coaching practice and are therefore positioned as prerequisites upon which sit the competencies demonstrated and applied with each coaching conversation.

The second domain is called Co-Creating the Relationship and covers the three competencies of Competency 3: Establishes and Maintains Agreements in Chapter 8, Competency 4: Cultivates Trust and Safety in Chapter 9, and Competency 5: Maintains Presence in Chapter 10. All three competencies focus on the importance of not just building an appropriate relationship with our client, but also on creating the environment and the conditions for the client to work in a safe, trusting and supported way. The concept of relationships also extends beyond the immediate client to other parties involved in the ultimate success of the coaching engagement. Specific attention is paid to how those relationships and associated agreements around them are established and maintained. The final aspect of the co-created relationship is how the 'being' of the coach influences and informs the relationship, and how the coach fully maintains presence with their client in service of their learning and forward movement toward their stated goals and outcomes.

Communicating Effectively is the third domain and compromises the two competencies of Competency 6: Listens Actively in Chapter 11 and Competency 7: Evokes Awareness in Chapter 12. Effective communication as a coach is a sophisticated blend of many advanced communication skills. However, in their simplest form, these two competencies focus on the depth and breadth of how a coach truly and deeply listens to their client on many levels. Based on such holistic listening, the coach can engage in dialogue with their client in a way that evokes the client's awareness, inviting them to consider what they are learning and noticing about themselves and their situation, and how this awareness can help them progress toward their goals.

Finally, the domain of Cultivating Learning and Growth comprises Competency 8: Facilitates Client Growth in Chapter 13. Here we explore how the coach invites the client to integrate their learning into forward movement beyond the coaching session or the overall coaching engagement.

Chapter 5: Introduction to the ICF Core Competency Model

Background

The International Coaching Federation (ICF) is the world's largest organization of professionally trained coaches, with members in more than 145 countries worldwide. The organization was first established in 1995 to provide a space for all coaches to support each other's development and help expand the profession of coaching. The ICF has grown rapidly during the past two decades, reflecting the development of coaching and its professionalization. The ICF launched a single credential of Master Certified Coach (MCC), the first 34 of which were awarded in 1998. The following year, the Professional Certified Coach (PCC) credential was added and the Associate Certified Coach (ACC) credential was introduced in 2004.

As an evidence-led organization, the ICF has reviewed the competencies twice using a job analysis process, drawing on experience and research from practitioners and academics. The purpose on each occasion is to ensure the ICF competencies reflect both developing practice and our growing understanding of the behavioural and psychological processes involved in coaching. The insights from these reviews are part of the wider process of the continuous improvement of credentialing, which includes the Coach Knowledge Assessment (CKA), assessment methods, and the curriculum standards for ICF-accredited training programmes.

The job analysis in 2018/19 was based upon a rigorous two-year coaching practice analysis. The research and evidence was collected from more than 1,300 coaches across the world, who represented a diverse range of coaching disciplines, training, backgrounds and coaching styles. The process is summarized in Box 5.1.

> **Box: 5.1: ICF Job Analysis**
>
> **ICF Updated Competency Model Phases**
>
> The study used a mixed-methods approach that is often used in job analysis and competency modeling. The ICF-HumRRO (Human Resources Research Organization) team completed the following phases of research:
>
> - Semi-structured interviews with six experienced coaches.
> - Workshop to gather written critical incidents in coaching.
> - Workshop to determine tasks, knowledge, abilities and other (coach-specific) characteristics (KAOs).
> - Survey to validate the tasks and KAOs.
> - Workshop to gather feedback on possible competency model update.
> - Updated competency model development and validation.
>
> A group of subject matter expert (SME) coaches were also asked to link coaching tasks to KAOs. This exercise is primarily used to assist in the development of credentialing assessments, rather than updating the competency model, and offers a holistic perspective to the process.

ICF Credential

The ICF offers a globally recognized, independent credentialing programme for coach practitioners. Using the term 'credential' to describe the designation the coach receives, reflects how the ICF awards a qualification that requires periodic renewal. This renewal approach assures clients of ICF-credentialed coaches that the coach is not only fit for practice and meets stringent education and experience requirements, but that they have also demonstrated a thorough understanding of the ICF Core Competencies. The renewal process verifies that the coach regularly undertakes continuing professional development activities to maintain and further develop their knowledge, while also reviewing their practice to ensure compliance with ethical best practice as it develops within the industry. An ICF credential is renewable every three years.

The ICF offers three levels of credential: Associate (ACC), Professional (PCC) and Master Certified Coach (MCC). Each requires different levels of coach-specific training, coaching experience and demonstrable evidence of the use of the ICF's Core Competencies.

Here is a summary of the requirements for an ICF credential at each level:

Associate Certified Coach (ACC)

- 60+ hours of coach-specific training
- 10 hours of mentor coaching
- 100+ hours of coaching experience following the start of coach training
- Coach Knowledge Assessment (CKA)
- Core Competence performance evaluation to ACC-level minimum requirements.

Professional Certified Coach (PCC)

- 125+ hours of coach-specific training
- 10 hours of mentor coaching
- 500+ hours of coaching experience following the start of coach training
- Coach Knowledge Assessment (CKA)
- Core Competence performance evaluation to PCC-level minimum requirements.

Master Certified Coach (MCC)

- 200+ hours of coach-specific training
- 10 hours of mentor coaching
- 2,500+ hours of coaching experience following the start of coach training
- Coach Knowledge Assessment (CKA)
- Core Competence performance evaluation to MCC-level minimum requirements
- Coaches are also required to hold a PCC credential before they can apply for the MCC credential.

More details about the requirements and application process for each credential level can be found on the ICF website.

ICF Coaching Core Competency Model

The ICF model consists of eight core competencies that sit under four domains (ICF, 2019b). This competency model reflects the latest work undertaken by the ICF in the 2018/19 job analysis noted above. The model was developed to support greater understanding about the skills and approaches used within today's coaching profession, as defined by the ICF. At the heart of the model are the ICF's core values of integrity, excellence, collaboration and respect.

> **Box 5.2: ICF Core Competency Model**
>
> **A. Foundation**
> 1. Demonstrates Ethical Practice
> 2. Embodies a Coaching Mindset
>
> **B. Co-Creating the Relationship**
> 3. Establishes and Maintains Agreements
> 4. Cultivates Trust and Safety
> 5. Maintains Presence
>
> **C. Communicating Effectively**
> 6. Listens Actively
> 7. Evokes Awareness
>
> **D. Cultivating Learning and Growth**
> 8. Facilitates Client Growth

The Coaching Core Competency Model (ICF, 2019b) and the ICF definition of coaching (ICF, 2007) are used as the foundation for the Coach Knowledge Assessment (CKA) (ICF, 2020), which is part of the assessment process for coaches applying for an ICF Credential. The eight competencies sit within four domains that represent the core characteristics of a coaching conversation. The domains and individual competencies are not weighted and do not represent any kind of priority, in that they are all considered core or critical for any competent coach to demonstrate. As such, this competency model also offers support for coaches to calibrate the level of alignment between the coach-specific training expected by the ICF and the training that a coach has experienced.

In transitioning from the original competency model, the job analysis validated that much of the original model (developed nearly 25 years ago) remains critically important to the practice of coaching today. Some elements and themes, which emerged from the data as being either new or of enhanced significance, have also been integrated into the updated Coaching Core Competency Model (ICF, 2019b).

These elements and themes will be discussed in more detail in the following chapters of this section; however, it is worth noting that the review process highlighted the following areas as paramount for the practice of coaching in today's world:

- Ethical behaviour.
- Confidentiality.
- Coaching mindset.
- Reflective practice and professional development.
- Expanded focus on the coaching agreement, including important distinctions between various levels of coaching agreements.
- Enhanced concept of partnership between the coach and the client.
- Cultural, systemic and contextual awareness.

The combination of the foundational components from the previous model with the new themes that emerged from the job analysis produced an updated model that reflects the key elements of coaching practice today and serves as a strong and comprehensive standard for the next phase of the evolution of the coaching profession.

An important point to make about this competency model is that the domains, the individual competencies, and their sub-competencies are not a checklist and are also not necessarily chronological. Although some aspects of the competencies lend themselves to the beginning or the end of a coaching engagement or session, most are seen as behaviours and qualities that the coach might display at any point throughout the coaching work. As such, this model is intended to describe features and characteristics of coaching that interplay with each other and should be viewed as a holistic body of work, as well its component parts.

The model plays an important role in the design and delivery of coach-specific training programmes that have been accredited by the ICF. Such programmes are required to demonstrate that at least 80% of the training is focused on the ICF Core Competencies. In this way, students are well educated and prepared for the relevant assessment process toward their credential application. In the same way that coaches are evaluated as part of the credentialing and renewal process, an ICF-accredited training provider also undertakes a performance evaluation, audit and renewal process to maintain their programme accreditation, thereby underpinning the rigor and consistency of quality assurance for students.

Useful Documentation

The ICF produces several documents as part of the development, assessment and credentialing process.

ACC, PCC and MCC Minimum Skills Requirements

The three levels of the ICF credentialing process are a reflection of the continuum of growth that each coach undergoes. Minimum skills requirements have been created by ICF to support coaches with preparation for either ACC, PCC, or MCC credentialing performance evaluation. The aim is to help coaches successfully complete their ACC, PCC, or MCC performance evaluation and also help them continue to develop their skill set as coaches.

This structure provides those who want to learn and apply these competencies, as well as those seeking a credential, with an understanding of what assessors evaluate in relation to each one. They outline the minimum level of skill necessary to successfully demonstrate an ACC, PCC, or MCC level of competency. They also offer an understanding of what behaviours might prevent successful completion of an ACC, PCC, or MCC performance evaluation process. These documents are also intended to help coaches answer questions such as:

- What does it mean to be an ACC, PCC, or MCC coach?
- What do ICF assessors listen for when they are evaluating an ACC, PCC, or MCC coach?
- What are my strengths and what are the skill-set areas that I need to grow to pass the ACC, PCC, or MCC performance evaluation?

Core Competencies Comparison Table

The core competencies comparison table is an adaptation of the Minimum Skills Requirements documents for each credential level and shows the rating levels at ACC, PCC, and MCC, including pass and non-pass criteria.

PCC Markers

Assessment markers are the indicators that an assessor is trained to listen for in order to determine which ICF Core Competencies are in evidence in a recorded coaching conversation, and to what extent. The 'PCC markers' are the behaviours that should be exhibited in a coaching conversation at the Professional Certified Coach level. These markers support a performance evaluation process that is fair, consistent, valid, reliable, repeatable, and defensible. The markers are useful as a benchmark and to help understand what is expected at PCC level and they are used as part of the mentor coaching process. However, they are not a tool for coaching, and should not be used as a checklist or formula for passing a performance evaluation or, indeed, as a checklist for coaching. Details of the PCC markers can be found on the ICF website (ICF, 2019d).

ICF Code of Ethics

The ICF is committed to maintaining and promoting excellence in coaching. Therefore, the ICF expects all members and credentialed coaches (coaches, coach mentors, coaching supervisors, coach trainers, and students) to adhere to the elements and principles of ethical conduct – to be competent and integrate the ICF Core Competency Model (ICF, 2019b) effectively in their work.

In line with the ICF core values of integrity, excellence, collaboration and respect – and the ICF definition of coaching (ICF, 2007) – the Code of Ethics (ICF, 2019a) is designed to provide appropriate guidelines, accountability and enforceable standards of conduct for all ICF members and ICF credential-holders who commit to abiding by that code.

The following chapters in this section will take each domain and competency in turn and provide an overview of that competency. In addition, we hope to bring the competencies to life in a practical way with examples and descriptions to help illustrate the essence of each competency and how they come together in a great coaching conversation. Finally, Chapter 33: Progressing Your Coaching Skills outlines some of the differences between ACC-, PCC- and MCC-level coaching, and Chapter 28: Continuing Professional Development shares many ways you can grow as a coach and develop your skills toward these credentials.

Conclusion

In this opening chapter for Section 2, we have introduced the background to the ICF's core competency model and the associated system for becoming credentialed as a coach at the three levels of ACC, PCC and MCC. Coaching is still a relatively 'young' profession, with the concept, definition and application of coaching evolving organically. We therefore also highlighted the key changes that emerged from the ICF's job analysis, which reflect the skills and actions of an effective coach in today's environment. The subsequent chapters in this section will offer a more in-depth exploration of what is intended by each competency and how they are demonstrated in coaching practice.

Chapter 6: Foundation Domain, Competency 1. Demonstrates Ethical Practice

The Foundation Domain is focused on how coaches should conduct themselves while coaching and in all interactions with related individuals. From a broader competency-development view, the competencies within the foundation domain would be considered a set of coach-focused competencies (i.e., describing who the coach 'is' and the 'being' of the coach), whereas the other three domains are focused on coaches' behaviour (i.e., what the coach 'does'). In the job analysis process, these two perspectives are typically framed as 'worker'-focused vs. 'work'-focused, respectively.

This domain has two competencies (Demonstrates Ethical Practice and Embodies a Coaching Mindset), the essence of which seek to highlight the level of professionalism that is expected from an ICF-credentialed coach. This professionalism is considered to be foundational to the coaching practice, upon which the competencies sit and are applied. The professionalism implied within this domain also particularly embraces two of the ICF core values: integrity and excellence.

Starting with this domain, we see straight away that good coaching is about much more than demonstrating a skill set; it is also about genuinely and consistently demonstrating a mindset that informs how we approach our work as professionals and also how we tend to operate as human beings. In this chapter we will look at the first of these two competencies, Demonstrates Ethical Practice, and address the competency of Embodies a Coaching Mindset in Chapter 7.

> **Box 6.1: Competency 1: Demonstrates Ethical Practice**
>
> Definition: Understands and consistently applies coaching ethics and standards.
> 1. Demonstrates personal integrity and honesty in interactions with clients, sponsors, and relevant stakeholders.
> 2. Is sensitive to clients' identity, environment, experiences, values, and beliefs.
> 3. Uses language appropriate and respectful to clients, sponsors and relevant stakeholders.
> 4. Abides by the ICF Code of Ethics and upholds the core values.
> 5. Maintains confidentiality with client information per stakeholder agreements and pertinent laws.
> 6. Maintains the distinctions between coaching, consulting, psychotherapy, and other support professions.
> 7. Refers clients to other support professionals, as appropriate.

Ethical practice, as defined within the ICF Code of Ethics (ICF, 2019a), is considered to be the foundation of the coaching relationship. Understanding the code and its consistent application is required for all levels of coaching and the standard for demonstrating a strong ethical grasp of coaching is similar and rigorous for all levels of ICF credentialing. In addition, this competency highlights seven sub-competencies for specific attention.

1. Demonstrates personal integrity and honesty in interactions with clients, sponsors and relevant stakeholders

This sub-competency is considered of paramount importance and is an overarching statement about how a coach is expected to behave, not just in a coaching session but generally as a practitioner in the profession of coaching. The scope of this expectation goes beyond the client and is extended to the sponsor of the coaching engagement and, indeed, all stakeholders. A sponsor is defined as "an individual (or entity), usually within an organization, who has a vested interest in a client's progress in coaching, is actively promoting the use of coaching for this individual and is likely providing funds for the coaching". A stakeholder is defined as "an individual (or entity), usually within an organization, who has an interest in a client's progress through coaching". These could be, for example, HR representatives, a broker who has arranged for the coaching engagement, or any number of other relevant third parties. The message here is simply that coaches are expected to operate with an intention of integrity and honesty at all times and this is exemplified in all sections of the Code of Ethics.

2. Is sensitive to clients' identity, environment, experiences, values, and beliefs

Sensitivity to these aspects of the client's being implies that the coach has several important qualities. The coach's capacity to be inclusive, non-judgmental, unbiased, and empathetic in their work with the client is paramount. In addition, the coach's ability to understand the effect of these elements on the client, the coaching work and the coaching relationship are significant. In this way, the coach engages and works with the client as a whole person and not just the coaching goals and topics they bring into sessions. As human nature leads us to judge and hold bias as part of our own moral, ethical or behavioural compass, self-reflection and self-regulation are important aspects of how a coach consistently demonstrates their integrity and honesty. For example, here are some questions for reflection:

- How do my own religious/spiritual beliefs have an impact on my coaching?
- How do they align (or not) with the beliefs of my client?
- What impact does our alignment/misalignment have on our coaching relationship and the coaching process?
- Is that helpful or unhelpful to the coaching relationship?
- How do I respond if my client shares a particularly traumatic experience?
- How is my response impacted if I have no frame of reference whatsoever for that experience?
- How is my response impacted if I have a strong frame of reference for that experience?
- Perhaps I have had a similar experience; is it possible that I might 'over-empathize'?
- How do I ensure that I stay present, open and sensitive when my own beliefs, perspectives, views and/or experiences are different or contrary to those of my client?
- How does my own 'view of the world' have an impact on my coaching?
- How fixed is my view?
- How do my own identity, environment, experiences, values and beliefs have an impact on my coaching, both generally and with my clients?

The reflective practice of coaching supervision is a useful and powerful resource for coaches to check-in and self-regulate around these qualities. The Code of Ethics also indicates that part of our integrity and honesty means seeking professional support if we feel unable to display these qualities with a given client and even to terminate the coaching relationship if we feel unable to resolve any differences or misalignment that might be present. You can read and learn more about the process and practice of coaching supervision in Chapter 29.

3. Uses language appropriate and respectful to clients, sponsors and relevant stakeholders

The inter-relation between these seven sub-competencies is hopefully already becoming apparent and, in this one, we see how our honesty and integrity – along with our ability to display qualities of sensitivity and inclusivity – can be exemplified in our language. The language of a coach is intended to strike a delicate and subtle balance between being considered and intentional, as well as spontaneous and intuitive, and at all times respectful toward all parties. This item is also an example of how the ICF core value of respect is contained within the code of ethics and competency model.

In order to use appropriate and respectful language, the first question is: do I know what is appropriate and respectful? This takes us back to the previous sub-competency and highlights why having awareness of and sensitivity to the client's identity and environment is important. Furthermore, we argue that attitude is of equal – if not more – importance than identity. For example, a coach may be aware of and sensitive to someone's identity; however, it is their attitude toward this identity that will inform how they engage with and coach the person, thereby informing the language they use and the behaviours they display in the coaching context. You will see more on attitude and the coach's 'mindset' in the next chapter.

4. Abides by the ICF Code of Ethics

The ICF Code of Ethics is considered core knowledge for coaching and is described in full in the appendices section; however, here is the purpose and an overview of the code:

To elicit the best in every ICF coach, ICF members and coaches are expected to commit to:

- Ethical behaviour as the foundation of the coaching profession.
- Continued learning in the field of coaching as required.
- Search for continued self-awareness, self-monitoring and self-improvement.
- Acting and being an ethical individual in all professional interactions.
- Full accountability for the responsibility undertaken as an ICF member and coach.

- Complete engagement with and commitment to the coaching profession, setting an example both to the profession overall and to the community.
- Uphold the highest standards in a manner that reflects positively on the coaching profession.
- Be fully present in every interaction in which we engage.
- Recognize and abide by the applicable laws and regulations of each country, municipality and local governing body.
- Provide a safe space for trainers, service providers, coaches and coaches-in-training to learn, excel ethically and strive to become professional coaches of the highest caliber.
- Embrace diversity and inclusion, and value the richness of our global stakeholders.

The importance of the ICF Code of Ethics is exemplified by the fact that it is part of the curriculum of ICF-accredited coach-specific training programmes, as well as the work that a coach completes with their mentor–coach prior to applying for their credential (and credential renewal at ACC level). The ICF also offers a complimentary online course on ethics and one of the ICF Communities of Practice (also complimentary to ICF members) is dedicated to ethical discussions and development.

Ethics are closely linked to personal morals and values. In many cases ethical decisions are not 'black and white' but instead multiple shades of grey. The ethical code provides a foundation from which to work, but a reflective mindset and process of inquiry is vital when it comes to thinking through ethical dilemmas that occur in practice. To help with this, in 2010 Liora Rosen, then Chair of the ICF Ethics Education Sub-Committee, developed a simple ethical review checklist (Figure 6.1).

Figure 6.1: Ethical Review Checklist

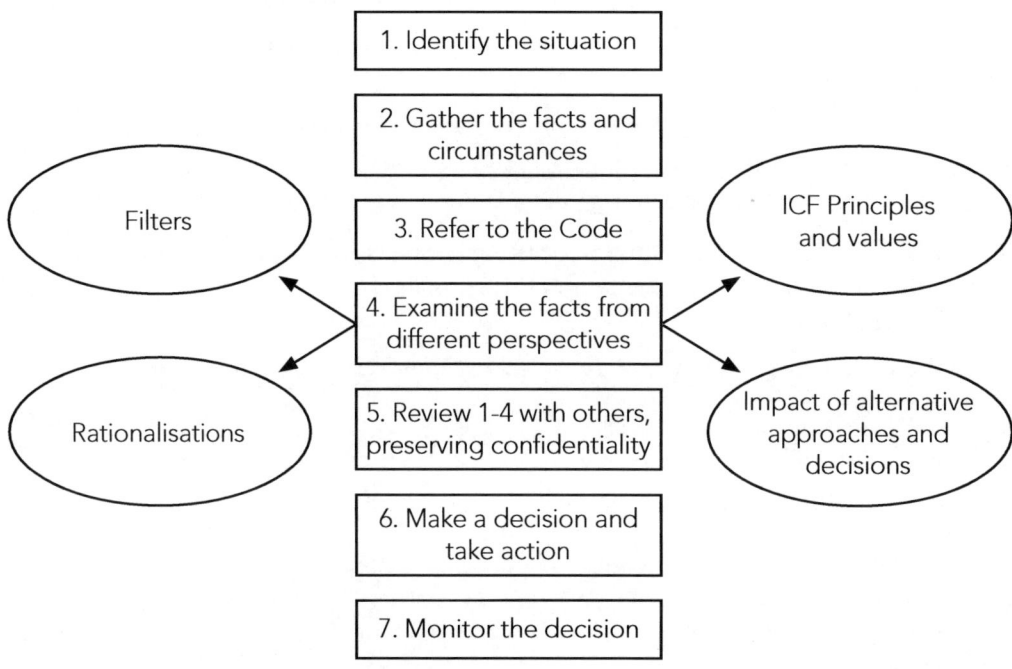

1. Identify the situation
2. Gather the facts and circumstances
3. Refer to the Code
4. Examine the facts from different perspectives
   - Filters
   - Rationalisations
   - ICF Principles and values
   - Impact of alternative approaches and decisions
5. Review 1-4 with others, preserving confidentiality
6. Make a decision and take action
7. Monitor the decision

The steps themselves are self-explanatory; however, Step 4 is worthy of some further narrative. This step involves exploring four distinct perspectives, the first of which is 'filters'. In this context, 'filters' refer to a wide range of sources of reference that we draw upon when making judgments and decisions about something. These filters can include (and are not limited to) references relating to our culture, ethnicity, religion, education, gender, age, geographic location and socioeconomic background, as well as our own needs, values, feelings and motives associated with the ethical issue in question. The nature and influence of these filters will inform how we perceive a particular issue or situation.

The second perspective is 'rationalizations', and this refers to the fact that it is human nature to support something that reinforces our own stance, attitudes, beliefs and values, etc. When considering this alongside the filters we use as our own personal and unique sources of reference or 'moral compass', we find that our biases (conscious and unconscious) inevitably play a part in how we judge a situation. For this reason, the model advocates the consideration of two further perspectives, as well as discussing the situation with others (Step 5) to gain a range of other inputs in service of a fair and objective review.

The third perspective is to reflect upon the ICF core values of integrity, excellence, collaboration and respect, and the extent to which they have been honoured or breached within the issue under consideration. The final perspective is to explore the feasibility and impact of some alternative approaches to the situation, in order to identify a possible way forward.

One of the best ways to learn and understand more about the ICF Code of Ethics is through discussion. By taking ethical scenarios and considering the steps in this checklist, a thought-provoking conversation with colleagues can highlight how our approach to such scenarios is likely to be influenced by our own experiences, values, beliefs and biases (conscious and/or unconscious).

Box 6.2 is an ethical case study for reflection.

Box 6.2: Ethical Case Study

One morning Joe, with whom you've been working for several months, arrives at your coaching meeting late, looking and sounding very serious and stressed. At first, he was tight-lipped, sharing only that he was extremely busy and under a lot of pressure to meet deadlines.

Suddenly he divulged that he was in trouble. There had been a significant error in quoting a price to a customer. He knew it would take hours of his time to get to the bottom of exactly how and why the error had occurred. As he felt pressured for time, he had simply assured the customer that he would not be financially penalised in any way and that Joe's organisation would absorb the financial costs of the error.

The next day in a meeting with the executive leadership team, the executives decided that the company would refuse to absorb any of the costs of the error and that the customer would be required to absorb the loss. The executives were unaware of the promise that Joe had made to the customer.

Joe feels trapped. The culture in the client's organization is to take time and care with such proposals and they therefore have less tolerance for rash mistakes and last-minute changes in direction or actions. His organization has a fast-paced and even 'aggressive' culture and decisions are made and changed frequently.

He wants your help deciding on a course of action. Your coaching conversation hardly began when he immediately settled on his solution: "I'm going to lie. I'm going to hide the numbers and somehow cover this thing up. It's my only way out."

As the coach of other managers for the same company, you've heard complaints about Joe not being honest in all of his business dealings and you have developed a close business relationship with the HR manager who is responsible for administering the coaching programme.

Although you feel confident that you have navigated confidentiality issues well up until this point, this situation is testing your agreements on confidentiality.

Here are some questions you might take a few minutes to consider:

- What is the ethical dilemma?
- What elements of the code does this refer to?
- What is your recommendation for resolution?
- Which aspects of the ethical review checklist most informed your thinking?

Here are some thoughts and references from the ICF Code of Ethics that could inform the ethical discussion and decision-making around this particular case study:

Part Four: Ethical Standards

Section I – Responsibility to Clients

Item 2: Create an agreement/contract regarding the roles, responsibilities and rights of all parties involved with my client(s) and sponsor(s) prior to the commencement of services.

- Who is the sponsor in this situation, and do you have a coaching service agreement with them?
- If so, what is your responsibility in honouring that agreement?

Item 3: Maintain the strictest levels of confidentiality with all parties as agreed upon. I am aware of and agree to comply with all applicable laws that pertain to personal data and communications.

- Has Joe broken the law?
- What type of breach does his lying imply, if any?
- What does your client's organization state about lying or misrepresentation of data, etc. in their company policy?
- Does this situation constitute a breach of their company 'law'?

Item 4: Have a clear understanding about how information is exchanged among all parties involved during all coaching interactions.

- What have you contracted for in the tripartite coaching service agreement around the exchange of information?

Item 5: Have a clear understanding with both clients and sponsors or interested parties about the conditions under which information will not be kept confidential (e.g., illegal activity, if required by law, pursuant to valid court order or subpoena; imminent or likely risk of danger to self or to others; etc.). Where I reasonably believe one of the above circumstances is applicable, I may need to inform appropriate authorities.

- If Joe lying does constitute an appropriate reason for you to breach your pledge of confidentiality, have you outlined this in your coaching service agreement and did Joe (and the sponsor) knowingly agree to that limit of confidentiality?

Section II – Responsibility to Practice and Performance

As an ICF Professional, I:
Item 17: Recognize my personal limitations or circumstances that may impair, conflict with or interfere with my coaching performance or my professional coaching relationships. I will reach out for support to determine the action to be taken and, if necessary, promptly seek relevant professional guidance. This may include suspending or terminating my coaching relationship(s).

You have heard complaints about Joe's honesty and you have a close business relationship with the HR manager responsible for administering the coaching programme.

- Is this enough to constitute a 'personal issue'?
- Do you have a bias (conscious or unconscious) toward Joe based upon what you have heard?
- Does the closeness of your relationship with the HR Manager impact how you view Joe and this situation?
- Is any of this enough to impair your performance as a coach in this situation?

At this stage Joe has not yet lied; he is talking about his decision to lie. How does that impact this situation and your potential response? Finally, are there any other parts of the Code of Ethics that you feel could be relevant or inform your thinking about this type of scenario?

In most cases, ethical breaches by coaches are the result of simple mistakes or lack of awareness, consideration or knowledge as opposed to deliberate or intentional breaches. What is important is that coaches take care to consider ethical matters within their coaching practice and also feel supported by sources of reference and guidance. Peer group discussions, communities of practice and special interest groups are all potential sources of such support (remembering that client and sponsor confidentiality need to be maintained while such discussions are being held). Ethical dilemmas and questions are also ideally placed to be taken into a conversation with a coaching supervisor as part of the coach's ongoing practice management and professional development. The ICF offers a mechanism for complaints about individuals or programmes to be reviewed, which is the Ethical Conduct Review Process and Programme Complaint Process. These are handled by the Independent Review Board (IRB).

In Chapter 23 we offer an alternative model to review ethical decisions; the APPEAR model (Passmore & Turner, 2018). Such models are useful heuristics to guide you through what can be difficult and challenging processes of managing ethical dilemmas and encourage you to think more widely and take account of the individual and unique circumstances in each case, as we seek to balance the needs of our client, the organization and our own moral, legal and contractual responsibilities.

5. Maintains confidentiality with client information per stakeholder agreements and pertinent laws

Confidentiality has always been an important feature of a coaching relationship and has been further highlighted as a paramount characteristic and frequently used task in the latest and current ICF Core Coaching Competency Model. To that end, it is raised several times within the ICF Code of Ethics (Box 6.3).

Box 6.3: Extracts from the ICF Code of Ethics

Part 2: KEY DEFINITIONS:
'Confidentiality'— protection of any information obtained around the coaching engagement unless consent to release is given.

Part 4: ETHICAL STANDARDS
Section I – Responsibility to Clients

Item 3: Maintain the strictest levels of confidentiality with all parties as agreed upon. I am aware of and agree to comply with all applicable laws that pertain to personal data and communications.

Item 5: Have a clear understanding with both clients and sponsors or interested parties about the conditions under which information will not be kept confidential (e.g., illegal activity, if required by law, pursuant to valid court order or subpoena; imminent or likely risk of danger to self or to others; etc.). Where I reasonably believe one of the above circumstances is applicable, I may need to inform appropriate authorities. →

> *Item 7: Maintain, store and dispose of any records, including electronic files and communications, created during my professional interactions in a manner that promotes confidentiality, security and privacy and complies with any applicable laws and agreements. Furthermore, I seek to make proper use of emerging and growing technological developments that are being used in coaching services (technology assisted coaching services) and be aware how various ethical standards apply to them.*
>
> **Section II – Responsibility to Practice and Performance**
>
> *Item 19: Maintain the privacy of ICF members and use of the ICF member contact information (email addresses, telephone numbers, and so on) only as authorized by ICF or the ICF member.*

(ICF, 2019a)

A couple of points are worthy of further emphasis. The phrase 'maintain strictest levels of confidentiality' means that a coach must take all steps possible to ensure that the content of the coaching conversations stays only between the coach and the client. This means taking great care with any coaching notes that may have been taken, ensuring they are unseen by others and are anonymized wherever possible. It also means taking care with any client data that may be stored on a laptop, iPad or other electronic equipment so that it is safe and secure.

Confidentiality also means not verbally sharing content from the coaching conversations with others. Here are a couple of examples of how this can be navigated:

- You might bump into your client's manager in the corridor and they ask how the coaching is going. It would not be appropriate to share any update without the client's clear, prior agreement. This is an important aspect of the tripartite contracting conversation when reporting, updating and confidentiality should be discussed and agreed. Moreover, we also recommend that it is, in fact, the client who does any updating and reporting. Direct updating between the client and the line manager allows for their workplace relationship to stay intact and also keeps the boundary of accountability for and within the relationship clear and separate from the coach.

- You want to discuss a client case with your supervisor. Part of your contracting process with your client should include sharing that you engage with a supervisor as part of your ongoing professional development. Your client should be informed that this means some client content may be discussed; however, the identity of the client is always kept confidential and the supervisor is also bound by the same Code of Ethics and confidentiality boundaries.

- You want to record or transcribe your client session so that you can use the recording for mentoring or assessment purpose. Once again, this should be contracted for with your client, who would need to give their permission for their session to be used for these purposes.

- You work with a virtual assistant (VA) who helps you schedule appointments, etc. The VA also needs to adhere to the Code of Ethics and the client informed of this as part of the contracting process. A tip here is that, when contracting with the VA, you share and ask them to sign a copy of the Code of Ethics so that you have that on file as part of your contracting documentation with them.

Although it is not stipulated in the competency model or the Code of Ethics that coaching agreements and contracts must be in writing, we highly recommend that they are. Documenting the key elements of your coaching engagement and then asking each party to sign that agreement is good professional practice. In this way, all parties are clear about what is expected of them and what their part is in the coaching engagement.

What is perhaps striking about these points is that, in most cases, the vehicle for addressing them professionally is the coaching agreement or contract. When teaching coaching students, we often hear ourselves say "all roads lead to the contract" and in many ways this is true. Thorough contracting is the key to setting a great foundation to the coaching engagement. We will take a closer look at coaching agreements in Competency 3; however, a final note worth making here is that confidentiality also links to privacy. Data privacy regulation is now much more rigorous and therefore it is important that a coach ensures they are complying with requirements such as the EU's General Data Protection Regulation (GDPR) and other data privacy requirements around the world. This must be made clear to clients and other stakeholders in all types of interactions.

6. Maintains the distinctions between coaching, consulting, psychotherapy and other support professions

In a credential application, a coach will pass this aspect of the competency if they engage in a coaching conversation that is focused on enquiry and exploration and based on present and future issues.

A pass would not be awarded if the coach focuses primarily on telling the client what to do or how to do it (consulting mode) or if the conversation is based primarily in the past, particularly the emotional past (therapeutic mode).
In addition, the ICF notes that if an applicant is not clear on basic foundation exploration and evoking skills that underlie the ICF definition of coaching, this

lack of clarity in skill use will be reflected in the skill level demonstrated in some other core competencies. For example, if a coach almost exclusively gives advice or indicates that a particular answer chosen or suggested by the coach is what the client should do, then trust and safety, coaching presence, powerful questioning, evoking awareness, and client-generated ideas/actions and accountability will also not be present and a credential application, at any level, would be unsuccessful.

7. Refers clients to other support professionals, as appropriate

As well as maintaining the distinctions between coaching, consulting, psychotherapy and other support professions, a coach must know when and how to refer their client to another support professional and take appropriate action. As always, thorough contracting at the beginning of an engagement is the best way to proactively establish clarity around what is and is not being offered within the coaching relationship and coaching service. This helps mitigate against confusion or misunderstanding and thereby potentially avoids the need for referral.

However, sometimes the coaching process uncovers information, requirements, expectations and circumstances that mean a different way of working would be more useful to the client. A couple of examples of this are mentoring and counselling or psychotherapy.

Sometimes clients engage with a coach when what they actually want is mentoring. It may be that their requirement is more one of receiving information, advice, guidance, ideas and strategies than one of exploring their own thoughts, feelings and behaviours to find their own solution to an issue or a goal. The first thing to consider is whether there is a difference between what they want and what they need. A client may want the coach to offer them solutions and answers because that is perhaps easier than working it out for themselves. In this case, the coach may encourage, partner with and even challenge the client to reflect for themselves in order to find their own solution, thereby staying in the role of coach.

However, it may be that what the client actually needs is indeed mentoring and there may have been a misunderstanding or miscommunication of the service being offered at the contracting stage. This is an example of when the coach may propose that a different way of working might be more useful to the client and explore with them their options for engaging with a mentor.

Interestingly, this is not as clear as it might appear, and it is not always a simple case of either coaching or mentoring. The reality is that many coaches wear a number of different hats: coach, mentor, trainer, facilitator, etc. as part of their professional portfolio. This means that, in practice, some coaches offer a blended service. From an ICF perspective, this is a perfectly acceptable way of working as long as two important criteria are met:

1. It is not appropriate to use an example of a blended service when submitting a client session recording for ICF assessment purposes. The assessment process is to establish that the coach understands and can apply the core coaching competencies and stay in coaching mode. Submitting a recording where the coach more than occasionally steps out of coaching mode is likely to fail an assessment.

2. When logging client hours for ICF credentialing and renewal purposes, the coach must only log those hours that have been contracted for and provided as coaching, and not those where a blended service was provided.

The other key area for potential referral is when counselling or therapy is more appropriate for the client. There may be a time when the client demonstrates certain behaviours or shares certain information or perspectives that indicate that another form of professional service or resource might be more appropriate and useful to the client. This is referenced in the ICF Code of Ethics under Part 3, Section I – Responsibility to Clients, Item 8: "Remain alert to indications that there might be a shift in the value received from the coaching relationship. If so, make a change in the relationship or encourage the client(s)/sponsor(s) to seek another coach, seek another professional or use a different resourc". Guidance on when and how to refer clients to therapy can be found in an ICF white paper *Referring a Client to Therapy: A set of guidelines* (Hullinger & DiGirolamo, 2018).

Some aspects of this competency are not directly assessed during a performance evaluation; in fact, it is more the absence of this competency that would indicate a non-pass result. When an assessor reviews a recorded coaching conversation as part of a credential application, there are two key disqualifiers, which are:

1. If the coach displays a clear ethical breach (i.e., of the ICF Code of Ethics); and/or
2. If the coach more than occasionally steps into a role other than that of coach (e.g., counsellor, consultant, teacher, trainer).

Conclusion

This chapter has introduced the Foundation Domain of the ICF Core Competency Model and the first competency: Demonstrates Ethical Practice. We have shared the competency definition and its sub-competencies and explored the essential elements and expectations for each one. We have seen how this competency places significant emphasis on integrity, professionalism, confidentiality and ethical conduct. Some of the factors that underpin a person's ethical platform have been described and an ethical case study was analyzed to highlight some of the many and varied considerations to take into account when faced with an ethical scenario. This case study has also been used to identify where the ICF Code of Ethics can assist in navigating and informing an ethical query. The code was shown to be a highly useful source of reference and guidance for coaches as part of our professional coaching practice. We have also included an ethical review checklist that offers simple guidelines on how to review and consider thoroughly an ethical scenario, its implications, and its possible solutions.

Chapter 7: Foundation Domain, Competency 2. Embodies a Coaching Mindset

The second competency in the Foundation Domain is Embodies a Coaching Mindset. This is a new competency that emerged from the most recent coaching job analysis conducted by the ICF, as well as a qualitative study of coaches' learning journeys completed by the ICF Academic Research team. Many of the core coaching tasks, knowledge and attitudes identified in the job analysis process included aspects of reflective practice (e.g., reflection, awareness and self-regulation). This has been identified and emphasized as critical 'self-work' that coaches must engage in.

The competency is described in Box 7.1.

> **Box 7.1: Competency 2: Embodies a Coaching Mindset**
>
> Definition: Develops and maintains a mindset that is open, curious, flexible and client-centered.
> 1. Acknowledges that clients are responsible for their own choices.
> 2. Engages in ongoing learning and development as a coach.
> 3. Develops an ongoing reflective practice to enhance one's coaching.
> 4. Remains aware of and open to the influence of context and culture on self and others.
> 5. Uses awareness of self and one's intuition to benefit clients.
> 6. Develops and maintains the ability to regulate one's emotions.
> 7. Mentally and emotionally prepares for sessions.
> 8. Seeks help from outside sources when necessary.

(ICF, 2019b)

A 'coaching mindset' is considered of sufficient importance to be a competency in its own right and is a key part of describing the coach's 'way of being'. In practice, it should be noticeably evident throughout the way the coach works with their client and other relevant parties. We note that, when an individual learns and is able to practice coaching skills, a transformation frequently occurs wherein the individual embodies these skills – they become an inherent part of the individual's personality and are consciously or unconsciously used in conversations throughout their daily lives. As such, a coaching mindset might be part of how the coach demonstrates all of the other competencies within this framework. As with Competency 1, Demonstrates Ethical Practice, the theme emerges once again that qualities such as professionalism, integrity, honesty and a coaching mindset are foundational to good coaching practice.

This competency is specifically outlined through eight sub-competencies:

1. Acknowledges that clients are responsible for their own choices.

This sub-competency immediately focuses on the fact that coaching is client-centered. Partnership and equality are important themes within the overall competency framework. However, within those principles there is also a clear intention and expectation that it is the client who sets the agenda and direction of the coaching work. The client is also responsible for generating their own ideas, actions and next steps. This acknowledgment is probably initiated right at the beginning of the coaching engagement when the coach explains to the client (and any other relevant parties) what coaching is, is not, and how it is different from other ways of working.

This type of acknowledgment continues throughout the coaching process and shows up in other competencies. Examples of this include when the coach:

- partners with the client in the creation of coaching agreements (Competency 3: Establishes and Maintains Agreements)
- demonstrates respect for and acknowledges the client's perceptions, suggestions and work in the coaching process (Competency 4: Cultivates Trust and Safety)
- invites the client to generate forward-moving ideas (Competency 7: Evokes Awareness)
- partners with the client to design goals, actions and accountability methods
- acknowledges and supports the client's autonomy in doing so (Competency 8: Facilitates Client Growth).

Some practical examples of the many things a coach might ask to evidence this sub-competency are:

- "What would you like to focus on today?"
- "How would you like to approach this?"
- "What are your options?"
- "What do you think?"
- "What will you do now?"
- "How do you feel about doing that?"
- "How committed do you feel about this?"
- "What will you do to ensure you that you honour your commitment?"

In practice, therefore, although the coach may explore, enquire, invite, notice, ask and challenge, these activities are done in complete service of empowering the client to take responsibility for themselves and, as per the ICF definition of coaching, be inspired to maximize their personal and professional potential.

2. Engages in ongoing learning and development as a coach.

Ongoing learning and development are fundamental to the ICF's philosophy of coaching. As outlined in Chapter 5, the renewable characteristic of an ICF credential underpins a proactive and intentional commitment to continuing professional development activities, which maintains and further develops the coach's knowledge, skills, attitudes and behaviours as a professional practitioner.

The credential renewal process requires that all coaches complete at least 40 hours of Continuing Coach Education across each three-year period that their credential is valid. This education is described on the ICF website and can come in various forms, including:

- ICF-approved training.
- Other training.
- Self-paced courses and other self-study.
- Mentor coaching.
- Coaching supervision.
- Research and teaching.

For those coaches who want to renew their credential at the ACC level, part of this development must include at least 10 hours of mentor coaching so it is clear that the coach is still fully understanding and applying the core competencies. At least three hours of development in coaching ethics is also required for coaches renewing their credential at any level, thereby re-emphasizing the importance of ethical practice and professional conduct. Learning and development opportunities are available from ICF Chapters and ICF-accredited training schools, such as the Henley Centre for Coaching and also via the ICF's Learning Portal. This ongoing learning and development is considered a core task and activity, as it is an important part of the 'self-work' coaches must undertake in order to better serve their clients.

From a practical perspective, taking a proactive approach to this requirement is highly recommended. We can count many, many examples of when a coach has approached us because their three-year credential period expires within the next couple of months and they are suddenly trying to complete 40+ hours of development. Not only is there an expectation of intentionality within the credentialing process, it is also much easier to complete this development in a meaningful and cost-effective way when it is planned ahead across the three-year periods. It is also this concept of intentionality that supports the self-work and ongoing learning that is at the heart of a 'coaching mindset'.

3. Develops an ongoing reflective practice to enhance one's coaching.

Reflective practice has been identified as a specific and significant activity within the area of ongoing learning and development as outlined in the sub-competency above. For these purposes, reflective practice includes three core tasks of reflection, awareness and self-regulation. Some forms of reflective practice are:

- Coaching supervision (see Chapter 29).
- Peer group reflection.
- Journaling.
- Mentor coaching.
- Observed coaching practice followed by debrief and feedback.
- Listening to recordings of client work.

As described in Competency 7, Evokes Awareness, the coach is facilitating client insight and learning for their client. In this case, the coach is role modeling this behaviour for their own insight and learning. Self-regulation can take several forms, including:

- managing one's own emotions within the coaching process
- the use of one's own intuition
- staying in coaching mode
- managing one's own inclination to tell, suggest, judge or 'fix' the client.

4. Remains aware of and open to the influence of context and culture on self and others.

A key area addressed within this sub-competency is that of bias – specifically, biases that a coach may bring into the coaching process and also the biases that clients may have regarding the coaching work and coaching process. Part of the coaching mindset, therefore, is for the coach to stay conscious to the possible (and probable) presence of biases (of self or others) and how this might influence and impact the work undertaken.

In practical terms, this can be evidenced by the coach owning, acknowledging, sharing and checking their own possible assumptions about the client and/or the work. For example:

- "I realize I am making an assumption here; however, I am wondering if…"
- "I'd like to check my thinking with you here. Is…?"
- "Please challenge or correct me if I'm wrong; however, you seem to me to…"
- "Tell me if this doesn't land, but I was thinking that perhaps…"

This sub-competency may also be demonstrated by the coach enquiring about or challenging the client's assumptions; this links closely to some aspects of other competencies, which will be explored in each relevant case. However, as far as the coach's biases are concerned, another important and valuable way to explore and address these is through the process of reflective practice, as noted in the previous sub-competency.

5. Uses awareness of self and one's intuition to benefit clients.

The use of intuition in the coaching process is considered very important and is also a skill to be carefully balanced and managed. Research on the use of intuition shows a vast range of results, from highly flawed to remarkably accurate, and still intuition can light a creative spark. Using intuition with careful judgment and good sense, along with a lack of attachment to one's own sharing, may well stimulate client awareness or learning.

The coach can share their intuition with the client in several ways, including:

- "I have a hunch that…"
- "I'm feeling a strong sense of [XYZ]; what do you think or feel about that?"
- "It strikes me that…"

6. Develops and maintains the ability to regulate one's emotions.

This links to sub-competency 2.3 and reflective practice is considered a valuable vehicle for regulating one's emotions. Reference to working effectively and appropriately with the client's emotions will be further explored in the chapters focused on Competency 5, Maintains Presence, and Competency 6, Listens Actively. However, in order to work effectively with our client's emotions, we must first be aware of our own and how to self-manage and self-regulate in such a way that our emotions do not get in the way of the client or the coaching process. In coaching supervision, this is sometimes called "where the personal intrudes on the professional" – you can read more about this in Chapter 29.

We will all bring a particular emotional 'state' to the coaching session, based upon how we feel at that time, and our emotions may also be influenced by what the client brings into the session. Our ability to regulate our emotions can change from moment to moment; we are expected to be mindful of this and continuously check our own responses and reactions to ensure that our emotions are not entering the process in an unhelpful way.

The self-awareness that develops as a result of ongoing learning, development and reflective practice is a useful quality that enables us to regulate our emotions. Some examples of when we might need to regulate our emotions are:

- You have a client who is really excited about Christmas and passionate about preparing for the festivities. What if your own relationship with Christmas is not so positive and you find it a period of sadness, loss or disappointment? How will you regulate your own reactions, responses and biases?

- Your client shares that they are getting divorced and you have just recently experienced a painful and acrimonious divorce yourself. How will you make sure that your own emotional experience does not creep into your coaching practice?

- Your client shares their excitement about an upcoming trip, which is the same trip you went on the previous year and was the most amazing experience of your life. How will you regulate your emotions so that your own 'story' does not take over the client's space?

If we are unable for any reason to regulate our emotions, it may even be appropriate to stop working with that client or suspend our coaching practice for a period of time. For example, if we are going through a challenging time – or the client brings up a topic that is particularly triggering and sensitive for us – we could simply be unable to sufficiently self-manage and be present for others. This is something that ideally should be explored with a coaching supervisor and is also addressed in the

ICF Code of Ethics in Part Four: Ethical Standards, Section II – Responsibility to Practice and Performance.

As an ICF professional, I:

Item 17: Recognize my personal limitations or circumstances that may impair, conflict with, or interfere with my coaching performance or my professional coaching relationships. I will reach out for support to determine the action to be taken and, if necessary, promptly seek relevant professional guidance. This may include suspending or terminating my coaching relationship(s).

7. Mentally and emotionally prepares for sessions.

This aspect really helps to bring Competency 2 together, as it highlights a practice that enables us to tap into our optimal coaching state or mindset. It draws upon all of the above aspects of this competency by consciously and intentionally preparing for our client work. This is an ongoing process, which is part of our continuous professional and personal development, but is also a specific activity in readiness for each coaching session. Output from the competency review process and also ICF research into how coaches spend their time highlight that good coaches demonstrate this practice.

Such preparation can take on different forms and will vary based upon the personal preferences of the coach. This could include activities such as going for a walk, taking some exercise, meditating, sitting quietly and reflection. We might also consider examples of when and how the coach can access their optimal coaching mindset:

- Are there days of the week or times of the day when the coach is 'at their best'?
- How many clients can the coach engage with in one day and still be fresh, professional, present and available for each one?
- How much space between client engagements does the coach need in order to be fully prepared for their next client?

DiGirolamo, Rogers and Heink (2016) wrote a useful paper on this topic.

8. Seeks help from outside sources when necessary.

The previous elements of this competency are designed to support the development of a good coaching mindset. However, we have already seen some examples of when and how our mindset could be impaired in a way that is not helpful to our client or the coaching process. In these cases, it is therefore important that a coach seeks the support needed to address this in whichever way is most appropriate. Coaching supervision is a useful source of support and is covered more in Chapter 29.

Conclusion

This chapter has introduced and outlined the new competency that has become part of the updated ICF Core Competency model. This addition underscores the importance of the being of the coach as well as the doing of coaching and the fact that our role as a coach extends beyond our direct interaction with our client and other stakeholders. We have explored each of the sub competencies and how they in turn link directly to and are in support of our ability to evidence other competencies within the model. We have also highlighted various ways that we can engage with and meet this competency as a valuable part of our ongoing development towards coaching maturity

Chapter 8: Co-Creating the Relationship Domain, Competency 3. Establishes and Maintains Agreements

This domain comprises the three competencies of 3. Establishes and Maintains Agreements, 4. Cultivates Trust and Safety, and 5. Listens Actively. It is a collection of competencies that relate to the logistics involved prior to and within coaching engagements and sessions, as well as those that lead to client growth and development.

This chapter focuses on Competency 3. Establishes and Maintains Agreements and positions three distinct levels of agreement as follows:

1. Agreements for the coaching relationship.
2. Agreements for the overall coaching plan and goals.
3. Agreements for the session goals and objectives.

These levels have emerged more formally in the most recent competency framework and reflect the ongoing development and maturity of the coaching process and profession.

> ### Box 8.1: Competency 3: Establishes and Maintains Agreements
>
> Definition: Partners with the client, and relevant stakeholders, to create clear agreements about the coaching relationship, process, plans and goals. Establishes agreements for the overall coaching engagement, as well as those for each coaching session.
>
> 1. Explains what coaching is and is not and describes the process to the client and relevant stakeholders.
> 2. Reaches agreement about what is and is not appropriate in the relationship, what is and is not being offered, and the responsibilities of the client and relevant stakeholders.
> 3. Reaches agreement about the guidelines and specific parameters of the coaching relationship such as logistics, fees, scheduling, duration, termination, confidentiality and inclusion of others.
> 4. Partners with the client and relevant stakeholders to establish an overall coaching plan and goals.
> 5. Partners with the client to determine client–coach compatibility.
> 6. Partners with the client to identify or reconfirm what they want to accomplish in the session.
> 7. Partners with the client to define what the client believes they need to address or resolve in order to achieve what they want to accomplish in the session.
> 8. Partners with the client to define or reconfirm measures of success for what the client wants to accomplish in the coaching engagement or individual session.
> 9. Partners with the client to manage the time and focus of the session.
> 10. Continues coaching in the direction of the client's desired outcome unless the client indicates otherwise.
> 11. Partners with the client to end the coaching relationship in a way that honours the experience.

(ICF, 2019b)

The fundamental purpose of this competency is to get clear agreement on the appropriateness and suitability of the coaching relationship and the work that is being done within that coach–client relationship for each session. The essential element of this competency is that the coach establishes and maintains agreement at all three levels.

Level 1: Agreements for the Coaching Relationship

- Explaining what coaching is and is not, and describing the process to the client and relevant stakeholders.

- Reaches agreement about what is and is not appropriate in the relationship, what is and is not being offered, and the responsibilities of the client and relevant stakeholders.
- Reaches agreement about the guidelines and specific parameters of the coaching relationship such as logistics, fees, scheduling, duration, termination, confidentiality and inclusion of others.
- Partnering with the client to determine client–coach compatibility.
- Partnering with the client to end the coaching relationship in a way that honours the experience.

Level 2: Agreements for the Overall Coaching Plan and Goals

- Partnering with the client and relevant stakeholders to establish an overall coaching plan and goals with associated measures of success for the coaching engagement.
- Establishing an understanding of the importance or significance of the coaching work and the client's commitment to the coaching engagement.
- Continuing the coaching in the direction of the client's desired outcome unless the client indicates otherwise.

In cases of coaching for and within organizations, when agreement is reached that coaching would likely provide positive results, agreements may be made between the coach and the organization for one or more engagements with specific or potential clients. In these cases, the discussions to reach agreement on some aspects of Levels 1 and 2 may be between the coach and the organization.

In cases where a coach engages with clients directly and an organization is not involved, the elements will be agreed upon directly between the coach and client. The activities undertaken at Levels 1 and 2 are often formalized into a written coaching 'contract', which is signed by the relevant parties involved.

Level 3: Agreements for the Session Goals and Objectives

Finally, in each session coaches frequently begin with an informal, verbal agreement regarding what will be covered in the session, including:

- Partnering with the client to identify or reconfirm what they want to accomplish in the session.
- Partnering with the client to define or reconfirm measures of success for what the client wants to accomplish in the individual session.
- Partnering with the client to define what the client believes they need to address or resolve in order to achieve what they want to accomplish in the session.

- Partners with the client to manage the time and focus of the session.
- Continuing the coaching in the direction of the client's desired outcome unless the client indicates otherwise.

One of the things we have noticed in our roles as coach trainers is that often this competency is not fully explored. It is the depth and extent to which the coach defines and explores the coaching agreement, and the client's desired outcome for the work, that is important. So let's now bring all of these guidelines and requirements together to get to the core of what is required for this competency. Levels 1 and 2 of Coaching Agreements focus on careful and thorough professional practice and are relatively self-explanatory. It is the competence a coach shows at Level 3 – i.e., establishing and maintaining the agreement during each coaching session – that is worthy of further exploration.

Newly trained coaches sometimes feel that they have to get to the goal of the coaching quickly so that they can get on with the 'real work' of coaching the client, and yet there is such rich territory in working more extensively and deeply with the client to understand what they want to achieve and why it is important to them. In fact, establishing the coaching agreement is something that can happen during the first half of a session, or can even take a full session to achieve clarity for the overall coaching engagement. This process does not have to be completed within the first few minutes of the conversation and, indeed, may also be revisited at any point throughout the session.

Although every coaching conversation is different and has its own unique trajectory and pace, a technique that we find useful when teaching this competency is to imagine a simple structure that holds true for any great story, book, report, project, essay or assignment – i.e., it has a beginning, a middle and an end. The same structure applies to coaching and it is important that all of these three phases are fully explored, for the extent to which we effectively work with one part will inevitably affect how we work with the other two. For example, thoroughly exploring the coaching agreement will undoubtedly inform the client – and therefore the coach – about the path the work might take. This structure also helps to establish the most appropriate path for the work to take and why, as well as identifying any potentially important surrounding circumstances, context or information that underpin the significance of the work for the client.

In addition, thoroughly exploring the coaching agreement also means that bringing the coaching conversation to a close and the next steps for the client will be enhanced by clearly knowing what it was that the client really wanted in the first place. In this way, you can both revisit that agreement to explore how the client will take this work forward into their life after the session in a way that maximizes their achievement of their goals and outcomes. We would even go so far as to say that it might be useful to spend a whole coaching session getting this foundational work done well, and a coach can evidence all of the core competencies within that process. Indeed, this is often a differentiator between beginner coaches and those who are more experienced and effective. Beginners tend to rush to get an agreement, whereas more experienced coaches understand the value of full exploration when developing agreements. Ultimately, our mantra is *'don't rush this!'*

Having established the need for thorough exploration of this competency, now let's look at some of the detail around how this can be done. The first thing we'd like to highlight here is the use of the words '… in the session' when describing certain aspects of this competency. When a client comes into a coaching session and the coach asks them what they would like to work on, it is quite possible that the client will begin to share information about something that they want to happen, achieve or change, etc., 'out there' in their life. Examples include:

- "I want to improve my relationship with my team"
- "I want to explore my next career move"
- "I want to be healthier"

Not only are these goals quite high level, they are also things that would ultimately come to fruition outside the coaching context as part of the client's daily life. Having understood what it is that the client wants to achieve 'out there', our role is then to explore the outcome from the piece of work that the client wants to accomplish in the coaching session. In this way, we not only know the 'out there' goal, we also now know the goal 'in here' for the piece of work that we will do together in the session.

This further exploration of goals not only helps to get clarity on the piece of coaching work, it also helps the client to consider really what it is that they want to achieve and work on. It is interesting how often the client may actually change or reframe the goal for the session based on important insights that may have arisen through this deeper enquiry. If we are working with a client for several sessions, we may have an overarching goal for the package of work (established in Level 1 or 2) but for each individual coaching session there would still be a specific desired outcome – the achievement of which brings them incrementally closer toward the overarching goal.

Another point to note is that, as with any process, sometimes the goal posts move and sometimes even the goal itself changes. For example, the coach is expected to notice if the direction of the conversation seems to have deviated from the client's originally stated goal, so that there is an opportunity to check in and either continue, change or realign that direction based upon what is most important or relevant to the client. The coach might say: "Now that this new area has emerged, what would be most useful to focus on?". Based upon these check-in opportunities, the coach should then continue the direction of the conversation in line with the client's desired outcome. A notable addition to the most recent description of this competency is the inclusion of the word 'maintains', which highlights this idea that agreements need to be revisited throughout the coaching engagement to ensure they are still relevant to the client and that the coaching is moving in the desired direction.

Defining measures of success is also a key aspect of this competency. Once again, this specifically relates to getting clarity on what the client wants to accomplish across the overall coaching engagement (Level 1 or 2) and then within each coaching session (Level 3). When the coaching engagement or session ends, how will they know that they have accomplished what they wanted? This is necessary for the client to feel a sense of achievement and progress. Also, where there is a sponsor (e.g., a line manager), it is a way of measuring the benefit of the coaching in terms of establishing a return on investment or a return on expectations for the work undertaken. As noted in the previous paragraph, there may be a need to reconfirm these measures if the goal or outcome for the session changes.

We then reach the part of this competency concerned with understanding the importance or meaning of the piece of work for the client. This is useful to establish for several reasons. This enquiry helps the client consider their level of motivation for and commitment to this topic. Understanding what it means to them also helps to demonstrate what difference this would make in their life if the issue were resolved or the goal were achieved. This in turn may highlight some of the client's values and the real reasons why this is an important conversation for them. This line of enquiry can also clarify the actual goal for the coaching session, if the client carefully considers what they want and why. This might be explored with questions such as:

- "What would it mean to you to resolve or achieve this?"
- "What is important for you in addressing this now?"
- "In achieving this, what would it lead to for you?"

The coach is expected to help the client consider what needs addressing to successfully achieve the session outcome. The analogy we suggest for this is planning a trip. We may decide that we want to travel from one part of the country to another and look at a route planner to consider how to get there. However, that planner is showing us a route and timings based on certain assumptions and averaged criteria. Therefore, do we simply head off on our way and hope for the best that we'll get there on time, with no challenges or interruptions? Or do we check what the weather forecast is or if there are any roadworks or other transport challenges, etc.? In the same way, the coach invites the client to consider any issues that might be relevant in service of the client's successful accomplishment of their goal.

Finally, establishing and maintaining the coaching agreement is also closely linked to how the coach partners with the client to manage the time effectively and bring the session or the overall coaching engagement to an appropriate close. From a session-by-session perspective, the coach is expected to partner with the client, not only to manage the focus of the session but also to manage the time so that the conversation has a beginning, middle and end. It is the coach's responsibility to manage the time and to check in with the client periodically to assess progress toward the stated goal and how the client would like to use the remaining time. In this way, the client can focus on their coaching work and the coach holds the coaching space through carefully tracking time. For example, the coach might ask:

- "We're about halfway through our time today, how are you doing in relation to your goal for today?"
- "We've got [XYZ] minutes left today, where would you like to focus now?"
- "How would you like to use the remainder of our time?"

This process of managing time is also relevant for the overall coaching engagement so that progress toward the client's overarching goals is noted and any adjustments the client may want to make are addressed.

Ultimately, the coaching engagement will come to an end and a vital part of this competency is that the coach partners with the client to end the coaching relationship in a way that honours the experience. The key word here is 'partners', and the coach is expected to co-create an appropriate way of ending that acknowledges and even celebrates the client's progress and achievements in the coaching process. This is where the beginning of the work closely relates to the end of the work and this competency links directly to some aspects of Competency 8: Facilitates Client Growth.

Chapter 9: Co-Creating the Relationship Domain, Competency 4. Cultivates Trust and Safety

The next competency in this domain is Cultivates Trust and Safety. Although this chapter focuses on Competency 4 specifically, its close relationship with Competency 5: Maintains Presence is significant. It is the combination of these two competencies, along with the depth and thoroughness of partnering undertaken in Competency 3: Establishes and Maintains Agreements, that truly co-creates the relationship with the client. Whereas the other competencies focus more on how the coach demonstrates their skills for the actual process of coaching, Competencies 4 and 5 particularly focus on how the coach creates, nurtures and maintains a good coach–client relationship to make the coaching process more effective. In this regard, the word 'cultivates' in the title specifically reflects that trust and safety is something that must be tended to throughout the relationship, rather than a 'one-time activity' by the coach.

The interrelatedness of all of the competencies is hopefully already apparent; however, it is worth noting here that Competencies 4 and 5 are highly intertwined with the other competencies and ideally form a thread that runs through the conversation, enabling an environment and a relationship that is conducive to an effective coaching experience and outcome for the client. Coaching is often described as a dance, in which the coach and client work elegantly together in rapport. The dance metaphor is a useful one, as there are several parallels with coaching. The client takes the lead and at first the dance can feel clunky, and we might tread on each other's feet or start to move in different directions. We might even feel as though one of us is dancing a waltz while the other is doing the jive! Part of the coach's skill here is to seek to work 'in step' with the client as quickly as possible, so that the work can be facilitated. For the purposes of assessment, these skills should be observed within the coaching session. However, in reality one would expect both of these competencies to be applied from the beginning of the coach–client engagement – for example, during a chemistry session.

> **Box 9.1: Competency 4: Cultivates Trust and Safety**
>
> Definition: Partners with the client to create a safe, supportive environment that allows the client to share freely. Maintains a relationship of mutual respect and trust.
> 1. Seeks to understand the client within their context, which may include their identity, environment, experiences, values and beliefs.
> 2. Demonstrates respect for the client's identity, perceptions, style and language, and adapts one's coaching to the client.
> 3. Acknowledges and respects the client's unique talents, insights and work in the coaching process.
> 4. Shows support, empathy and concern for the client.
> 5. Acknowledges and supports the client's expression of feelings, perceptions, concerns, beliefs and suggestions.
> 6. Demonstrates openness and transparency as a way to display vulnerability and build trust with the client.

(ICF, 2019b)

Thus, the essential elements of Competency 4 are that the coach:

- creates a safe, supportive environment
- respects the whole person of the client
- acknowledges the work of the client in the process.

What is being examined in this competency is the coach's respect for the client and their contribution to the work, as well as creating a safe space for the client to do that work. Given that this competency is intended to co-create the relationship and be evident throughout the coaching conversation, there is an expectation that multiple examples of these skills will be observed during the piece of work. These skills may be evidenced directly through the language or actions of the coach but also indirectly by the coach's way of being. For example, the friendly exchange of language that can occur between the coach and client when they are in rapport and have a comfortable relationship with each other is a valid way of demonstrating this competency.

Initially, one would expect to notice the coach seeking to understand their client better and get to know them as a person, as well as gaining clarity on what they are bringing into the coaching process. The focus here is on the *who* of the client and not only on *what* they are bringing. This aspect links to elements of the previous competency, Establishes and Maintains Agreements, where the coach may have invited a deeper enquiry into the significance, importance and timing of the client's chosen coaching topic. This is how the coach begins to know and understand the person bringing the topic, as well as the topic itself. In this competency, the process of relationship-building continues via further exploration of other aspects of the client that may be relevant to the work, including their associated environment, experiences, values, beliefs, needs and expectations – and even their own sense of identity in relation to their topic or goal.

Once the coach and client know each other a little better, the process of acknowledgment and respect is facilitated. Acknowledging and demonstrating respect for the client's work in the coaching process might be evidenced by comments such as, "You seem to have given this a lot of thought" or, "It strikes me that you have already put a lot of effort into this topic". The coach can support the client's expression by continuously inviting them to share their opinion and to say more about their feelings, perceptions, concerns, beliefs, and also their suggestions for how they might move forward. These acknowledgments and invitations are coupled with respect for the client's style of expression and language.

Sometimes the focus of a coaching conversation may enter into areas that are quite sensitive for the client. This competency also requires the coach to acknowledge this sensitivity by checking in and seeking permission to further explore in that direction. This respectful, sensitive probing, which leaves the client a choice, is an important feature in building a strong and safe coach–client connection. A high level of respect and rapport can also be shown by how the coach appropriately adapts to (or matches) the client's way of speaking and, in the case of face-to-face coaching, how the coach relates to the client with eye contact and body language.

Another aspect of acknowledging and respecting the client's work in the coaching process is to support, encourage and champion the client's courage and/or willingness to make changes in service of accomplishing their goal. This might also include acknowledging the challenges they face while making those changes. This type of acknowledgment could be evidenced by comments such as, "I know that it took courage for you to take the risk and do something different" and, "You really seem to be gaining momentum now with this new habit". Being aware and inclusive of the client's life, history, work, values, beliefs, etc., is yet another way of demonstrating respect and can be seen in a comment such as: "I know how important this is to you and how you have struggled with this in the past. I now notice how confidently you are working through these situations as they arise."

We should point out that showing support, empathy and concern does not mean rescuing or looking after. A core feature of how these three qualities are used in coaching is the extent to which the coach creates an equal relationship with the client and recognizes the coaching principle that clients are creative, resourceful and whole. Therefore, they do not need us to 'save' them, 'fix' them or do anything that disempowers them or results in their own sense of resourcefulness being limited or undermined in any way. This observation also closely relates to a competency we have already covered in a previous chapter, Competency 2, Embodies a Coaching Mindset.

It is necessary, then, to frame and offer acknowledgment so that it does not come across as praise or approval from the coach. To illustrate this point, we draw upon a model from transactional analysis called Ego States (Stewart & Joines, 1987), in which the coach seeks to establish an adult-to-adult relationship with the client as opposed to a parent–child type of relationship. To that end, the coach is expected to offer empathy, when appropriate, instead of sympathy, to express confidence in the client's capabilities, and to notice the client's strengths and achievements. The coach should also demonstrate patience while the client is processing their work and not judge them or their behaviour.

Support that is offered in this equal, non-judgmental, non-fixing way can be not only enormously helpful but also highly empowering for the client; inviting them into a safe space where they can truly tap into their resourcefulness and creativity to overcome challenges and make the changes they want to accomplish their goals. Examples of this could be:

- "You can do this. You have achieved so much already."
- "I feel your sadness, how do you want to be with this right now?"
- "Congratulations on making this breakthrough."

Encouraging and allowing the client to fully express themselves is a key part of this competency and also another way of demonstrating respect and support as we create a trusting environment. It could also be shown in a direct way by the coach actually asking the client to "Tell me more…" or "What are you thinking about this?" The common theme here is that the client should do most of the talking, without interruption from the coach. The client is also invited to share more, when appropriate, in support of forward movement toward their outcome for the session.

Finally, trust and safety is built through the coach demonstrating openness and transparency as a way of displaying their own vulnerability. This is evident if the client feels able to agree or disagree with the coach and could sound something like: "Tell me if this doesn't resonate with you, but what I notice is…"

In the next chapter, we will look at the competency that completes the trilogy in the domain for effectively co-creating the coaching relationship.

Chapter 10: Co-Creating the Relationship Domain, Competency 5. Maintains Presence

We continue to look at how the coach co-creates the relationship with their client and, in this competency, the focus is on the extent to which the coach is curious about what the client is saying and who the client is. The quality of this partnering is also significant in terms of how much the coach actively seeks input from the client around the content and direction of the conversation, as opposed to offering content and direction themselves. The competency is described in Box 10.1.

Box 10.1: Competency 5. Maintains Presence

Definition: Is fully conscious and present with the client, employing a style that is open, flexible, grounded and confident.

1. Remains focused, observant, empathetic and responsive to the client.
2. Demonstrates curiosity during the coaching process.
3. Manages one's emotions to stay present with the client.
4. Demonstrates confidence in working with strong client emotions during the coaching process.
5. Is comfortable working in a space of not knowing.
6. Creates and allows for silence, pause or reflection.

(ICF, 2019b)

Essential elements of this competency are that the coach:

- maintains full focus on the client
- demonstrates curiosity
- manages emotions
- creates space for reflection.

Presence is exemplified in the first sub-competency by the coach being able to remain focused, observant, empathetic and responsive to the client. The following sub-competencies then offer examples of how the coach can demonstrate the quality of presence. Some key themes at the heart of this competency are the extent to which the coach truly partners with their client, staying grounded and open even when faced with challenge, complexity and uncertainty, and the extent to which the coach works with the client beyond their coaching topic. Sometimes this is called 'coaching the person' and not just the topic. Partnering has already been positioned as critical within the competencies covered so far and it is this focus on partnering that enables a highly effective coaching conversation.

Partnering:

- Shows respect and equality.
- Engenders trust and safety.
- Empowers the client.
- Helps to hold the client accountable for the work in the coaching process (see more on accountability in Chapter 13).
- Underpins autonomous and developmental thinking and positive change for the client.

In practice, the coach can demonstrate this partnering in several ways. First, the coach invites the client to co-design the focus and direction of the session with comments such as:

- "Where would you like to start?"
- "How would you like to approach this?"
- "Where would you like to go next?"
- "How can I best work with you today around this topic?"

Partnering is also experienced when the coach invites the client to disagree with the coach. This could be through the coach comfortably moving from their own frame of reference to that of the client – for example: "What my intuition says is... However, I may be wrong; what do you think about…?" The coach could also invite the client to disagree by offering their perspective without attachment: "What is your reaction to what I just offered? Please feel free to disagree with it."

Another facet of partnering occurs when the coach plays back options or possibilities expressed by the client and then invites the client to choose what to do. What is significant here is that the client has agency and is the one who not only sets the agenda, but also the direction and approach the work will take in the coaching process. For example, the client might share several options for how they would like to move forwards after the session and the coach may play them back by paraphrasing and clarifying, before inviting the client to choose which direction is going to be most useful. This might sound something like: "You have outlined options A, B and C; what do you want to do?" This approach is also helpful if the client brings several possible coaching topics into the session. Additionally, this playback is useful if and when the client is exploring possibilities that could potentially be in conflict – for example: "I'm hearing that you want to take a six-month break and you are also intrigued by this new project. What would be most fulfilling for you at this time?"

Coaching is intended to support the client's growth and development beyond the coaching conversations and beyond the specific topics they bring into coaching, so partnering with them is one of the keys to unlocking that growth and potential. Specifically, the coach can encourage the client to formulate his or her own learning as opposed to doing it for them. In this way, the coach champions the client's capability to assess their own experience by asking questions such as:

- "What do you notice as you describe that situation?"
- "What does that tell you?"
- "What are you learning as you hear yourself describe that experience?"

Now let's look at the other key aspect of this competency, which is 'coaching the person'. At an ACC level of coaching, the coach is likely to hold a focus that is limited to the topic that the clients bring in to coaching. At PCC and even more so at MCC level, there is an expectation that the coach will not only hold and work with the client's topic, but also focus on how the client thinks, feels, learns, relates and creates. This might also extend to the client's values and beliefs – i.e., how they view the world and how they see or want their place in the word to be. For example, the coach might ask: "How might this new project align with the values you shared earlier?" or "What are the beliefs and values that you will honour when you have that conversation?"

When coaching the person, the coach is also demonstrating empathy and responsiveness and showing they fully observe what is happening in the coaching process. This could be noticing and enquiring about client emotions or feelings, such as: "I'm sensing some disappointment and I'd like to check… How is this for you?" or "I can see your emotion and I know this is important for you. Would you like to explore this further?"

This brings us to the topic of the client's emotions and, in particular, strong emotions. The coach is expected to appropriately hold the space for the client to fully express themselves and this may include expressing a strong emotion. This links back to the belief we hold that the client is creative, resourceful and whole. A client expressing emotions (e.g., crying) does not necessarily become un-resourceful, lacking in creativity or broken! Rogers (1980) stated: "I regret it when I suppress my feelings too long and they burst forth in ways that are distorted or attacking or hurtful". Part of what coaching can offer is a place for emotions to be expressed and explored in service of forward movement and growth. It is therefore important that the coach can offer a space where it is OK to express emotions. To illustrate this, we make reference to a concept called Life Positions, which originated from the work of Eric Berne (1962), who founded a psychological approach called transactional analysis. Aspects of Berne's work were further developed by Franklin Ernst (1971), who proposed a model called the OK Corral. In this model, there is a healthy and functional position where both the coach and the client hold the perspective of: "I am OK with me and you are OK with me". This means that, although the client may be emotional or tearful, they are still OK at their core and the coach and the client can still get on with the coaching work at hand, as opposed to the coach assuming that the client needs to stop – or, indeed, that the coach needs to stop – because of the emotions present at that time. This aspect of working with emotions is natural and comfortable for some coaches, and less so for others. In this case, an opportunity for the coach's valuable growth might be in exploring this aspect of their work and their own responses to emotions in others. This links directly to sub-competency 3: Manages one's emotions to stay present with the client and also to many aspects of Competency 2: Embodies a Coaching Mindset.

Another way to coach the person (as well as the topic, thereby demonstrating that we are focused, observant and responsive) is by exhibiting curiosity with the intention to learn more about the client. Curiosity is shown by the coach genuinely enquiring about the client's agenda and facets of the client as a person, as well as regularly seeking input from the client around their ideas and perspectives.

It is also relevant at this point to state that coaching is not therapy and there may be a time when the client's level and nature of emotion indicates that another form of resource might be more appropriate and useful to the client. This is referenced in the ICF Code of Ethics Part 4. Ethical Standards, Section I – Responsibility to Clients, Item 7: *Remain alert to indications that there might be a shift in the value received from the coaching relationship. If so, make a change in the relationship or encourage the client(s) / sponsor(s) to seek another coach, seek another professional or use a different resource.* As previously outlined in Chapter 6, guidance on when and how to refer clients to therapy can be found in an ICF white paper called *Referring a Client to Therapy* (Hullinger & DiGirolamo, 2018).

Sometimes the coach's presence is noticeable in its absence. The absence or reduction of our presence with our client may be due to certain factors – including strong client emotions, which we have just explored. Another factor that can challenge our presence is the 'need to know'. In so many walks of life, what we know seems to be important, we are conditioned and encouraged to know, and we are – in many circumstances – valued by what we know. Academics, subject matter experts, and specialists are paid because of what they know. Leaders are supposed to know what to do during organizational change; doctors are expected to know what is wrong with their patients. However, if we consider the humanistic approach (see Chapter 16), it may be that our knowledge can in fact be a distraction and even get in the way of the client being able to do their own work.

The humanistic approach embraces the belief that people have a 'self-righting reflex' and, given the right conditions, will be able to achieve their goal. A new coach may struggle with this concept as it is often quite a significant mindset shift from the social conditioning we have experienced around knowledge in other aspects of our lives. It can feel almost counter-intuitive to think that we add value by not knowing. As we develop in our coaching practice, we come to realize that we do not know exactly what is going on for our client or, indeed, ultimately what is best for them – nor is it our role to do so. They are the subject matter expert on their life and our role is to be comfortable enough to be with them as they navigate their unknown – not trying to solve or fix, but simply to create and offer them the space and time to think by being utterly present, deeply listening and supporting their thinking and feeling with some clean, simple yet thought-provoking questions and observations.

One example of this challenge might be a person who has had a successful career in their field and decides to leave corporate life and become a coach. Although they clearly grasp the theory of coaching and understand the competencies on paper, they might simply not be able to resist the urge to offer, to suggest, to fix, to drive, to direct. Their conditioning from years of being valued for what they know in their professional career and their own perception of how they add value can be tied up and intertwined with that conditioning. This can mean that the coach's own agenda and beliefs begin to seep into the work and in fact add no value, as they end up getting in the client's way. We have heard many new coaches say things such as:

- "I didn't *do* anything"
- "I'm just not sure how *I added value*, really"
- "I'm struggling to help my clients get to their goal"; or even
- "How can *just listening* help them? Surely, I need to *give them* something, otherwise what value am I being to them… and they are paying me for that!"

This shift in our own mindset is also closely linked to coach maturity, which we have explored in Chapter 1. Developing the capacity to be comfortable with not knowing may also involve some personal work (perhaps with our own coach or a coaching supervisor) for us to explore our own beliefs about knowing and what it means for us to know or not know, and how we perceive ourselves to have value as a coach. As coaches, our value can be enormous, but it may be more a question of how we define and perceive that value.

This competency also entails the extent to which the coach creates or allows space for silence, pause or reflection. This is an important aspect of the client being able to express themselves fully and for them to engage freely in the thinking and feeling processes needed for that fullness of expression. This space – the 'coaching space' – is what then enables the client to make sense of their thoughts and feelings. This meaning-making process links closely to Competencies 7, Evokes Awareness, and 8, Facilitates Client Growth. Space for the client could be encouraged simply by the coach staying quiet and allowing the client to share, pause, and then share more as their thoughts unfold and come to the surface. By way of illustration, we draw upon the comparison to a game of table tennis. In table tennis, we hear the constant tap, tap, tap, tap as each player hits the ball and passes it back over to the other side. Often when people are first learning to coach, the conversation sounds a little like this as the dialogue is exchanged between the coach and client through a stream of questions and answers with little space in between. One of the things that we know about how we process information and communicate best, is that it is the space in between the dialogue that makes the difference. It is during this space that the words just spoken are truly listened to, rather than just heard. It is also in this 'coaching space' that we digest and process the words and begin to formulate our response. What is noticeable in coaching conversations with more experienced coaches is that the 'game' slows down. It's almost as though the table tennis ball becomes momentarily suspended in the air somewhere between the two players before it lands, and the other person speaks again. In this way, the client has the space to really hear themselves and gain insights from their own expression and the coach has the space to truly listen to their client and then take the time to consider what to say or ask next, based upon what they are hearing, noticing and experiencing in the coaching process.

It is important for the coach to give the client sufficient time for reflection, time to answer questions, and simply give them time to think (Kline, 1999). Kline proposes that the quality of someone's thinking is directly comparable to the quality of the listening they receive. All too often, coaches feel that they have to add value by asking great questions or offering some powerful insight. They can therefore get caught up in their own agenda and desire for performance when all the client needs is the space and time to think for themselves and be deeply heard and listened to.

This is an important part of how the partnership (and the 'dance') between coach and client can become transformational when inviting the client's own wisdom to come forward.

Chapter 11: Communicating Effectively Domain, Competency 6. Listens Actively

We now look at the first of two competencies concerned with the effective communication of the coach and methods of evoking awareness in the client.

> **Box 11.1: Competency 6: Listens Actively**
>
> Definition: Focuses on what the client is and is not saying to fully understand what is being communicated in the context of the client systems and to support client self-expression.
>
> 1. Considers the client's context, identity, environment, experiences, values and beliefs to enhance understanding of what the client is communicating.
> 2. Reflects or summarizes what the client communicated to ensure clarity and understanding.
> 3. Recognizes and enquires when there is more to what the client is communicating.
> 4. Notices, acknowledges and explores the client's emotions, energy shifts, non-verbal cues or other behaviours.
> 5. Integrates the client's words, tone of voice and body language to determine the full meaning of what is being communicated.
> 6. Notices trends in the client's behaviours and emotions across sessions to discern themes and patterns.

(ICF, 2019b)

On reading this description, you may notice there are some themes that have already been introduced in the competencies covered so far:

- The client's broader context.
- Seeking and listening to understand.
- Probing and integrating client's way of communicating for greater clarity and depth of meaning.
- Noticing and exploring voice, verbal language, energy and body language.
- Playing back.
- Noticing and exploring trends, themes and patterns.

The above themes also form a thread that is intended to run through the coaching conversation in a natural, intuitive and appropriate way.

The key elements of this competency are that the coach:

1. Engages in holistic listening.
2. Reflects back to ensure shared understanding.
3. Integrates understanding of the client to support communication.

In essence, this competency is about the coach's ability to truly hear what the client is presenting about who they are and their situation or coaching topic. This ability is evidenced in how the coach responds to what the client presents and how the coach uses the information and language shared by the client to co-create a structure and direction for the conversation, including potential areas of exploration.

At a basic level this implies all of the great active listening skills that we know well:

- actively demonstrating attention
- showing genuine interest
- paraphrasing
- summarizing
- mirroring
- seeking clarity
- encouraging the client to share
- withholding judgment
- refraining from pushing their own ideas and agenda.

On top of these skills, we then add another layer of listening that engages both the client and the coach in a deeper exploration of the meaning of what is being presented, which offers greater insight and awareness in service of the client's forward movement.

One of the ways to initiate this deeper listening is by asking questions or making observations that are truly reflective of what the coach knows about the client and their situation or topic. This may appear to be an obvious suggestion; however, it is not always so easy to do in practice. It can be easy for the coach to find themselves in a place where they have a question they want to ask, and the client is still talking. The coach's energy then becomes focused on waiting for the client to stop so that they can ask their question. We have heard this called 'question queuing' and it is something that takes the coach's energy, attention and presence away from listening to their client because they are more focused on their own agenda of asking their question. Many times, when listening to recordings of coaching sessions, we have even heard the intake of breath by the coach, who is literally waiting for the client to finish so that they can allow their question to come out. This creates a different environment for the client to work in compared with the one that allowed for space for the client to express themselves fully as described in Competency 5.

Questions or observations that reflect what we have learnt about the client show that we draw upon information given by them previously – for example: "In our last session you mentioned how important rest was for you at the moment; what is the impact of this new project on that?" In this way, the coach 'notices trends in the client's behaviour and emotions across sessions to discern themes and patterns'. By using cumulative information from listening across sessions, the coach can come to understand the broader context and full meaning of what the client is saying. This deeper, broader aspect of listening is sometimes overlooked by less experienced coaches and is also one that, once developed, helps the coach to build and maintain their coaching presence with the client.

Deeper listening also involves deeper enquiry. This enquiry might be about the client's use of language and the client's feelings, or patterns the coach has noticed, as well as how the client processes. For example, the coach might ask about language: "You have mentioned freedom a few times, what does freedom mean to you?" For feelings, the coach might ask: "How do you feel when you think about that freedom?" For a deeper enquiry into how the client processes, it could sound something like: "How will honouring your value of freedom support you in achieving your goal?" Enquiry into a client's emotions can also link to some of the points discussed in Competency 5 around working with client emotions. For example, the coach might ask about or reflect back the client's emotions by noticing their mood, tone, body language, energy, etc. In this instance, the coach could ask: "When you talk about this, your face lights up and you smile broadly; what does this mean for you?" or "I notice your tears; what's going on for you right now?"

What is also important about this is that it helps the coach to check and take care with their own possible assumptions about what the client is saying. When a client mentions 'freedom', it can be quick and easy for the coach's own mind to go directly to what freedom means for them, as so often we process what someone else is saying by using ourselves and our own lives as a point of reference. In coaching, the danger with this is that we may then act upon those assumptions. What freedom means to the coach may be quite different to what it means for their client. Although we may think we are speaking the same language, in fact we are not; everyone has their own unique way of choosing words and terms to accurately express the real meaning of their thoughts and feelings. The care we take when choosing our words is exemplified when we struggle to 'find the right words' and so it is vital that the coach carefully listens to the words their clients share, as they will have been chosen for a reason. The phrase 'words create worlds' comes to mind.

Noticing and exploring energy shifts is a powerful way to invite deeper listening and communication with the client. There would need to be a noticeable shift in the client's energy for this to be relevant, of course. However, the coach is expected to demonstrate their presence by sharing observational feedback with the client when the client's body, physical rhythms or posture change. A further nuance to this level of enquiry is to explore the client's tone of voice, pace or volume of speech, and other changes to vocal qualities. As with energy shifts, changes in the client's vocal qualities are a way for us to demonstrate our deeper level of listening through observational feedback. For example: "When you talk about that event your speech speeds up quite a bit and your voice gets higher; what do you think that is about?"

Finally, in addition to listening for language, feelings and voice qualities, the coach may also ask about the client's behaviours and how the client perceives the world in terms of their environment, beliefs and values, etc. For instance, the client may share a particular situation and the coach might further probe the client's actions, reactions and/or responses to people, places and events. What is noteworthy here is that these questions are not intended to simply elicit data – e.g., what did he do and what did you do and then what did he do? The focus of the coach should be on exploring the process that was happening before, during or after certain behaviours, with questions such as:

- "What were your thoughts and feelings that led you to react in that way?"
- "What was the impact of your actions in that meeting?"
- "How do you want to be when you have that conversation?"

How the client perceives his or her experience can be determined by asking questions about the client's beliefs, assumptions, values and perspectives, such as:

- "What assumptions might you be making about this?"
- "From where you stand, what is your perspective?"
- "What is your belief about this?"

What is evident in this chapter is that listening involves questioning. Listening in the coaching relationship is not a passive activity, we listen actively. Our listening as a coach has a purpose and this means asking questions to probe, enquire and explore so that the true meaning of what the client is communicating is fully expressed, conveyed and understood.

Chapter 12: Communicating Effectively Domain, Competency 7. Evokes Awareness

The second of the two competencies concerned with the coach's effective communication is Evokes Awareness. The competency and job analysis process identified and analyzed certain 'kernels', which emerged as highly effective characteristics in the coaching process. These included:

- the client being open to change or learning
- the coach listening to the client
- the coach using appropriate coaching methods and approaches to cause the client to shift.

Box 12.1: Competency 7: Evokes Awareness

Definition: Facilitates client insight and learning by using tools and techniques such as powerful questioning, silence, metaphor or analogy.

1. Considers client experience when deciding what might be most useful.
2. Challenges the client as a way to evoke awareness or insight.
3. Asks questions about the client, such as their way of thinking, values, needs, wants and beliefs.
4. Asks questions that help the client explore beyond current thinking.
5. Invites the client to share more about their experience in the moment.
6. Notices what is working to enhance the client's progress.
7. Adjusts the coaching approach in response to the client's needs. →

> 8. Helps the client identify factors that influence current and future patterns of behaviour, thinking or emotion.
> 9. Invites the client to generate ideas about how they can move forward and what they are willing or able to do.
> 10. Supports the client in reframing perspectives.
> 11. Shares observations, insights and feelings, without attachment, that have the potential to create new learning for the client.

(ICF, 2019b)

The key elements of this competency are that the coach:

- asks to elicit new insights
- shares observations to support new learning
- supports the client in reflection and reframing.

We start by looking at powerful questioning as an important coaching tool that causes the client to shift. Sometimes coaches think that a powerful question is one that 'blows the socks off the client'. To understand what constitutes a powerful question, we point our attention toward the ICF definition of coaching: "Partnering with clients in a thought-provoking and creative process that inspires them to maximize their personal and professional potential" (ICF, 2007).

The process of powerful questioning relates directly to the 'thought-provoking' part of this definition. We know that we are typically creatures of habit and that our habits extend to thinking habits as well as behavioural ones. There is a saying of disputed origin: "If you always do what you've always done, you'll always get what you've always got". This really underlines the relevance of this tool in coaching. If the client's current behavioural and thinking habits were working well for them in the situation they have brought into coaching, they probably would not need or want coaching on it. The fact that they have brought this topic means that they are most likely experiencing some sort of challenge or complexity around it that would be best supported by expanding their thinking, their perspectives and therefore the choices they feel they have in that situation. This is the function and purpose of this tool; not to 'blow the client's socks off', but rather to ask clear questions that help the client to explore issues, their part in those issues, and how they are behaving. These questions are intended to help the client to move forward toward their desired outcome for the coaching conversation.

There are some common patterns in the effective use of powerful questioning, including the focus or types of questions that can be asked, the nature and quality of those questions, and the purpose of powerful questions.

Taking the focus or type of questions first, words such as 'evoke', 'explore', 'beyond', 'generate' and 'reframe' are noticeable. Therefore, the types of questions that are powerful are those that challenge the client and invite them to go beyond the boundaries and limitations of their habitual thinking to discover new ways of considering their situation, issue or goal. This can be done in several ways. The coach can ask questions about the client's way of thinking, their assumptions beliefs, values, wants and needs, etc. For example:

- "What choices have you considered so far?"
- "What is important for you about that?"
- "What assumptions are you making about this situation?"
- "What will you consider to make a decision?"
- "What do you really want?"

These expansive questions might also focus on inviting the client to consider new ways of thinking about themselves and even challenge their current thinking so that they can see the situation from a different angle. In this way, the coach's questions invite the client to move away from their current 'story' and look toward new and different possibilities. This can be demonstrated by questions such as:

- "Is that belief really true?"
- "How could you challenge your view about this?"
- "How might you think differently about yourself in this situation?"

Apart from exploring the client's thinking and how they view themselves, powerful questions can also focus on expanding their awareness of the situation they are bringing into coaching. With these types of questions, the coach is inviting the client to look at the situation from different perspectives. The questions are intended to support the client to reframe the situation to one that is more empowering for them. Examples of such questions are:

- "If it were six months from now and this were resolved, what do you notice?"
- "What is a different way of looking at this?"
- "What do you notice when you put yourself in their shoes?"
- "What else?"

Finally, it is also important for the coach's questions to invite the client to direct their attention and thinking toward their goal. Here, the coach is inviting a vision of what success might look like and asks the client to imagine their desired future. This may also include working with time by inviting an enquiry that starts from the future and works backward to the present moment. These questions help the client to create new scenarios and possibilities that would enable the successful accomplishment of their goal. Examples of these types of questions might be:

- "How do you want things to be in a year from now?"
- "What would the ideal outcome look like for you?"
- "What could you change today that will move you closer to that goal?"; and the 'miracle question'
- "What if you had a magic wand, what would you change?"

The miracle question can be useful as it directly challenges the limitations imposed by habitual thinking. Often something is only impossible because of the way we are thinking about it and, once our thinking is unlocked through these powerful questions, so many more options and possibilities become available to us.

As seen above, the focus on the future and what is possible also links closely to the client's ideal view of self. A question such as "What if anything were possible?" speaks directly to the concept of exploring fantasy life outlined in Chapter 21 and the psychodynamic approach. Boyatzis's Intentional Change Theory (2008) and the discovery of the 'Ideal Self' also reinforces a focus on the benefits of exploring the client's hopes, dreams, and vision of success to open up the scope for what is possible in the client's thinking.

Future focus is at the core of the forward-moving philosophy of coaching. Whereas the competency of Listens Actively (see Chapter 11) focuses a great deal on listening to the client and their current view of the world, their situation, and their view of self, the competency of Evokes Awareness is much more about shifting that view into what may be possible. Questions are important for both of these competencies; however, the intentions and outcomes for each are distinct.

As we discuss these different types of questions, we refer back once again to the ICF definition of coaching: "Partnering with clients in a thought-provoking and creative process that inspires them to maximize their personal and professional potential" (ICF, 2007).

By provoking new and expanded thought, the coach is able to support the client to access their innate creativity – something that may have been left dormant or impeded by their previous thinking habits. To that end, the role of the coach goes beyond being someone who asks 'powerful' questions to the essential idea of the coach helping the client gain new insights. Once their creativity is unlocked and the client can see more options, possibilities and choices, their energy can be more positively directed toward accomplishing their goals, leaving them feeling more inspired and fulfilled.

Moving to the nature and quality of the coach's questions, these should be as clear and concise as possible. Through conciseness, the client can hear and process the question more easily, meaning that their mental energy is maximized and not distracted by complicated, lengthy questions that take time and energy to understand, let alone process and respond. This is further supported by the coach's questions being primarily open ended – asked one at a time, rather than multiple questions – and at a pace that allows the client time to listen, think, reflect and respond (remember, this isn't a game of table tennis!). The acronym WAIT (Why Am I Talking?) is helpful here to remind the coach that their questions are intended to evoke new thought, not interrupt or demonstrate the coach's performance or agenda. We definitely advocate a philosophy of 'less is more' and the coach is encouraged to take their own time to reflect so that they can carefully consider, formulate and ask their questions in as few words as possible for maximum positive impact on the client.

The quality of the coach's questions can on occasions be enhanced by appropriately mirroring the client's language and frame of reference. Questions being clear and concise are qualities that Nancy Kline (1999) notes when describing incisive questions, which we have covered further in Chapter 16.

The coach is also expected to consider the client's experience, context and communication style in order to understand and notice what is working so that they can then adapt and work with the client's style. This may be learning by doing, reflecting, experimenting, visualizing, etc. For example, the coach might ask:

- "You mentioned that you had caught a glimpse of that future, what can you see?"
- "How would you like to approach this part of the work?"
- "What would you like to do now?"
- "You said you are firing on all cylinders; what is that like?"

In the final analysis, the coach's questions should neither be leading nor contain a conclusion or direction from the coach. This is a clear way of demonstrating the extent to which the coach is keeping to and holding the client's agenda vs. their own and is evidenced with questions such as: "From the options you have outlined, which path do you want to take?", "What ideas do you have?" and "What conclusions are you drawing from this?"

Ultimately, the purpose of powerful questioning is to help the client explore new and different thinking that opens up new and different possibilities, while empowering them to make those choices and take steps toward accomplishing their goal. What is important to remember, however, is that these questions need to be customized by what we have heard and learnt about the client and their situations. Although several examples of questions are suggested in this section, we strongly caution against thinking about these questions as a list of options. Every coaching conversation is unique and the best way to ask a powerful question is to be deeply connected to the client and the conversation. Be fully present, listen with all of the senses and ask questions that arise directly from what is being heard and learnt in the coaching process. Formulaic coaching is in itself a thinking and behavioural habit and is the very thing that we are inviting our clients to do differently.

Now let us consider another significant and useful tool in coaching for evoking awareness. The use of metaphor and/or analogy is a way of working with the client's language to create the relationship, communicate effectively, and evoke awareness. One of the roots of this word is the Greek *metapherein*, which means 'to carry over' – i.e., to transfer meaning. Metaphor is an important way that we give meaning and structure to what we say. Although our speech may be structured, measured and logical, our mind and thoughts are more random, fast and multifaceted. Language is therefore used to express what is going on inside and metaphor is used to share how we give meaning to our experience. Working with the client's shared metaphor(s) is a rich way to communicate and engage with the client to more deeply understand what something truly means to them. Consider the question "How are you?" What is evoked if the answer is "I'm on Cloud 9" or "I feel like I'm trapped in a dark cave and I can't find my way out"? These metaphors and symbolic language offer an opportunity to draw upon great coaching skills and enquire about the client's use of language and what it means for them – all customized by what we have heard through deep presence and listening.

Silence is also a really useful way to evoke awareness and, once again, the inter-relatedness of the competencies is clear. The coach's ability to allow silence and space, to pause for reflection, consideration and meaning-making, offer a powerful opportunity for expansion of the client's awareness. As such, silence is also highlighted and covered more fully in Chapter 10, Competency 5: Maintains Presence.

Another aspect of this competency is the extent to which the coach's questions, intuitions and observations have the potential to create new learning for their client. The key word here is *potential to create*. A coach cannot guarantee that the client will take to learning; however, the role of the coach in this competency is to offer contributions that have the potential for this learning to be evoked. Indeed, this is one of the places in coaching where the coach may in fact offer occasional mentoring or consultancy-type interventions by sharing their own ideas to evoke insight and forward movement. (Although it should always be in service of the client's agenda, as opposed to indulging the agenda or ego of the coach.) Examples include:

- "May I share my perspective on this? Please let me know if it's helpful or if you disagree."
- "I think of you as a highly creative thinker; what happens when you think of yourself that way too?"
- "You appear to be limiting your options here; what do you think?"

Part of this activity may include the coach sharing observations, insights and feelings, without attachment, which have the potential to create new learning for the client. The idea of coaches giving advice is always a controversial topic. We know from years of anecdotal evidence and listening to recordings of coaching sessions that many coaches do this – and frequently with positive results. Evidence of this was seen at all stages of the competency and job analysis process and two important criteria have been identified:

1. It is acceptable to share observations, insights or feelings with clients after getting permission to do so, as long as there is no attachment to it.
2. The sharing must broaden (rather than narrow) the range of options or views for the client.

Therefore, such interventions by the coach are expected to serve the client's forward movement or learning – not the coach's agenda. This means that the interventions seek to expand the client's thinking, potentially challenging it and supporting the client in new and different ways of considering and interacting with their issue. This type of intervention means that the coach is described as 'unattached' to their offering and is communicating in a way that enables self-discovery for the client, as opposed to the coach holding a sense of being right or 'knowing' what the client needs. Such unattached observations, intuitions, comments, thoughts and feelings might sound something like:

- "It sounds like you are much more satisfied with that solution."
- "I'm hearing disappointment; is that right?"
- "I am wondering if there's still something missing for you; how are you feeling about it?"

Chapter 13: Cultivating Learning and Growth Domain, Competency 8. Facilitates Client Growth

This final competency sits under the domain of Cultivating Learning and Growth and epitomizes the overarching function and purpose of the coaching process. The specific use of the words 'learning' and 'growth' immediately tells us that coaching is not just about solving a problem, working on an issue, reaching a goal, or addressing a challenge. It is about much more than that. On one level, it is about using the coaching process to work with what the client brings into the session in order to establish specific, positive and forward-moving outcomes. On another level, coaching focuses on how the client can fully leverage their experience of addressing their topic in a way that maximizes their personal and professional potential in a much broader sense. In this way, coaching most definitely has a micro and macro level of focus in many ways (Box 13.1).

Box 13.1: Micro–Macro Focus of Coaching	
Micro	Macro
Topic	Person
Current	Future
Topic/situation	Where and what else?
Behaviour	Being
Solving a 'problem'	Building capacity and maximising potential

> **Box 13.2: Competency 8: Facilitates Client Growth**
>
> Definition: Partners with the client to transform learning and insight into action. Promotes client autonomy in the coaching process.
>
> 1. Works with the client to integrate new awareness, insight or learning into their worldview and behaviours.
> 2. Partners with the client to design goals, actions and accountability measures that integrate and expand new learning.
> 3. Acknowledges and supports client autonomy in the design of goals, actions and methods of accountability.
> 4. Supports the client in identifying potential results or learning from identified actions steps.
> 5. Invites the client to consider how to move forward, including resources, support and potential barriers.
> 6. Partners with the client to summarize learning and insight within or between sessions.
> 7. Celebrates the client's progress and successes.
> 8. Partners with the client to close the session.

(ICF, 2019b)

The key elements of this competency are that the coach:

- Facilitates learning into action.
- Respects client autonomy.
- Celebrates progress.
- Partners to close the session.

Having supported the client to achieve expanded thinking and greater awareness in the previous competency, the essence of this competency is focused on how the client is then invited to consider what learning and insights they are drawing from their work in the coaching process and how these might be applied and integrated for their benefit beyond the coaching conversation. In simple terms, this is about how the coach helps the client leverage their enhanced awareness, thereby facilitating growth as a result. Furthermore, the forward movement implied in the coaching process means that this competency also focuses on next steps and their associated planning and implementation.

What is being looked for and evaluated in this competency is the coach's ability to promote client autonomy and let them create, claim and determine how to use the new learning that arises from the coaching conversation (and across the coaching process). There is also a focus on how the coach partners with the client to create the potential for that new learning and growth to take place.

Part of this might include the coach inviting the client to explore what they are learning from the session about their coaching topic or issue, with a question such as: "Having explored this topic today, what are you learning about the situation?" However, in the spirit of not wishing to become formulaic in our coaching style, coaches are encouraged to draw upon many other ways to offer this type of enquiry. For example:

- "What insights are you gaining about…?"
- "What conclusions are you drawing about…?"
- "What is changing now that you have explored this further?"

This type of enquiry might also be about what the client is learning about themselves, how they might behave differently as a result, or how they perceive themselves now in their situation. Some more questions:

- "What have you learnt about yourself as a leader today?"
- "What will you do differently now that you have made these decisions?"
- "How will your insights impact the way you want to be as a parent?"

This competency also examines how the coach invites the client to explore beyond the learning around their specific coaching issue to their broader environment and their goal 'out there' in their life (from micro to macro). Thus, this competency really opens up the possibility for the coaching process to offer growth and development opportunities to the client that are focused on them as a person and not limited to the resolution of their issue. Such broader learning and its application might be explored by the coach asking questions such as:

- "Where else might this insight be of use to you?"
- "How might you apply this learning more broadly?"
- "How are you going to use the learning from today in your intention to be more proactive at work?"

In addition to these questions, the coach may facilitate growth by offering their own observations about the client or the client's situation and partnering with them by seeking the client's further input or exploration. This could be offered at relevant points throughout the session and could involve noticing tone of voice, body language, emotions or patterns of thought and language. For example: "I notice that your shoulders dropped, and you sighed heavily when you said that, what is that about?" or "I notice you talking much more confidently about this today, what is different?"

In essence, what is important in this competency is that the coach explores and invites an enquiry about learning, insights, conclusions and decisions, etc. This is done without attachment and in a way that evokes self-discovery for the client and not telling or teaching by the coach. In this way, the client is more naturally propelled to a place of forward movement as a result of the learning and this facilitates a conversation about next steps after the session.

It is important to note here that, although this is the final competency, the process of partnering and enquiry that facilitates learning and growth does not necessarily have to show up only at the end of the coaching conversation. Insights, learning, awareness, observations and decisions, etc., might naturally surface at any point within the coaching conversation.

The process of establishing learning, insights, conclusions and decisions, etc., naturally lends itself to a focus on next steps. This competency therefore also addresses how the coach brings the coaching session (and potentially the overall coaching engagement) to a close in a way that is meaningful and forward-moving for the client. We spoke in Chapter 7 about a good coaching session having a beginning, a middle and an end. We might even think about this as forming a third, a third and a third of the time for the session. Now, in reality, the middle is likely to be more than a third of the session; however, it does highlight the importance of not underestimating the time needed to thoroughly work with the client on the beginning and the end aspects of their work. So often these two aspects are squeezed into the first and final two minutes of the coaching session when in fact they offer the opportunity for significant insight and progress for the client when done well. Setting a strong and thorough foundation to the work at the beginning of the session (and the overall coaching engagement) will help to facilitate bringing the session (or the overall coaching engagement) to closure and it is that closure that we will now explore.

Fundamentally, this competency expects the coach to help the client apply and carry forward the results of the coaching session. A necessary part of enabling the results to be carried forward is the coach enquiring about the client's progress toward their goal. This may be done intermittently – e.g., "We are about half way through the session now; how are we doing in terms of progress toward what you wanted to take from this session today?" – and also in a specific way, such as: "At the beginning you said your motivation was at 4 out of 10, and you wanted it to be at least 8 out of 10. "Where are you right now?"

Another aspect of this competency is how the coach partners with the client around what the client will do after the session to move forward toward their ultimate goal. This enquiry is intended to support the client to explore and decide upon additional thinking, behavioural changes, actions, experiments, self-reflection, research or further assessment that the client will engage in to continue with their progress beyond the coaching conversation. Note that there are several ways for 'next steps' to be realized and a tangible action is not always necessarily what is most appropriate. Thinking may well be the perfect next step; in which case the coach can enquire about the focus and nature of the thinking and how it will be in service of the client's forward movement.

The development of next steps is intended to be a co-created process between coach and client as the coach helps the client to decide upon steps that are going to inspire them to maximize their potential and fulfil their goal. This may include the coach offering encouragement to the client and being a champion of support and belief in the client's ability to take such steps. It may also include the coach offering acknowledgment for the work the client has done so far and even sharing with the client an 'If not now, when?' challenge to help them take the steps they have concluded will lead them toward their desired outcome. The coach may potentially offer a suggestion to the client, as long as it is done without attachment, supports and honours the client's autonomy, is in service of the client's agenda and forward movement, and is aligned with the client's style.

Designing goals for when the coaching is complete could include the coach exploring the likelihood of an action occurring after the session, as well as how the client feels about taking that action and their willingness to commit. We can again consider the ICF definition of coaching: "Partnering with clients in a thought-provoking and creative process that inspires them to maximize their personal and professional potential."

The key word this time is 'inspires'. Although next steps may challenge the client, the intention is that they can find the resources necessary (from within themselves and/or with the support of others) to take those steps because they are inspired to do so in service of maximizing their potential, as opposed to feeling they 'should' do something. The partnering aspect is important so that the client feels a sense of self-ownership and that their plans post-session are congruent and accessible to them. This partnering should also include identifying potential obstacles and developing mitigating strategies, as well as considering what types of support the client might need to help them take the action. In some ways, this process could be compared to the development of a project plan, which can look great on paper when designed within the confines of the project manager's office. However, when taken out into the real world, the plan can fail almost before it has begun because there was no risk analysis or implementation planning undertaken to ensure its viability and success. This phase of the coaching process therefore supports the client to leave the session with a robust plan that will lead them toward success.

The coach also supports the client to reach a level of commitment to their goals and plans (including mechanisms to apply and measure that commitment) for which they can hold themselves accountable. Apart from establishing accountability, two other aspects of this competency are that the coach partners with the client to bring closure to the session (as opposed to being directive) and that the coach holds both the bigger picture of the coaching work, as well as what the client wants to achieve in each session. In this way, the coach helps to hold the client accountable for their overall progress toward their stated outcome, thereby underpinning the process of supporting them to maximize their personal and professional potential.

As you can hopefully appreciate, the exploration and work undertaken within this competency is rich territory for the client to move forward, develop and grow in ways that transcend the boundaries of the topic they brought into coaching. Therefore it is important that this aspect is given sufficient time and space within the coaching process and is not something the coach 'shoe-horns' into the end of the conversation when they notice the that session time is coming to a close. In Chapter 7 we looked at Competency 3, Establishes and Maintains Agreements; we explored how important it is to allow sufficient time and space to fully explore the client's goals for the coaching process so that the work has a solid and clear foundation. In the same way, this final competency is a vital part of the coaching process that underpins and enables the work done in the session to carry over into new patterns and habits moving forward. We noted earlier that coaches often rush through establishing the coaching agreement, and this is also often the case for this final competency. Part of a coach's responsibility to their clients is to manage the time boundaries set for the coaching sessions and, far too often, coaches run out of time to work with this part of the coaching process adequately and find themselves squeezing in questions such as "We've got two minutes left, what are you going to do after the session?" in a rather inelegant, clumsy and forced way.

The recommendation, therefore, is to remember the simple concept of beginning, middle and end so that the coaching session is balanced and paced, allowing for full and rich exploration of all aspects of the client work.

Reviewing the Eight Core Competencies

Having considered each of the eight core competencies and, by way of bringing this section to a close, we would like to offer a few final thoughts to bring these competencies together. It has been noted before that coaching is sometimes described as a dance and this embodies both the partnership between coach and client and also the intertwined way in which the coach applies the core competencies. Although we have covered each competency individually, it is important to remember that they are not a checklist and they are not chronological in their occurrence. Some aspects of some competencies lend themselves to the beginning or the end of a coaching session; however, the reality is that they all interrelate and form a continuous and cohesive thread throughout the piece of work.

Here are a few examples of how these competencies work together:

1. A thorough exploration of the client's goals for coaching (Competency 3) not only provides the foundation for the work but also allows the session to be brought to a relevant and elegant close with appropriate next steps in place (Competency 8).

2. Complete and active listening (Competency 6) enables well-placed and appropriate observations and interventions from the coach (Competency 7).

3. Clear thought-provoking questions (Competency 7) evoke awareness that can be harnessed into important learning for the client (Competency 8).

4. Harnessing learning allows for the client to make choices and decisions that naturally lead to actions and next steps (Competency 8).

5. As the 'dance' progresses, the quality of the coach–client relationship (Competencies 4 and 5) runs throughout the coaching process to create the optimal conditions for impactful positive change for the client.

6. When the dance and flow of these competencies have a strong professional and ethical platform (Comptency 1) and an embodied coaching mindset (Competency 2) the conditions are set for the client to fully benefit from the power of coaching!

Section 3: Approaches to Coaching

Section 3 is a collection of nine chapters exploring a variety of different psychological approaches that offer useful insight and application for the process of coaching.

We begin with the universal eclectic approach, which draws upon some of the most popular models of psychology. In each case, we offer the background and an overview of these approaches followed by specific examples of how they are relevant and can be applied to coaching. In Chapter 14 we share the Universal Eclectic Framework (UEF) and offer reflections on the key features of this framework, including person-centred, behavioural, cognitive-behavioural, Gestalt, systems theory, psychodynamic, evolutionary and biological.

Chapters 15–21 each look at a different psychological approach. We intend to offer an overview of the history and origins of these approaches and how they developed. For each one, our key area of focus is on how the principles and philosophies of these approaches can be easily and clearly applied to coaching in both a conceptual and practical way. Each approach includes tools and models that key figures in the field have developed, which bring the theories to life. We also highlight how some of these principles are embedded within the language of the ICF Core Competency Model.

Chapter 22 is the final chapter of this section and explores the idea of integration. The ability to flex and adapt to the uniqueness of our clients and, indeed, the uniqueness of each coaching conversation means that good coaching practice draws upon multiple resources. This results in an integrated approach that is naturally, organically and intuitively present within the coaching relationship and conversation. The seven streams integrated coaching model is shared as a way of showing how these different approaches come together.

Chapter 14: The Universal Eclectic Coaching Approach

In this chapter we review the Universal Eclectic Coaching model, which draws on the eight most popular models of psychology and applies these to coaching. We look at each of the psychological models and how they can be applied to coaching, with a focus on the most popular approaches used – i.e., person-centred, behavioural, cognitive-behavioural, Gestalt, systemic, solution focused and psychodynamic.

Eclectic Coaching

Looking back in history, psychologists and philosophers have shared a common interest in understanding how humans learn. A whole variety of theories have sprung up, each with its own focus. The Greek philosopher Socrates used questions as a way of helping his students to learn, although his provocative questions ultimately got him into trouble. Other writers have suggested alternative approaches. BF Skinner argued that rewards can act as a stimulus for learning, whereas David Kolb argued that our experiences in the real world are the key component for learning. He suggested that by reflecting, theorizing and testing these out, adults can begin to understand the world in new and different ways.

The Universal Eclectic Coaching model covers eight major psychology approaches: person-centred, behavioural, cognitive-behavioural, Gestalt, systems, psychodynamic, evolutionary, and biological. The model was developed by Alison Hardingham (2006) as the British Eclectic Model and subsequently developed during her time at Henley Business School into the Universal Eclectic Model.

Not all coaching approaches fit neatly into the eight segments of the model, and the model does not cover all psychological approaches. But the model does offer one way of thinking about, and trying to categorize, the multiplicity of coaching approaches that are now available.

The Universal Eclectic Model begins by considering how each theory explains how humans learn and develop. The learning is often described through a related theory of learning or change. The development of such theories has often been followed by a coaching approach that applies the theory to the environment of one-to-one work. In many cases the ideas were originally applied to counselling, such as psychotherapy and CBT. However, some approaches don't naturally fit one-to-one work – for example, evolutionary approaches view change as taking place over millennia as opposed to months.

In other chapters we explore these different approaches in more depth. We focus on the approach and explore its roots, its application in counselling, and its adaptation to the world of coaching. Here we aim to give a brief overview of each different approach and how it has been applied to coaching.

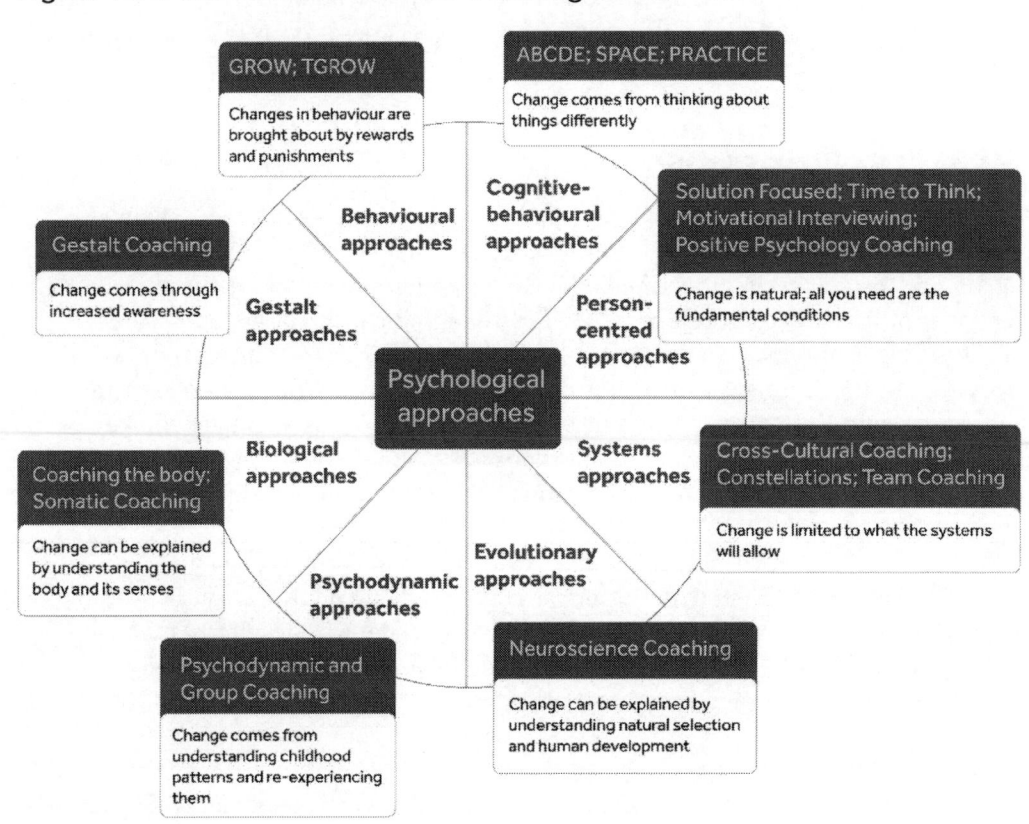

Figure 14.1: The Universal Eclectic Coaching Model

GROW; TGROW
Changes in behaviour are brought about by rewards and punishments

ABCDE; SPACE; PRACTICE
Change comes from thinking about things differently

Solution Focused; Time to Think; Motivational Interviewing; Positive Psychology Coaching
Change is natural; all you need are the fundamental conditions

Cross-Cultural Coaching; Constellations; Team Coaching
Change is limited to what the systems will allow

Neuroscience Coaching
Change can be explained by understanding natural selection and human development

Psychodynamic and Group Coaching
Change comes from understanding childhood patterns and re-experiencing them

Coaching the body; Somatic Coaching
Change can be explained by understanding the body and its senses

Gestalt Coaching
Change comes through increased awareness

Central: **Psychological approaches**

Segments: Behavioural approaches; Cognitive-behavioural approaches; Person-centred approaches; Systems approaches; Evolutionary approaches; Psychodynamic approaches; Biological approaches; Gestalt approaches

(Reproduced with permission from Henley Business School, 2020)

Person-Centred

The person-centred approach assumes that change is natural, provided the 'fundamental conditions' of warmth, genuineness, and unconditional positive regard are present. These fundamental conditions – sometimes called the 'necessary and sufficient' conditions – are expressed through the coach–client relationship. Within this relationship, development, growth or healing can take place. The essential tool for the coach or therapist is thus the quality of the relationship, ensuring clients experience the warmth and empathy offered by the coach. As a result, tools are a less commonly used within person-centred approaches. The focus is on the relationship, and how the coach uses listening and displays empathy toward their client.

Within coaching, one approach that embodies the person-centred philosophy is Nancy Kline's Time to Think (Kline, 1999), which we cover in Chapter 16.

Behavioural

Behavioural approaches emphasise the importance of rewards and punishments. The belief is that animals, including humans, can be stimulated by rewards such as food or a pay rise, and through this the animal or human begins to associate the reward with the stimuli. This was illustrated by Ivan Pavlov, who trained his dogs to associate the reward of food with the ringing of a bell, and the work of BF Skinner, who worked with pigeons and rats and trained them to follow patterns of behaviour through the use of food rewards. The behaviourists believed it was not possible to understand fully the 'black box' of the mind and thus it was better to focus on what we could see – e.g., human behaviour. If the individual's behaviour was 'appropriate', it did not matter what people thought or believed, as all we can see was the behaviour and not their thoughts.

Behaviour-based approaches underpin much of modern organizational management. They form the theoretical basis for the use of competency frameworks and are commonly used in development, such as appraisals ratings.

In coaching, the GROW model is a typical example of a behaviour-based approach (Whitmore, 1992). The GROW model, as we discuss elsewhere, is focused on human behaviour, although it has drawn from other models over time to add scaling and an exploration of faulty thinking. We cover more on GROW and the behavioural approach in Chapter 15.

> **Box 14.1: GROW – Commonly Used Questions**
>
> What topic do you want to focus on today?
>
> What's your goal for the session?
>
> What's the reality of the situation you are facing right now?
>
> What options do you have that will move you closer to this goal?
>
> What do you want to take away from our conversation as your way forward?

Cognitive-Behavioural

The cognitive-behavioural approach believes that learning, development and change take place as a result of an interaction between behaviour, cognition, emotion, and an external trigger. Commonly used models within this approach are ABCDEF and the Current Bun model.

The coach will use the ABCDEF model to help the client work through the difficult situation, challenging their unhelpful beliefs, and working to help the client to establish new more evidenced-based, logical and enabling beliefs. We explore the ABCDEF model and the cognitive-behavioural approach more in Chapter 17.

> **Box 14.2: ABCDEF Model**
>
> A = Activating event
>
> B = Beliefs (the views we hold about something)
>
> C = Consequences (our reactions, behaviour, emotion, thoughts, physiological)
>
> D = Disputing statements (statements we tell ourselves that are helpful and evidenced-based)
>
> E = Effective new beliefs (a new understanding/belief about the Activating event)
>
> F = Future action

Gestalt

Gestalt assumes that increases in awareness are key to change. By becoming more aware of ourselves, our environment and our clients, we can begin to observe the patterns and the wider environment in which we are operating.

Gestalt regards the individual as a totality of mind, body, emotions and spirit, with each person being unique. In therapy this means Gestalt practitioners focus on the present moment and on immediate thoughts, feelings and sensations. They then bring these into the session to deepen understanding. The aim is to build client's self-confidence and to help them live more in the present moment.

In coaching this translates into:

- Paying attention to the body, as well as the mind.
- Being aware of the content and the environment.
- Using metaphors and images.
- Using enactment such as Chairwork to explore ideas.

We explore the Gestalt approach further in Chapter 18.

Systems

Systems approaches are useful for helping the coach to recognise they are situated within a specific role, team, organisation, economic sector, national and historical context. These systemic factors, or content, all influence how the individual client and others act.

Oshry (2007) brings this alive in his organizational systems work, noting that most employees identify as being subject to one of four conditions or systemic circumstances.

Even in the most complex, multilevel, multifunctional organisations, each of us is constantly moving in and out of these conditions. In each one there are unique opportunities for contributing to total system power; and in each there are pitfalls that readily lead us to forfeit those contributions.

To bring this alive in our coaching work, the coach invites the client to:

- reflect on the importance of the organizational context

- draw on family metaphors to help clients recognise the inter-relationship between elements
- help clients to become more politically astute.

Techniques such as Force Field and Constellations also help clients consider the systemic forces at work and develop plans to manage these. This involves asking clients to identify, list and assess the strength both the forces for change (the desired outcome) and those resisting change (the desired outcome).

We explore the systemic approach, Oshry's work and the Force Field Model in more depth in Chapter 20.

Psychodynamic

Psychodynamic psychology is concerned with the dynamic unconscious. The belief is that as humans, much like an iceberg, most of our feelings and behaviours are driven by instincts and thoughts that are outside our awareness (i.e., unconscious).

This can manifest itself in many ways – as defenses, projection, denial, projective identification and acting. The role of the psychodynamic coach is to help clients be more aware of these mechanisms, to understand their origins and triggers, and identify ways to manage these defenses if they are considered unhelpful.

The psychodynamic approach is explored in more depth in Chapter 21.

Evolutionary

Evolutionary psychology is concerned with explaining why humans have evolved in the way we have. Given Darwin's theory on 'natural selection', why have certain traits or aspects of human thought, feelings and behaviour survived? What benefits do they confer?

In coaching terms, these psychological theories have informed neuroscientific coaching. By helping clients to understand the brain, its structure, function and operation, clients can be more aware of how the brain as a device can both help and hinder their pursuit of their goals.

Biological

Biological explanations of human behaviour are informed by genetics and how our genes determine human behaviour. There remains considerable debate about the balance between nature (genes) and nurture (environment and relationships). The general consensus suggests that about 60% of human behaviour is determined by our genes, with 40% responding to environmental factors. Even with 40%, this leaves huge capacity for clients to make a choice about their behaviour. Biological theories inform approaches such as somatic coaching. Somatics is concerned with the whole body, helping clients to be more bodily aware, and through observation of bodily sensations to be more sensitive to their own changing emotions and thoughts.

> **Box 14.3: Applying the Universal Eclectic Coaching Model**
>
> An initial phone conversation between the coach, Ross, and the client, Sandra, led Ross to recognize that a person-centred approach would be useful. Although Sandra had requested a challenging conversation about career aspirations, Ross felt that he was needed during the conversation. Sandra was anxious about coaching and about her role in the company. Ross looked to draw on the 'necessary and sufficient conditions' to help provide a relational platform on which the future work could build.
>
> Ross spent the first hour of the session listening to Sandra's story. Ross was warm and highly affirming, reflecting back what he heard both in terms of words and feelings.
>
> Once the relationship was secure, Ross moved towards cognitive-behavioural approach. Sandra was inclined to see her lack of leadership promotions as a sign she was less capable than other managers. Ross encouraged Sandra to explore these limiting beliefs and used chaining to identify and help Sandra challenge her core view of herself as 'unworthy' to be a leader in the organization.
>
> As the work continued Ross decided Sandra would benefit by thinking about the system in which she worked. The organization leadership was male-dominated and there were a limited number of female role models. Sandra felt this was demotivating and having a negative impact on her relationship with the organization. Ross used the Force Field analysis technique to explore how the organization currently limited her scope for leading (Systemic). This was followed by some Chairwork (Gestalt) to help her plan for a difficult conversation with her boss and Human Resources, who have made public commitments to increase the number of women in leadership roles in the organization. The use of that technique was in itself challenging for Sandra, as she had never tried anything like that before. It increased her urgency for change and provided her with a script to take away and explain her perspective in a way that her boss and HR could understand, so they could offer some positive suggestions for change.
>
> During the final phases of the coaching assignment Ross drew upon behavioural technique, inviting Sandra to observe other senior female leaders and 'model' their approach to leading, as well as to think about what role she was modelling for other female employees, who may be looking to Sandra as their role model to champion change.

Lessons about how to use the model

The first thing worth noting is that, like most used in coaching, this model is invisible to clients. The aim of the model is to provide a heuristic or map for the coach to guide their approach to working with clients.

What the client will see is the behaviours that the coach employs and the tools the coach selects. The coach needs to know the tools well enough to select the most appropriate tool for the client, as opposed to selecting their favourite three or four tools for every client. The best coaching is co-created in the moment; it is led by the needs of the client and delivered in partnership with them through a collaborative process.

If you do want to introduce a tool and you are unsure, or you think the tool may be well outside the comfort zone of your client, one way to do this is to describe the use of the tool as an 'experiment'. You can model the idea that it is possible to try out new tool and monitor the impact before deciding whether to continue or repeat their use more widely. This has the benefit of reducing the pressure on the coach of 'being perfect', and simply tests and evaluates the technique using a cycle of practicing, observing, reflecting, and adapting for the next iteration of the cycle.

Finally, before adding the technique to your repertoire, it's worth testing it five or six times with different clients and in different situations. Use a reflective journal to make notes of how and when you used it and what your client fed back to you about how the tool landed. Mastery re-emerges only through repeated application and reflection.

Conclusion

In this chapter we described the Universal Electic Model and provided brief insights into eight different psychological perspectives on learning and change, and how these perspectives have been applied by different writers and thinkers to coaching. The Universal Eclectic Model is one way to think about using different evidenced-based approaches in our coaching practice. As you will see with the Integrated Model in Chapter 22, it is not the only way. Ultimately, we believe each coach needs to find their own way to draw together a range of different approaches and integrate these for their clients, often changing and adapting to meet their clients' needs.

Chapter 15: Behavioural Approach and the GROW model

The GROW model is possibly the most popular coaching framework in use across the world. Its popularity is due to the combination of its simplicity as a 'four box model' combined with its power to summarise a step-by-step route to problem-solving, making use of psychological theory along the way.

The tool was originally developed by Sir John Whitmore, Graham Alexander, and Alan Fine, during their time working as organizational consultants in the UK. Its origins are in behavioural psychology, with a strong goal focus and desire to set, achieve and measure outcomes. GROW can be integrated with other coaching techniques and is also used beyond coaching as a problem-solving process.

Behavioural Psychology

The GROW model is considered to fit within the behavioural psychology tradition, given its focus on what people do as opposed to what people think. Few models developed through practice are a perfect fit to theory. GROW is no exception. However, throughout the years the model has drawn techniques from other models, such as scaling from solution-focused therapy and perceptual positions from Gestalt.

The model, however, fits within the behavioural psychological school and the work of researchers such as Skinner, Pavlov and Watson during the 1930s. Their interest was in understanding how others learned through an objective, quantified approach to explaining and predicting behaviour. These ideas were developed in parallel with modern management, which looked to psychologists for ideas on how to improve efficiency and the movement from craft production to modern manufacturing techniques. The outcome was Taylor's scientific management (Taylor, 1911), which subsequently provided the core platform for human resources practice in the past century.

The GROW Model

The model consists of four phases, which are deployed flexibly by the coach (Alexander, 2016; Whitmore, 2017). The coach may start with the Goal, moving to Reality, but can return to the Goal to further clarify and refine the goal before progressing to the Options stage.

Phase 1: Establishing the Goal

The first phase involves the coach working with their client to establish a goal. This may start with a general exploration of the wider purpose for the conversation, taking into account the brief from the sponsor and contextual factors. It may move into an exploration of the specific goal and the focus for the individual session. In some models the preliminary discussion of the topic has seen the model re-labelled as T-GROW.

During this phase the coach's aim is to help their client to set a clearly defined, measurable and meaningful goal for the session. The more clearly defined it is, the more meaningful it is for the client and more likely that progress can be made. As a result, it is helpful to encourage clients to define clear measures of success and milestones, but also to think about how important the goal is and how it connects to other objectives.

Sometimes the goal that emerges needs to be amended or clarified. The model is meant to be flexible and adaptable to the requirements of each client, so it is possible for the coach to step back into the Goal stage if more work is needed to clarify or refine the goal.

Box 15.1: Goal: Some Helpful Questions

- "We have an hour together. What do you want to leave the room having achieved in that time?"
- "What are you hoping to achieve through this goal?"
- "Why is this goal important for you now?"
- "How will you know when you have achieved the goal?"
- "When are you aiming to achieve this by?"

Phase 2: Exploring the Current Reality

In the second phase, the coach encourages the client to explore the current situation as it relates to their chosen topic. Sometimes clients may want to move to action quickly, and skip over an exploration of the issue – i.e., what they have tried before and why this has not worked. During this phase the coach's aim is to help their client to stand back and, through open questions, take time to reflect on all the ramifications of the situation. In addition to broadening and deepening their client's understanding, the reflective time will provide a foundation for the next phase, generating and evaluating Options.

During the reality discussion it will be helpful for the client to explore what they have tried so far, blockages to achieving the desired outcome, reviewing the situation from a number of different stakeholder perspectives, identifying likely causes and effects, and thinking about impacts on the client's performance and that of their colleagues. As these aspects are discussed possible solutions may begin to emerge from these considerations. However, it is important for the coach to help their client to 'park' these and remain focused on their exploration of the reality.

At this stage it can be easy for the coach to start following their own line of enquiry, gathering evidence to prove their hypothesis. It's important for the coach to remember that the coaching conversation is in the service of the client. This means questions should not be focused toward evidence collection but rather deepen the client's self-awareness and insight.

Box 15.2: Reality: Some Helpful Questions

- "What have you done so far to move toward your goal?"
- "What have you learned from these efforts?"
- "What is happening now?"
- "What is working well right now?"
- "What constraints have stopped you moving toward your goal?"

Phases 3a and 3b: Generating and Evaluating Options

The Options stage is best seen as having two sub-parts. We have labelled these as 3a Option Generation and 3b Option Evaluation. It's important not to get these tangled, as moving to an evaluation of the first two or three pros and cons may limit the generation of subsequent often more creative and unusual solutions.

As with the Reality phase, it is helpful to create the space for clients to explore, brainstorm or use idea writing to generate as many ideas as possible before starting to evaluate the pros and cons of each.

If a detailed picture has been created during the Reality phase, the client will have a good foundation for generating ideas. It can be helpful to encourage them to think of 'off-the-wall' ideas, as well as those that may seem more obviously feasible. Using techniques such as VIP and Post-Its (discussed in Chapter 34) can be helpful in generating more ideas. Sometimes there is the kernel of something useful in what may at first seem a crazy impossibility.

They might come up with ideas that are completely novel, or the options they generate may be adaptations of – or can help to confirm – existing thinking. What is important here is that the coach supports the client through open questions to expand the options. We find that clients can find this more difficult to do themselves and the role of the coach here can be particularly helpful in expanding their thinking.

Once there is a feeling that multiple options have been generated, the second part of this phase is to evaluate the options. Depending on the client's preference this can be undertaken formally, using a pre-determined set of criteria generated by the client – or, more informally, talking about each option's benefits and risks.

Box 15.3: Options: Some Helpful Questions

- "What could you do to move toward your goal? What else could you do? And what else?"
- "If you were the Chief Executive of Google, what would you do?"
- "Have you encountered something like this before? What worked then that might work now?"
- "Think of someone who does this kind of thing really well. What do they do that you could try?"
- "You have five minutes to write down as many ideas for solving this as possible."

Phase 4: Wrap-Up/Will/Way Forward

By this point in the conversation the client will have generated a score of ideas, a number of which are feasible solutions in their own mind. The W phase involves helping the client to select the specific option (or options) they are motivated to take forward. The development of the 'action plan' needs to be something they feel confident about and capable of progressing. The plan also needs to acknowledge how to move forward, including resources, support and potential barriers (see Chapter 13 for a full discussion of Facilitates Client Growth). It is often helpful to focus on the support that the person can draw on as they progress with their plan.

This support team may offer motivation, resources, or be able to hold the individual to account. Finally the client can be invited to identify the actionable first steps they wish to take.

The W can also stand for Will. We have found it helpful to also invite the client to consider their motivation to act. You might ask them to scale this – for example, "On a scale of 1–10, how motivated are you to start progressing with this plan immediately?" What we find is clients who score less than 6, or who use phrases like "I am definitely thinking about this" or "I would really like to do this" have yet to commit. We suggest further work is required with these clients to ensure they are committed to any actions in their plan.

It is worth recognizing that in some conversations the outcome or goal will not be a series of specific actions but rather learning or insights. These are equally valuable.

At this stage it's also worth acknowledging the work the client has done so far in building their plan through an affirmation statement: "Well, that's some great work you have done in thinking through this challenge and coming up with a plan that you are taking away."

The final step is to invite the client to reflect on their work within the session as a mechanism to develop further insight about themselves and meta-learning. The use of two or three questions at this stage add value to the session for the client and enable them to better understand how the GROW framework may be something they can take away and use as a tool to think through other issues.

In Box 15.4 we have summarized some of the questions that the coach might use at this stage of the model, which are consistent with the approach in Competency 8.

Box 15.4: Wrap-Up: Some Helpful Questions

- "Which of all the options you have come up with will you take forward?"
- "What support do you need from your organization?"
- "How will you go about getting this support?"
- "What's the first step you're going to take?"
- "On a scale of 1–10 (where 10 is high), how committed are you to your plan of action?"
- "What insights has this conversation provided for you?"
- "What have you learnt that you can apply to similar leadership challenges?"

The T-GROW diagram (Figure 15.1) summarizes the stages of the approach from an initial conversation about the topic, to a focus and clarification of the conversational goal, a review of the current reality, before considering the alternative options and their associated benefits and risks, then moving to close the conversation with a way forward.

Figure 15.1: T-GROW Model

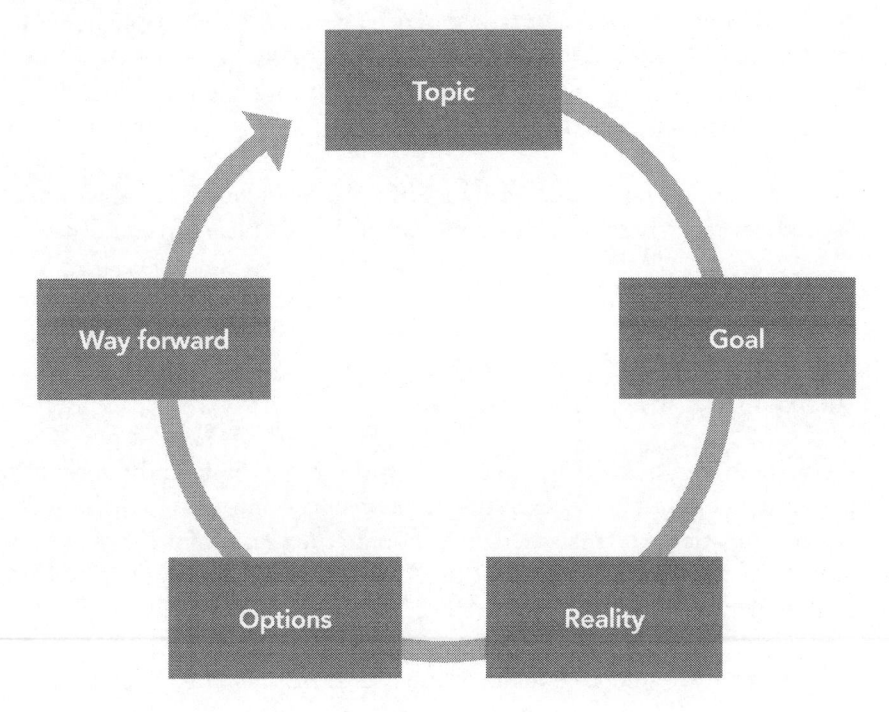

Conclusion

The GROW model has become one of the most popular coaching models in the world because of its simplicity. It's easy to remember and, when followed, creates a useful structure for a problem-solving conversation, either as a coach or as a self-coaching tool. In this chapter we have explored the GROW model of behavioural change. We described the stages of the model and discussed potential traps for the coach at each stage. We have also provided a series of questions at each stage as a handrail for the new coach.

Chapter 16: Humanistic Approach and the Time to Think Model

The humanistic approach (sometimes called the person-centred approach) is in some ways at the heart of coaching. This approach embraces the belief that within all of us is a 'self-righting reflex'. This links well to coaching, where we hold the perspective that our clients are creative, resourceful, and whole. It also relates well to the idea that if we can discover this aspect of ourselves, we can achieve any goal. The Time to Think model (Kline, 1999, 2009) applies these principles to coaching conversations, with a focus on the relationship, suggesting that the role of the coach is more often to get out of the way than to intervene with multiple questions, insights or reflections.

In this chapter we explore the humanistic approach, its implications for the coaching relationship, and how we can bring this alive in our coaching work through the Time to Think approach.

The Humanistic Approach

The humanistic approach is sometimes called the 'third force' as it challenged two previous psychological schools of thought – i.e., behaviourist and psychodynamic. Some psychologists felt those two were somewhat limiting whereas the humanistic approach focuses on the whole person and the uniqueness of each individual. This way of working is also directed toward development, growth and progress as opposed to the perceived pessimism or pathology associated with approaches such as psychoanalysis. Therefore, the emphasis with humanistic psychology is on choice and agency and the person's ability to make healthy conscious choices given the right circumstances.

Humanistic psychology first developed in the late 1950s and early 1960s and became popular during the 1970s and 1980s. It is underpinned by some basic assumptions:

- People have free will.

- People are basically good.
- People are motivated to self-actualize.
- The individual's subjective experience is most important.
- Challenges scientific methodology.
- Rejects comparative psychology (study of animals).

Carl Rogers was central to the therapeutic aspect of this approach and two other key contributors to this field were Abraham Maslow and Mihaly Csikszentmihalyi. Rogers initially developed the approach and, building upon the assumptions, focused on the principle that people are their own best experts and, as such, are the best source of reference for their well-being and development. A core theme to humanistic psychology is our 'actualizing tendency', which is a motivational drive leading to growth, development and autonomy that can also be described as the 'self-righting reflex' noted in the introduction. This concept of self-actualisation was first coined by Rogers and further developed by Maslow (1968) when it was positioned at the top of a human being's hierarchy of needs. Csikszentmihalyi (2002) also engaged with this concept in his work on how the combination of certain conditions allows us to achieve and experience a state of 'flow', leading to sensations of deep concentration, enjoyment, fulfilment and happiness. In essence, self-actualization is a natural human process that, given the right conditions, will motivate the individual to grow and reach their full potential. Part of the role of the practitioner, therefore, is to enable the client to feel a stronger and healthier sense of self so that they may access and realise their self-actualization tendency.

Sometimes the humanistic approach can be linked with an existential approach to explore the client's sense of self, their purpose and the meaning of life.

Relationship is Central

The humanistic approach is relationship-based. It can be argued that all forms of coaching (in addition to other modalities such as therapy, consultancy and mentoring) are relationship-based; however, the humanistic approach is considered to be highly non-directive. In this way, the principles and assumptions that underpin this approach are honoured. The humanistic approach would propose that it is the non-directive nature of the relationship that enables the process of self-actualization. Characteristic of – and in keeping with – this non-directive relationship, Rogers believed that change is a natural human process and that there are six necessary and sufficient conditions for positive change.

> **Box 16.1: Necessary and Sufficient Conditions for Change**
>
> 1. Coach–client psychological contact (the relationship must exist and be one that feels safe to the client)
> 2. The client is incongruent (incongruence exists between the client's experience and their awareness of that experience)
> 3. Coach congruence, or genuineness (the coach is authentic, deeply present with their client, not acting, and is able to draw upon their own intuition and experience to facilitate the relationship and the client's progress)
> 4. Coach holds unconditional positive regard for their client (the coach acts without judgment, disapproval or approval and champions an increase of self-regard in their client)
> 5. Coach has empathic understanding (the coach demonstrates empathic understanding of the client's inner world and their concerns, thus increasing and evidencing their unconditional positive regard)
> 6. Client perception (the client perceives and experiences the coach's unconditional positive regard and empathy)

Time to Think Model

A key contributor to the application of the humanistic approach in coaching is Nancy Kline and her work titled Time to Think (1999). The subtitle to Kline's book is Listening to Ignite the Human Mind, and this epitomizes the idea that the coach's contribution is largely centred on the belief that their client is indeed creative, resourceful and whole, and therefore has a self-righting reflex. As such, the role of coach is to honour that belief by building a safe and empathic relationship and then get out of the client's way, creating space and time for them to think so that they may access and utilize their own inner resources.

With this approach, the coach listens to the client without judgment, allowing the client to come to insights themselves. The role of the coach is to ensure that all of the client's thoughts and feelings about their topic are being considered and that the coach fully understands the concerns of the client in a way that is non-directive and brings a degree of warmth, acceptance and empathy. The coach employs strong skills of active listening, going at their own pace for the client to uncover their insights and make choices that will lead them to fulfil their potential.

Origins of the Time to Think Model

Inspired by her own mother's capacity for listening and deep presence, along with her own studies in the fields of education, counselling and philosophy, Kline observed that everything we do depends for its quality on the thinking we do first. Thinking comes first; therefore, to improve action we must first improve thinking. She had co-founded a school to help teenagers think for themselves and consistently observed the difference when students thought clearly and for themselves and when they did not. What was less obvious was what enabled them to do so. Age, gender, background, intelligence and experience seemed to make little difference. However, one differentiator began to emerge and that was how they were being treated by the people with them when they were thinking. Kline and her colleagues discovered that when someone is trying to think, much of what the 'listener' hears and sees is the effect that they themselves are having on the 'thinker'. They decided that if it were possible to identify what was *thinking–enhancing* behaviour, it could be learnt and therefore taught to others. During the following years, Kline and her colleagues identified and described the components of this *Thinking Environment*.

As the concept of the Thinking Environment evolved, Kline remembered and compared some of the qualities she experienced with her mother, whose listening had such a profound and positive impact for her. These included:

- Naturally keeping her eyes on the other person.
- Being at ease in her own posture, settling in to listen carefully.
- Her tone and sounds she made while listening.
- Laughing with, never at.
- Conveying equality and encouragement.
- Comfortable and relaxed with the other person's emotions and feelings of fear.
- Occasionally and unintrusively giving information needed.
- Affirming, not criticizing.
- Not interrupting.
- Showing joy when the person discovered an insight.

At the heart of these behaviours was attention. Later, a client of Kline's summed this up as: the quality of a person's attention determines the quality of other people's thinking. Kline and her colleagues proposed the following two statements:

1. Everything we do depends upon the thinking we do first.
2. Our thinking depends upon the quality of our attention for each other.

In this case, the most important thing we can do is listen to people so well and so carefully, giving them attention so respectfully that they may think for themselves clearly and in a new way.

Although attentive listening is crucial, Kline also noticed that there are times when this is not quite enough. Some blocks to thinking need more than just deep attention alone to enable the person to move beyond them. It seemed clear that the answer had something to do with questions; however, it was not known what type of questions or in fact what the blocks to thinking generally were about. After two more years of study, it became clearer that the blocks were almost always associated with assumptions being made by the thinker. These assumptions were largely unconscious and yet were being framed or experienced by the thinker as 'truths'. Of all the possible blocks to thinking, it was found that assumptions were the most powerful and troublesome.

Kline's ongoing work uncovered three types of assumptions with several subsets and concluded that being able to recognize them would help to remove them. Over time, certain questions were found to work in the removal of the assumptions. These were developed into a process called *incisive questions*, which – when combined with the best possible attentive listening – can enable the human mind to move past the barriers of assumptions toward new, different and previously inconceivable ways of thinking.

The Thinking Environment

Eventually, the essential behaviours that comprised the thinking environment became clear and 10 ways of being together and treating each other were identified.

Box 16.2: The Ten Components of a Thinking Environment

1. Attention: Listening with respect, interest, fascination and without interruption.
2. Incisive questions: Removing the assumptions that limit thinking and ideas, freeing the mind to create new and different thinking.
3. Equality: Treating each other as thinking peers. Giving equal turns and attention, keeping arrangements and boundaries.
4. Appreciation: Practicing a five-to-one ratio of appreciation to criticism, encouraging and enabling the person to feel safe to wander and delve into deep free thinking.
5. Ease: Offering freedom from rush or urgency so that the thinking process has space and time to emerge and evolve. →

6. Encouragement: Moving beyond competition. Internal competition and judgment make new, high-quality thoughts impossible. With no inner competition, there is no inner conflict, thereby allowing free thinking to happen.
7. Feelings: Allowing sufficient emotional release to restore thinking. Feelings cloud judgment and so the full expression of those feelings creates space for thinking to be restored and for free thinking to happen.
8. Information: Providing a full and accurate picture of reality. Information can help to build up thinking and when faced with the clarity of full facts, the mind can wander and explore strategies and solutions.
9. Place: Creating a physical environment that says back to people "You matter".
10. Diversity: Adding quality because of the differences between us.

Incisive Questions

The three kinds of assumptions Kline identified are:

1. Facts
2. Possible facts
3. Bedrock assumptions about the self and about how life works

Incisive questions are designed to remove these assumptions by a combination of memory and simplicity. It is important to remember how the thinker has described their assumption, in the exact words they used. When applicable, it is also important to remember what words or phrase they have used for the positive opposite of this assumption, again in their exact words.

Regarding simplicity, one of the simplest and cleanest incisive questions starts with: "If you knew…" What makes a question incisive is that it cuts cleanly into the assumption and removes it. It replaces the assumption with a new, freeing assumption; a new truth that is based on positive choice.

The incisive question typically has three parts:

1. Hypothesis: "If you knew…"
2. Followed by a freeing true assumption: "…that you are perfectly skilled for this task…"
3. Attach the new assumption to the goal: "…how would you respond to your boss's request?"

If you knew + freeing assumption + goal = incisive question

By asking the incisive question once, you may hear one idea. By asking it again, you will hear another. Repetition of the question, in exactly the same wording and format, is recommended and can give rise to many free and flowing ideas that had been previously blocked by the limiting assumption.

The tense used is also an important characteristic of the incisive question. For example: "If you knew that you *are* perfectly capable." By using the present tense, we are stating the positive new assumption as a truth. The hypothetical parts of the question are the first three words ("If you knew…") and in the last part, when asking for their ideas about their goal ("…how *would* you respond to your boss's request?"). Here the verbs are hypothetical because we are just supposing. We are not demanding that the thinker believe it, we are inviting them into playful speculation. This playful speculation provides mitigation against the thinker feeling defensive or resistant, allowing them to think freely and imaginatively without fear of judgment or commitment to act. It is this playful sense of possibility vs. requirement that opens up the space for ideas to emerge and action to follow.

The best incisive questions are those that emerge carefully and organically from the dance of the coaching conversation; however, some useful examples have been collected that also show how the three parts are a consistent feature.

Box 16.3: Time to Think Useful Questions

"What do you want to think about?" "What are your thoughts?"

(Maintain total attention to how the person's thinking is developing)

"What more do you think?" "What more do you think, feel, or want to say?"

(Repeat this 'more' stage of questions until there is an unequivocal signal that the person has got to the end of their thinking so far. This may be eye contact and a statement such as *"I think that's it"*)

"What more do you want achieve from this session?"

(Repeat the goal using the person's own words. If necessary, the coach might ask the client *"please can you say that in fewer words"*)   →

> A question that enables further thinking:
>
> *"What are you assuming that is preventing you from…?"*
>
> (Enter their words for what they want to achieve)
>
> *"What else?"*
>
> *"Is it true?"*
>
> (Explore the truth behind the limiting belief)
>
> *"If it is not true that [enter their words for the assumption], what are your words for what is true and liberating?"*
>
> *"If you knew that [enter their words for what is true and liberating], how would you [enter their words for what they want to achieve]?"*
>
> Listen to the answer.
>
> Ask the question again if required, until it has generated all the thinking it is going to.
>
> End with appreciation.

The Humanistic Approach and the ICF Core Competency Model

Many of the principles of the humanistic approach can be found within the ICF Core Competency Model. For example, these include:

Competency 2: Embodies a Coaching Mindset

- Acknowledges that clients are responsible for their own choices.
- Uses awareness of self and one's intuition to benefit clients.
- The overarching definition of this competency is also relevant: Develops and maintains a mindset that is open, curious, flexible and *client-centred*.

Competency 4: Cultivates Trust and Safety

- Seeks to understand the client within their context, which may include their identity, environment, experiences, values and beliefs.
- Demonstrates respect for the client's identity, perceptions, style and language and adapts one's coaching to the client.
- Acknowledges and respects the client's unique talents, insights and their work in the coaching process.
- Shows support and empathy for the client.
- Acknowledges and supports the client's expression of feelings, perceptions, concerns, beliefs and suggestions.
- The overarching definition of this competency is also relevant: Partners with client to create a safe, supportive environment that allows the client to share freely. Maintains a relationship of mutual respect and trust.

Competency 5: Maintains Presence

- Remains focused, observant, empathetic and responsive to the client.
- Demonstrates curiosity during the coaching process.
- Creates or allows space for silence, pause and reflection.

Competency 6: Listens Actively

- This whole competency is relevant. The definition is: Focuses on what the client is and is not saying, to fully understand what is being communicated in the context of the client systems, and to support client self-expression.

Competency 7: Evokes Awareness

- Asks questions about the client such as their way of thinking, values, needs, wants and beliefs.
- Asks questions that help the client explore beyond current thinking.
- Helps the client identify factors that influence current and future patterns of behaviour, thinking or emotion.
- Invites the client to generate ideas about how they can move forward and what they are willing and able to do.

Competency 8: Facilitates Client Growth

- Acknowledges and supports client autonomy in the design of goals, actions and methods of accountability.
- Celebrates the client's progress and successes.

Conclusion

In this chapter we have looked at what is the humanistic or person-centred approach. We have described the roots of humanistic psychology and how it is based upon certain assumptions that embrace the wholeness of the person and a human being's actualising tendency toward growth and potential, given the right conditions and environment. We have noted how this approach challenged other psychological schools of thought and highlighted who have been the main developers and contributors to this field. Although this approach has its origins in the therapeutic setting, there are many aspects of this approach that have direct relevance and are applicable to the context of coaching. An understanding of human needs, how we achieve a state of 'flow' and Rogers' necessary and sufficient conditions for change are all useful concepts in the coaching space.

We have seen how Kline's Time to Think model offers great insight into how and why the skills of deep listening, presence, and incisive questions build upon the work of Rogers and create conditions for change to occur by helping the client remove limiting assumptions thereby releasing and freeing new and creative thought. Finally, we have seen how this humanistic approach is reflected in some of the competencies within the ICF Core Competency Model.

Chapter 17: Cognitive-Behavioural Approach and ABCDEF Model

Cognitive-behavioural coaching (CBC) emerged from cognitive-behavioural therapy (CBT) and the work of therapists like Arnold Lazarus, Aaron Beck and Albert Ellis in the 1960s and 1970s and was developed by writers such as Windy Dryden in the 2000s. The approach aims to help clients recognize the connection between their thoughts, feelings and behaviours. It has been developed by coaches such as Stephen Palmer and Michael Neenan to work with non-clinical issues. The aim was to move away from unhelpful thoughts toward more evidence-based, performance-enhancing thinking, and in so doing improve performance or well-being. In this chapter we explore CBC as a tool that can help clients enhance their personal resilience, better manage stress, support them during organizational change, and address faulty thinking.

Cognitive-Behavioural Model

Cognitive-behavioural therapy argues that for change to take place in a client's behaviour, the client needs to understand the forces that are acting on them and triggering the behaviour. These forces may be driven by the individual's emotion ("I threw the cup across the room because I was angry") or due to thoughts ("I threw the cup across the room because I thought my neighbour's cat was about to pee on my kitchen floor").

The development of CBC builds on the early work of Albert Ellis (1962), Aaron Beck (1976) and Arnold Lazarus (1981), who developed CBT, rational emotive behavioural therapy (REBT), and multimodal therapy for work with their clients – as well as more recent writers such as Windy Dryden, who has written extensively on CBT.

Ellis looked into the relationship among conscious thought, emotions, behaviour, and happiness. He developed REBT on the premise that one's beliefs influence the emotional and behavioural outcomes linked to a particular event. For instance, if an individual believes that they are a bad presenter, and public speaking is part of their job, they might feel anxious when they need to undertake this task. This anxiety, linked to the belief they are a bad presenter, is likely to have a negative impact on their performance during a presentation. Ellis suggested that challenging and reframing such beliefs and replacing such thoughts with more logical – or evidence-based – thinking would be helpful for clients.

Beck argued that automatic thoughts (i.e., repetitive and systematically incorrect thought patterns) are responsible for negative emotions such as depression and anxiety. This internal critical dialogue could impact negatively on an individual's self-esteem, self-efficacy, and overall self-worth. His cognitive-behavioural approach suggests that this internal dialogue can be changed by bringing it into awareness, challenging its credibility, and reframing it more positively and constructively. Cognitive distortions (or thinking errors) are another contribution of Beck's cognitive therapy and refer to people's use of distorted or incomplete data to make conclusions that are inaccurate (Beck, 1976).

Some examples of thinking errors are:

- All-or-nothing thinking – also known as black-and-white thinking.
- Catastrophizing – anticipation of the worst possible outcome only.
- Disqualifying or discounting the positive – seeing this as accidental or lucky.
- Labelling oneself – thus accepting a limit to the possible outcome.
- Mind-reading – assuming one knows what others are thinking or are intending to do without any evidence supporting this view.

Following its development in therapy, CBC emerged in the 2000s (Williams *et al* 2014; Palmer & Williams, 2016). This model has followed a similar approach: helping clients see links between thoughts, feelings and behaviour; helping clients recognize automatic and incorrect thinking patterns; and challenging these by developing more logical and evidence-based thoughts.

More recently, the 'third wave' of CBT has also influenced the development of new CBC practices and models, including acceptance and commitment coaching (Anstiss & Blonna, 2014), mindfulness-based coaching (Hall, 2014), and compassion-based coaching (Anstiss & Gilbert, 2014). The effectiveness of cognitive-behavioural approaches has been extensively validated through research in counselling and more recently in a growing number of coaching studies (Bozer & Jones, 2018).

Cognitive-behavioural coaching is goal-directed, focused on the present, and takes place within a limited and defined period of time (Neenan & Palmer, 2001). It holds the same premise as CBT with its focus on emotional, psychological and behavioural blocks to performance. By understanding how their beliefs can lead to negative perceptions, the coach works with the client to develop greater awareness of thoughts and emotions, and their impact of behaviours. Using a cognitive-behavioural approach the coach aims to help their clients (a) make better progress toward realistic goals; (b) enhance self-awareness of the relationship between thoughts, feelings and behaviours; (c) develop more effective thinking; (d) strengthen their internal resources and resilience to support their action plan; and (e) develop their ability to self-coach (Williams *et al*, 2014; Palmer & Szymanska, 2019).

Cognitive-Behavioural ABCDEF Model

There are various CBC models including SPACE (Social Context, Physiology, Action, Cognition, Emotion) (Williams & Palmer, 2013) and PRACTICE (Problem Identification, Realistic Goals, Alternative Solutions, Consideration of Consequences, Target Most Feasible Solutions, Implementation of Chosen Solutions, Evaluation) (Palmer, 2007). We will focus on the most popular CBC tool, which is the ABCDEF Model (Palmer, 2002). The model uses six steps that the client moves through to gain insight into the relationship between their thoughts, feelings and behaviour, and to develop a new, more effective outlook (see Figure 17.1). The six steps are:

- an activating event (or awareness of the issue)
- beliefs and perceptions (rational or irrational) about the activating event
- consequences (emotional, behavioural and physiological)
- disputing or examining beliefs
- effective new beliefs (response or emotional state)
- future focus.

Figure 17.1: The ABCDEF Model

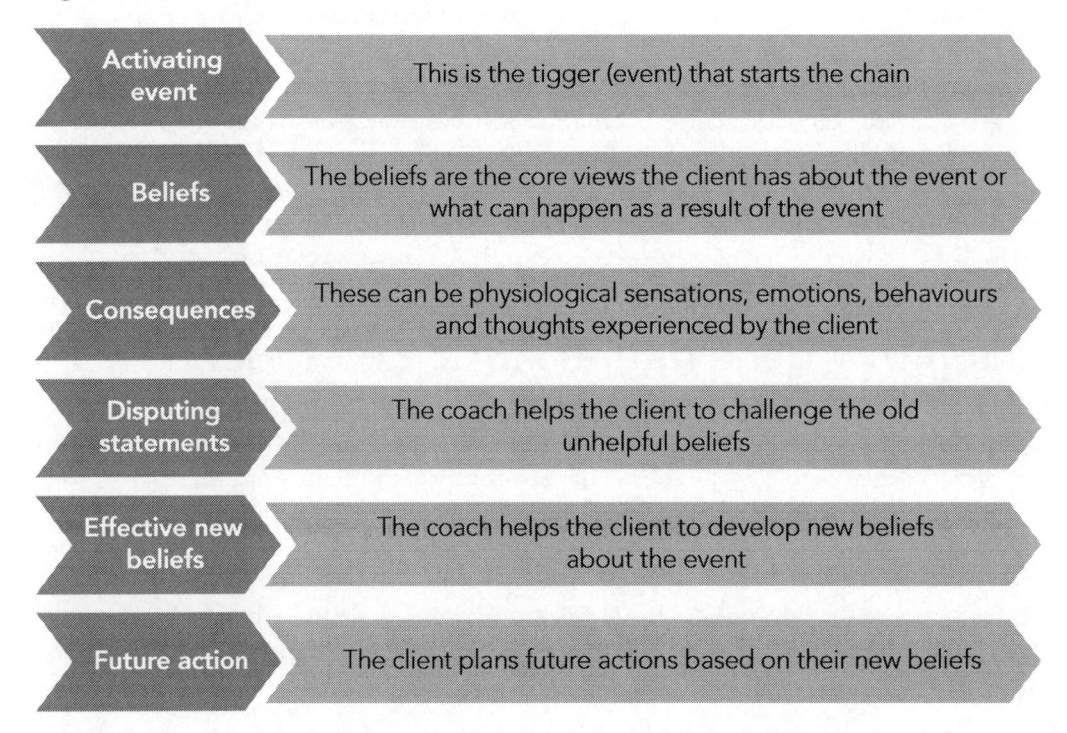

Activating event	This is the tigger (event) that starts the chain
Beliefs	The beliefs are the core views the client has about the event or what can happen as a result of the event
Consequences	These can be physiological sensations, emotions, behaviours and thoughts experienced by the client
Disputing statements	The coach helps the client to challenge the old unhelpful beliefs
Effective new beliefs	The coach helps the client to develop new beliefs about the event
Future action	The client plans future actions based on their new beliefs

There are a number of different approaches to using the tool. A popular one is to invite the client initially to describe the event (A) and move to exploring the consequences (C). Most clients find it easier to explore what happens to them in terms of the sensations and emotions they experience after describing the events and how they behaved in the moment. Clients are generally less able to describe their thought processes without help. It is thus best to explore beliefs after encouraging clients to talk about consequences (Client: "I could feel the hairs on my arm standing up," or "My heart was racing"). The sensations may be followed by an exploration of the client's emotions (Client: "I knew I was really scared about what would happen next"). Having established the emotion, it is then possible to explore thoughts (Coach: "What were you thinking was going to happen?"). Clients may talk about initial thoughts, but it is often helpful to get them to think more critically and in more detail. Many clients hold a series of beliefs; by chaining down through these layers of beliefs, we can help clients establish their core belief. These are commonly about self-worth, self-esteem, or how the client feels they will be judged by others. But we must be careful not to make assumptions about the client and their thought patterns. Each client is different, and we need to remain open and curious, as discussed in Chapter 4.

When the thoughts associated with the trigger and the underlying beliefs have been identified, the coach can begin with the client to challenge these unhelpful beliefs. In most cases the belief is irrational, illogical, as well as being unhelpful. Thus it is useful at the disputation stage to encourage clients to recognize this. We can do that by asking clients how logical the belief is, and what the evidence is for the belief. It is common in CBT for the therapist to invite clients to complete a chart to help identify how frequently these unhelpful beliefs are undermining their efforts. In Table 17.1 we illustrate how clients might complete this between sessions.

Table 17.1: Example of ABCDEF

Activating event	Consequences	Beliefs	Disputing statements	Effective outlook	Future plan
I saw a rat in the yard eating some waste food	It makes my flesh creep (sensation) I ran inside (behaviour) My heart rate went up (sensation) It was disgusting (emotion)	Rats are dirty I might catch a disease I might become ill and die	The rat was more scared of me than I should be of him I was some way away from the rat People don't die of the 'plague' these days	If I see a rat, it will probably run away if I move toward it I can take a broom and hit it if it does not move I can contact the rat catchers to deal with the rat	In future I will always put food waste in the bin If I see a rat I will call the ratcatchers to come and deal with it I will always keep my front door closed I will have a broom by the front door that I can hit the rat with if it does not run away

A blank version of this table is available for clients' use in Chapter 35: Resources, or it can be downloaded from www.pavpub.com/becoming-a-coach-resources.

Once the unhelpful beliefs have been disputed through evidence-based perspectives, new beliefs can be identified by the client. With a series of helpful new beliefs, the client can then test these out in the real world and move on to implement their new plan.

What we have found in our own practice is that old beliefs are not like a light, i.e., easy to switch off. Old beliefs can be intrusive and pervasive, haunting the client despite the new strategy and the knowledge that the old thinking is unhelpful and irrational. To overcome this, we encourage clients to see a movement toward the new beliefs as a process that can take weeks, months, or years. If the client beats themselves up when the old beliefs hang around, this only serves to reinforce unhelpful core beliefs that they are 'not any good' or are 'unworthy'. Therefore, in the intervening time and while new thinking and beliefs are 'gaining ground', we encourage clients to be compassionate toward themselves, to thank their old beliefs for reminding them of the risks while reassuring the old beliefs that it will be okay, as the new beliefs are here to help.

Box 17.3: ABCDEF: Useful Questions

1. Tell me about what happened? (Activating event question)
2. What were you feeling in your body when you saw the spider [or whatever is the trigger event]? (Consequences question)
3. What emotion would you associate those sensations with? (Consequences question)
4. What were your thoughts at time? (Consequences question)
5. What would it mean for you if that happened/what did you imagine happening next? (Belief question)
6. And what would that mean for you if that happened/people thought that? (This question can be repeated several times to chain toward the core belief)
7. What's the evidence for that belief? (Disputing question)
8. How helpful is that belief? (Disputing question)
9. How logical is that belief? (Disputing question)
10. What thoughts might be more helpful to hold about this situation? (Effective outlook)
11. Given this new set of beliefs, what would you want to do to move closer to the goal we started to discuss? (Future planning question)

Conclusion

Cognitive-behavioural therapy has developed into CBC. The approach can help clients better understand the relationship between their emotions, beliefs and behaviours. In this chapter we have explored the application of CBC using the ABCDEF model and how the approach can help clients become more effective thinkers and remove internal blocks to actions, performance and success.

Chapter 18: Gestalt Approach and Chairwork

The Gestalt approach aims to help clients reconnect with their 'whole selves', to understand their physiological reactions to the issues as well as their thoughts and feelings, and how these affect them in the here and now. Gestalt coaching encourages clients to identify and reflect on their patterns of behaviour and, through their insights, test out new ways of being before implementing these changes to their lives. In this chapter we aim to explore the Gestalt approach and how it can be adapted to work with coaching clients. We focus specifically on Chairwork, a tool that can be used to help clients take alternative perspectives and express their thoughts and feelings to other stakeholders within the coaching conversation.

The Model

The word gestalt has its origin in the German word meaning 'form' or 'pattern'. In terms of psychology, the Gestalt perspective explores how meaning takes shape in human perception. One well-known example of this type of research is the illusion. Examples include the 'old woman–young woman' image, 'Rubin's Vase', the waterfall, and Penrose stairs, all of which illustrate how our brain can make sense of information presented to us in more than one way – although on first inspection we sometimes find it hard to see more than one image in these illusions.

Figure 18.1: Rubin's Vase

These ideas about wholeness and the relationship between parts were developed by Fritz Perls in his work with clients during the 1940s and 1950s. For Perls, Gestalt offered a way of being that led to the development of presence with his clients. Unlike behavioural or cognitive-behavioural coaching, Gestalt coaching does not offer a specific model like GROW or ABCDEF. Instead, like humanistic approaches, it focuses more on the relationship and uses this as a basis for exploration of the self.

Key aspects within Gestalt are how beliefs, values and attitudes affect people's relationships, how they respond to change, and therefore impact on the organization and its stakeholders. The approach aims to promote discovery, whereas more rational approaches (e.g., cognitive-behavioural) are less effective in helping clients bring together their diverse thoughts and feelings about a topic.

Frequently, when coaches talk about Gestalt coaching they immediately think of Chairwork, but there is much more to it. Using a Gestalt perspective involves talking about the 'figure of interest', which means the particular thing that a person is focused on at a moment in time. When someone has an incomplete picture, they will seek to complete it with their own perceptions. Gestalt provides an opportunity to bring different perceptions together to provide a deeper and more complete perspective.

Overall, Gestalt is "founded on the notion that human nature is organized into patterns and wholes, and that the whole is more than the sum of its parts" (Gillie, 2008). 'Figure' and 'ground' are key terms in Gestalt coaching. As explained above, the figure is the focus of the client at that moment in time. Coaches are likely to see different figures emerging during the coaching session so it is the role of the coach to explore the figure, but also the ground – or the context – from which the figure emerges. The work of the coach is to help the client develop full awareness of the figure and the ground.

> "The aim of the Gestalt approach is for the person to discover, explore and experience his or her own shape, pattern and wholeness. Analysis may be a part of the process, but the aim of Gestalt is the integration of all disparate parts. In this way people can let themselves become totally what they already are, and what they potentially can become. This fullness of experience can then be available to them in the course of their life and in the experience of a single moment." (Clarkson, 1989, p. 1)

Gestalt-based coaching is underpinned by a number of related concepts:

- **Present-centred awareness:** Awareness is seen as curative and growth-producing. The coaching process follows the client's experience, staying with what is present and aware. It is essential that the coach is fully aware moment by moment, and this is aligned to mindfulness. Practicing mindfulness is one way this level of present-centred awareness can be developed.

- **Emphasis on the unique experience of the individual:** Individual experience consists of emotions, perceptions, behaviour and body sensations, as well as memories and ideas, and is honoured and respected as being true for each individual.

- **Creative experimentation:** The collaborative efforts of the client and coach promote growth and discovery through experimental methodology in which the coach 'tests' out hunches against the client's experience and modifies accordingly.

- **Relationship:** Relationality is central to the change process. Presence, dialogue, and the visibility of the coach characterize the co-created relationship of client and coach (Toman *et al.*, 2013).

How to Use Gestalt Coaching with Clients?

There are a number of ways in which to use Gestalt coaching:

Awareness: This can be used in terms of identifying what is going on 'in the moment' as data for the coaching conversation. It can take a couple of forms – for example, after noticing something about the client, the coach may say: "When you were talking about your line manager you were frowning; what were you thinking? What were you feeling?" This can help bring to the client's attention something they hadn't thought about. The coach can then use their own awareness to challenge or support, or as a line of enquiry to help deepen the client's awareness.

Alternatively, the coach may reflect back something they notice about a feeling they have: "I am feeling anxious at the moment, and I wonder what that might mean." Or, if the client says they are feeling a certain way – e.g., anxiety in a certain situation – the coach may then encourage them to explore this by asking: "Where in your body does the anxiety sit? What physical sensations do you have?" Asking clients to explore body sensations brings a much deeper awareness. Many coaches focus on the cognitive and rational thoughts when a greater awareness of bodily sensations can bring new data and insight, thereby opening the door to change.

Tools and Techniques

Chairwork

Chairwork is possibly the best known technique drawn from Gestalt and is now widely used within other approaches, sometimes using different names such as 'Perceptual Positions' or 'Empty Chair'. The approach can be used with clients in a range of circumstances but works well when the client has a strong stance on a topic, but others might hold a different perspective or interpretation of events. It works particularly with clients who are experiencing conflict in the workplace.

The coach begins by placing an empty chair near to the client and inviting them to imagine the person they are in conflict with is sitting in this chair. It's helpful for the client to provide some background to the relationship, and how each of the parties is feeling and what has happened recently between them. The Typical Day technique might be useful to understand the relationship and its typical interactions in preparation for Chairwork. This involves asking the client to describe in as much detail as possible a typical day when working with, or being with, this person. What is important is to focus on the detail and not to race through the story providing a summary.

Returning to the empty chair, the coach invites the client to 'bring the person into the room' by describing this individual as vividly as possible – e.g., what they look like, what they might be wearing, what smell might be present, how they would be sitting, how they move. The next stage is to invite the client to speak to the other person – to say whatever they want and need to say, however they want to say it. It is helpful to remind the client of the confidentiality clauses, which mean they can say whatever they want with no consequences.

The client may speak for a few minutes, or longer. This may be a calm explanation of their opinion or a torrent of emotion. The engagement depends on the client's style and hidden relationship between them and the other person.

At the end of the communication, and a period of holding the silence, the coach can follow this up with, "What more would do you want to say?" The coach can repeat this until it is clear that the client has finished everything they want to communicate to the other person. For some clients this can be a cathartic experience, releasing built-up tension and things they had always wanted to say. The coach can then pause at this stage and invite the client to reflect on how they now feel about the other person. This exploration can again take a few minutes or half an hour.

The next step is to invite the client to sit in the other person's chair. It's useful if the client thinks about the other person's posture and style. Invite the client to reflect: What do they see? How do they feel? What do they hear? What might they say in response to what they have just heard? This part tends to be shorter but is equally as powerful because the client sees the world from the other perspective. We find it helpful if the client addresses the empty chair as themselves, using their own name, and staying in the role for as long as possible.

A third (and optional) step is to invite the client to move away from the two chairs and occupy a new perspective, standing outside and at some distance from the relationship. Explain this new perspective as someone who is outside of the relationship and therefore independent from it. Independence is necessary as some clients want to select someone who shares their viewpoint, which offers little to broaden the client's understanding of the whole. This position provides a third perspective. In some cases, this perspective (person) does not have a view, or even awareness that there is an issue. This lack of awareness can itself be interesting to explore and provides insight about the bigger picture.

The final step is to ask client to return to their original chair and reflect on the different perspectives. What do these perspectives tell them about the whole? How might they want to move forward? Occasionally it can be beneficial to give the client another opportunity to speak to the Chair – to act out, or rehearse, what they might say to the other person, as a way to move the issue forward.

This approach works particularly well in a workplace conflict situation and also when clients have relationship challenges. The approach offers a wider perspective to clients and provides them with an 'experience' (talking to the empty chair) that changes the nature of their own subjective experience and perceptions about the other person.

Box 18.1: Chairwork Useful Questions

1. "What would you like to say to X?"
2. "What else would you like to say?"
3. "Now imagine you are X. Position yourself in the chair as they sit. Think about how they speak and the words they use. Now what will X say in reply?"
4. "What else would they say?"
5. "Now imagine that we are moving the other side of the room. Imagine we are an independent and slightly ambivalent third person (Y), outside of the relationship. What would this person say to you both?" →

6. "What else would they say?"
7. "As we return to your original Chair, what does it feel like to be X?"
8. "Why might X feel like they do?"
9. "As you think about the perspective from across the room, what might those outside feel about the situation?"
10. "As you reflect on what was said and these different feelings, how do you now make sense of this situation?"
11. "What would you like to do next?"
12. "Can I invite you to say a few words, based on what you have just said? Imagine that X is sitting in front of you now."

Conclusion

Gestalt is a valuable additional psychological approach that invites clients to consider other perspectives in their attempts to better understand the whole. It can help clients gain a fresh perspective through the techniques like Chairwork. It has been invaluable in working with interpersonal conflict and in supporting the enhancement of workplace relationships. Overall, it can really support the client when rational approaches have not worked or are not suited to the client or the presenting issue.

Chapter 19: Solution-Focused Approach and the OSKAR Model

Although many other psychological approaches to behavioural change focus on the problem, the solution-focused approach challenges this mindset. The technique has its origins in Brief Solution-Focused therapy, which avoids analyzing the problem and instead encourages a focus on identifying solutions. Solution-focused coaching, like many of the other approaches described in this book, has migrated from therapy but its future orientation and solution focus make the transfer from therapy to coaching an easy one. In this chapter we briefly explore the model and how it can be applied in coaching through the OSKAR framework.

The Model

The solution-focused approach has its origins in the work of Steve de Shazer, Insoo Kim Berg and Yvonne Dolan in Milwaukee's Brief Family Therapy Center in the US. The Milwaukee counselling team was interested in how they could have more of an impact by enabling more clients to access their services. They investigated the idea of reducing the number of counselling sessions but increasing the intensity of each session. Over the course of about 20 years, the team identified what was most useful to clients in their work. This led to the development of Brief Solution-Focused counselling. In its purest form the approach uses three 50-minute therapy sessions, which discouraged clients from talking about their past failures and focused attention of future actions. Research evaluations by the Milwaukee team suggested success rates as high as 86%, which are similar to rates achieved by other approaches over the course of 30 or 60 sessions spanning 6–18 months (de Shazer, 1991).

Solution-focused coaching can help clients focus on what they can do to put things right, rather than what's wrong, and what can be achieved rather than what may be considered desirable, or even unrealistic or unachievable.

This 'forward-orientated solution approach' contrasts with the majority of other psychological approaches. The traditional technique has been to encourage individuals to look back at the past – i.e., to focus on understanding the problem and to explore its cause through understanding the trigger and beliefs (cognitive-behavioural approaches), understanding their strategies for denial and defenses (psychodynamic approaches), or simply providing a space for the client to reflect and share their thoughts within a supportive, non-judgmental relationship (person-centered).

Solution-focused practitioners argue that a problem orientation is more likely to lead to blame, resistance and conflict, whereas focusing on a solution is much better suited for creating a collaborative environment where any past problem is overcome by the will of reaching a common goal. This view is supported by coaching research that has confirmed solution-focused questions are more effective than problem-focused questions (Grant & Gerrard, 2019).

As the basic principle of the solution-focused approach is to help clients identify and design their solutions rather than analyze and solve problems, the coach needs to remain future-focused, i.e., paying attention to the client's notion of how they want their life to be different in the future. The coach also needs to trust that the client is the expert; they are the one who is finding their own best solution, as opposed to what the coach might consider to be the right solution. The coach should also encourage the client to focus on their strengths and resources, reflecting upon and thinking through how they have solved problems in the past, and when they have been at their best. Finally, having identified a desirable outcome, the coach helps the client to recognize that progress towards a miracle in the real world is achieved by small steps.

Of course, it can be cathartic to talk about the problem and vital for the client, but the skill of the coach is to help clients move from what is often labeled as a 'problem island' to a 'solution island'. The purpose of the coach is to help the client identify the simplest and easiest path to achieving their objective.

OSKAR Model

The OSKAR model is a framework that can be used to structure a solution-focused coaching conversation (Jackson & McKergow, 2007; Dierolf, 2013). The model is similar to GROW, providing a series of letters as a handrail to structure the conversation and help the coach stay on track.

The model incorporates a number of the commonly used tools in a solution-focused approach, including scaling. Other commonly used tools are the miracle question, which we have included in our techniques section in this book.

> **Box 19.1: OSKAR Useful Questions**
>
> 1. Outcome:
> - What is the objective of this coaching?
> - What do you want to achieve today?
> - What does success look like?
>
> 2. Scaling:
> - On a scale of 0–10, with 0 representing the worst it has ever been and 10 the preferred future, where would you put the situation today?
> - You are at N now; what did you do to get this far?
> - How would you know you had got to N+1?
>
> 3. Know-how and resources:
> - What helps you perform at N on the scale, rather than 0?
> - When does the outcome already happen for you – even a little bit?
> - What did you do to make that happen? How did you do that?
>
> 4. Affirm and action:
> - What is already going well?
> - What is the next small step?
> - You are at N now; what would it take to get you to N+1?
> - What else could you do to move to N+1?
>
> 5. Review:
> - What is better?
> - What did you do that made the change happen?
> - What effects have the changes had?
> - What do you think will change?

Tools

Although the solution-focused approach is fairly simple, it can be more difficult to put into practice (Grant, 2016). The coach typically draws on a list of frequently used tools, which we discuss below.

Exclusive focus on solutions: The coach avoids being drawn into discussions about the problem. They listen until there is a hint of a solution and use this as the element to reflect back to direct the conversation forward. This avoids the session drifting into therapy or a focus on the past.

Explicit goal: The coach ensures every conversation has a clear goal from the start, with a clear measure of success.

Scaling: The coach uses coaching to help the client reflect on and evaluate their experience. This could entail asking the client to evaluate how close they are to achieving their goal: "On a scale of 1 to 10, with 10 being the complete solution, and 1 representing the worst, where would you say you are?" Or it can be used to clarify goals: "What does a 6 look like? How would you know you were there?" Or plan small steps: "So what would be different if you were at a 6.5?"

Exceptions: No matter how bad a situation is, there will usually be a time when things went well or at least were not so bad. The coach invites the client to focus on such a time and switches the client's thinking toward a more positive orientation, with the aim of moving forward: "Tell me about a time when the team worked well on a task."

"Do more of what works": Once the client has identified times when the problem is less pronounced, the factors in this situation can be identified and the client encouraged to do more of this, and thus by implication do less of what they find does not work.

Affirming: The coach looks for ways to acknowledge and affirm the client through genuine positive feedback. The coach aims to 'catch the client doing it right' and reflects this back. Such feedback can help clients build self-esteem and confidence. This can be incorporated into a more detailed framework for a real coaching conversation.

Reframing: The coach may help the client during the conversation to reframe their thinking in order to open up more possibilities and draw the client toward the resources they have available.

Client: "I really hate my job"
Coach: "It sounds really unpleasant. Tell me about which parts of the job are the least unpleasant for you."

Miracle question: This technique is most commonly associated with the solution-focused approach but has multiple variations. The classic question developed by de Shazer (1989) invited the client to think about an overnight miracle: "Let me ask you a strange question, which many people find helpful. Imagine that when you go to sleep tonight a miracle happens and all of the difficulties you have been having in this role disappear. Because you are asleep, you don't know that a miracle has happened. When you wake up in the morning, what will be the first signs for you that a miracle has happened?" This may be followed up with: "So, what would you be seeing if that were so?"

However, both Adler and Erikson developed variations of this question within their own work. These can provide the basis for questions, depending on your client and their perspective:

- "What would be different if all your problems were solved?" (known as Adler's Fundamental Question) (Adler, 1925)
- "If you have a crystal ball and looked into the future, explain how what has happened has come about?" (known as Erickson's Crystal Ball technique) (Erickson, 1980)

For all of these reasons the solution-focused approach fits well with coaching and the ICF competencies. In Box 19.2 we provide an illustration of solution-focused coaching and how some of these questions might sit together.

Box 19.2: Example of Solution-Focused Coaching

1. Acknowledge/validate problem

"This sounds like a real issue for you at work, which is causing you quite a bit of stress"

2. Compliment and affirm

"From what you said you have been coping with this well, and still managing to meet most of your objectives"

3. Exception

"It sounds like quite a few problems are affecting the team's performance. Tell me about a time when the team did work well together."

4. Reframing

"It's great that you can see some of the weaknesses in your team. Tell me about some of the team's strengths?" →

> 5. Miracle question
>
> *"Let me ask you a strange question, which many people find helpful. Imagine that when you go to sleep tonight a miracle happens and all of the difficulties you have been having in this role disappear. Because you are asleep, you don't know that a miracle has happened. When you wake up in the morning, what will be the first signs for you that a miracle has happened?"*
>
> *"So, what would you be seeing if that were so"?*
>
> 6. Scale goals:
>
> *"On a scale of 1 to 10, where 1 is complete team dysfunction and 10 is a high performing team hitting all their goals, where are you now?"*
>
> *"What would need to change for you to score this as a higher number?"*

Conclusion

The solution-focused approach is a useful model that can deliver fast-paced change when time is limited. Its focus on the solution as opposed to the problem can increase clients' self-ratings of positive effect, increase self-efficacy, decrease negative feelings, and lead to the generation of more action steps.

Chapter 20: Systemic Approach and Force Field Model

A system is a "perceived whole whose elements 'hang together' because they continually affect each other over time and operate toward a common purpose" (Senge *et al.*, 1994).

A systems approach can describe how the client's scope of attention might expand beyond that of their immediate goal and extend to include factors such as their role, the team, the organization, industry sector, economic sector, and even national, cultural and historical background. Having some level of understanding of and sensitivity to these factors will help the client recognize that they are situated within a specific and unique context. Such factors might be considered 'forces' that influence how they and others act. By understanding these forces, clients can recognize and manage the factors that they can control while learning to appreciate and understand they are sometimes only part of a wider system that they and others cannot control.

The Systemic Approach

Systemic approaches can be traced back to the 1970s and the work of writers such as Peter Checkland, a UK academic, who was interested in 'soft systems' and the challenges faced by managers within the systems. The Soft Systems Methodology (SSM) was developed from earlier systems engineering approaches and its primary use was the analysis of complex situations where there were divergent views about the definition of a problem and therefore its possible solutions. The situations were described as 'soft problems', such as "How to improve the provision of healthcare services" or "How to address the issue of homelessness among young people". That is, these are complex situations where the specific issue to be addressed may not be immediately clear or even wholly agreed upon. As such, the SSM approach seeks to explore the systemic considerations of a situation, as opposed to applying a more linear form of problem-solving.

More recently other writers have explored systems thinking from a range of different perspectives. Oshry (2007) has brought many of these ideas to life through his work examining organizational systems and the role that different characters play. As a playwright, as well as a consultant and writer, he described some of these characters as Tops, Middles, Bottoms and Customers. He notes that many people play different roles; sometimes at the same time but in different relationships, sometimes over time during the course of their careers. What is notable is that one can identify certain common challenges and themes associated with playing a certain role.

Tops have designated responsibility (accountability) for some piece of the action whether it is the whole organization, a division within it, a department, a project team, or a classroom. They are usually tasked with implementing a vision. They have all the responsibility but feel that no one does as they ask. They can feel that others are not listening, that they are being ignored and, as a result, can become isolated. Bottoms are usually embedded deep within a team with a remit to carry out tasks; they think higher-ups ought to be taking care of and providing them with information but fail to do so. They feel as though they are kept in the dark from wider communications and what is going on in the broader organization. Middles experience conflicting demands from all sides. Bottoms demand resources and information, while Tops demand action. Middles feel they can never satisfy both groups and struggle to balance delivery and meeting targets alongside the need for the training, resources and information needed to achieve that delivery. Finally, Customers are looking to some other person to provide a product or service in order to move ahead but feel continually let down by the 'system'.

The principle of this work is that even in the most complex, multilevel, multifunctional organizations, each of us is constantly moving in and out of Top/Middle/Bottom/Customer conditions. In each of these roles there are unique opportunities for contributing to total system power; and in each there are pitfalls that readily lead us to forfeit those contributions.

The Systemic Approach in Coaching

The systemic approach in coaching offers a powerful additional scope of attention and consideration when working with our clients. To bring this alive, writers like John Whittington (2012) have developed approaches that are well suited to use in one-to-one conversation (such as constellations), whereas others have focused on systemic team coaching approaches (Hawkins, 2017; 2018). These approaches help clients consider and work toward their coaching goals through an exploration of the context and system within which they find themselves.

In coaching, the concept of a system could include areas such as the client's job role, the team, the organization, industry sector, economic sector and the national, cultural and historical background. Each of these aspects can imply or even impose explicit and implicit 'rules', such as legal or regulatory constraints, or simply 'how we do things around here' – i.e., the organization's culture. Whittington's approach identifies an uncomplicated path or way to understand and navigate what can be a potentially complex situation for the client. This is done by identifying the key components in the client's system and creating a constellation.

The first stage of every constellation is mapping, which gives clients access to the system-level information and enables them to see their place in that system. The mapping process can allow what is beyond words to be articulated. It also allows clients to go a step further by testing options and ideas to explore the impact they would have on themselves, their goals, and the system itself. Once mapped, the coach can invite the client to explore the relationship between different parts or characters, including the client and their network, as well as non-human entities such as projects, roles and cultures.

This enquiry enables what is implicit and unconscious to surface and be more fully understood. By creating a physical representation, the coaching conversation can come alive in a new and dynamic way and help clients to plan how they manage the system and themselves within that system. The constellations approach to systems coaching is not only useful for one-to-one client work. Creating and developing constellations is a powerful way to work with teams and groups – shedding light on team and group dynamics, patterns and processes in order to build more effective working practices and relationships.

Peter Hawkins has popularized how the concept of coaching can contribute to team development. Hawkins proposes that team coaching combines individual coaching and consulting with inspiration from sports coaching. High-functioning sports teams respond to stressful moments instantly because they practice their responses and therefore execute as a team rather than a collection of individuals. In an increasingly complex business and organizational world, leadership teams must work together across departmental divides, professional disciplines, and geographic borders. They must also contend with and navigate some of the other systemic "lenses" already noted. As a result, in order to develop high-performing teams, leaders need to address seven challenges:

1. Balance the needs of various constituents
2. Handle tactical jobs and strategy
3. Cope with conflict

4. Wear multiple hats
5. Develop perspective
6. Manage virtual employees
7. Prioritize the connections rather than the parts

This last point embraces the concept of team coaching in that it focuses on the behaviour of the team more than the work of individual members of the team. Team coaching is therefore still a one-to-one process as opposed to a one-to-many process – one coach, one team.

Hawkins advocates that in leadership team coaching coaches must effectively apply eight skills.

Box 20.1: Hawkins' Eight Skills of a Leadership Team Coach

1. **Storming** – The coach supports the team as its members learn to work together.
2. **Team building or forming** – Coach and team focus on its mission and goals.
3. **Team facilitation** – One member takes ownership of the process so other members can focus on the job.
4. **Team process consultancy** – The coach observes how the team works together.
5. **Team coaching** – The coach helps the team learn.
6. **Leadership team coaching** – The coach assists the team in understanding its impact on the organization's constituents and stakeholders.
7. **Transformational leadership team coaching** – The coach helps the team change the organization into its next incarnation. "One CEO described this as having to navigate the ship through stormy seas while rebuilding the ship at the same time."
8. **Systemic team coaching** – The coach focuses on factors that improve or detract from a team's performance.

This final skill involves the kind of organizational factors that we have already referenced, and is underpinned by a team coaching process called CID-CLEAR.

> ## Box 20.2: Hawkins' CID-CLEAR Team Coaching Process
>
> - **Contracting 1** – The coach holds an initial discussion about the team's understanding of coaching, and everyone works toward an agreement about what the coach's job entails.
> - **Inquiry** – In this data-gathering phase, the coach learns about how the team works.
> - **Diagnosis and design** – The coach analyzes the data from the first two steps.
> - **Contracting 2** – The coach and the team create a contract describing the team's goals for the coaching process.
> - **Listening** – The coach examines the issues identified in the previous step, while remaining alert to verbal and nonverbal feedback.
> - **Explore and experiment** – The coach and the team construct new ways of behaving that address the issues they have identified.
> - **Action** – The team takes the knowledge it has gained and puts it into practice, sometimes using 'SMART (specific, measurable, actionable, realistic and timely)' action steps.
> - **Review** – In this final step, the coach and team examine how the process unfolded and make plans for the next stages.

A leadership team must consider the organization's tasks and processes and the intersection of internal and external concerns. This requires practicing five cyclical disciplines, which the team coach can play a significant role in supporting:

1. **Commissioning:** Team members define the group's purpose and establish how it will measure success. To coach a team in the commissioning stage, the coach gathers data about the goals of the organization's transformation plan, how the team enacted the plan, and what the members thought of the results.

2. **Clarifying:** The team develops and defines its mission, goals, values and processes. In this stage, the coach helps the team examine why it operates, where the organization focuses, what values mold the organization, and what the team hopes to become. This discussion helps team members own their goals and prepare to execute the resulting plan.

3. **Co-Creating:** The team monitors how it functions as a whole, celebrates its achievements, and corrects any malfunctions. To achieve co-creation, the coach looks at the team's objectives and the measures it uses to assess success. The team coach can observe meetings or help the team members process the results of their work to help them stay on track.

4. **Connecting:** The team focuses on how each member connects with external stakeholders. In the connecting phase, the coach helps team members look

outward to see how the constituents of the organization perceive the team's goals and results.

5. **Core-Learning:** Team members assess their performance and draw lessons from their experience. The coach gives the team members feedback on their performance and what they can change in the future.

Finally, Hawkins proposes that an effective team coach will develop the following capacities:

1. Self-awareness
2. Self-ease
3. Staying in the partnership zone
4. Appropriate authority, presence and impact
5. Relationship engagement
6. Encouragement
7. Working across difference
8. Ethical maturity
9. A sense of humour and humility

Force Field Model

One model based within systems thinking that can be used by most coaches is the Force Field model. The Force Field helps clients to consider the systemic forces at work and develop plans to manage these. This involves asking clients to identify, list and assess the strength of both forces for change (the desired outcome) and those resisting change (the desired outcome).

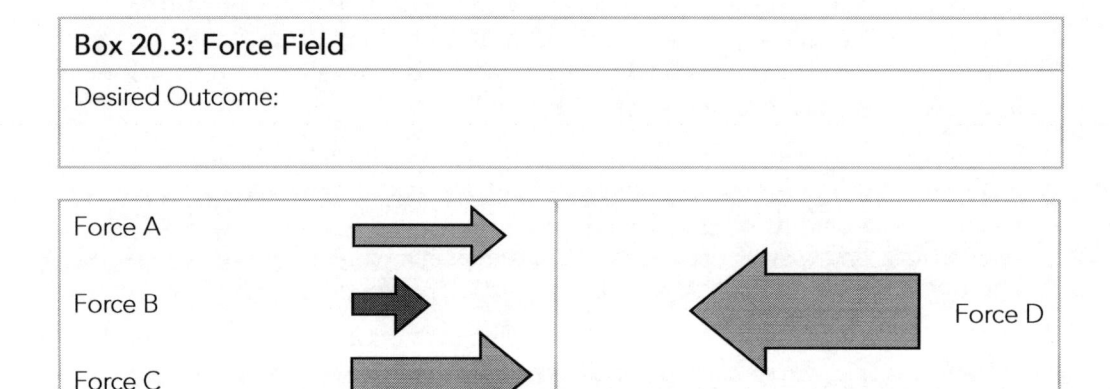

Box 20.3: Force Field

Desired Outcome:

Force A
Force B   Force D
Force C

The model is based on the work of Kurt Lewin and the forces for change (Lewin & Dorwin, 1951). The model invites clients to think about the forces within their system that are pushing for and resisting change. It invites clients to map these forces, reflect on the power of each respective force, and consider what actions can be taken to manage, mitigate or magnify the key forces.

Step 1. Identify the drivers

This step is about becoming confident that there is enough energy and support for the stated goal, and about seeing where that energy and support will come from.

Once the coach has got the client to state their goal, the coach then encourages the client to think about the 'drivers' that will help them progress toward that outcome. 'Drivers' are any forces that support the goal or push you in the right direction. They can be commitment and enthusiasm (from the client, their team, and other people's), lobby pressure from others, events, and so on.

Start by identifying all the "drivers" for your outcome – for example, by asking yourself some of the following questions:

- What difference will this change make to me? What will I get out of it?
- What will the organization get out of it?
- What difference will this change make to people in my team, customers, suppliers, shareholders and other stakeholders?
- What's in it for them? (e.g., your boss, your colleagues, your subordinates and your family and friends)
- Who wants me to make this change? Why?
- Does this change fit with any other changes that people and/or the organization are making?
- Are any events coming up that are particularly relevant to the change I want to make?
- Has anything happened recently that supports the need for me to make this change?
- Are there people who support and invest in me, who might be interested in helping me to achieve the objective?

2. Identify the resisters

Once the drivers have been identified, the next step is to invite the client to consider the 'resisters'. The resisters are the people, feelings, events and forces that will hinder the achievement of the goal. Here are some questions to help you identify them:

- What sacrifices will this change require me to make? What will I have to give up? How much will it cost me?
- What negative consequences will my trying to achieve this objective have for others? And if I am successful, are there people who will lose something as a consequence?
- What are the 'obstacles' to my change, and how powerful will their resistance or indifference be?
- Does this change conflict with any other changes that people and/or the organization are making?
- Are there any events coming up that will get in the way?
- Why haven't I made this change before?
- Do I have the resources I need to achieve the change? (e.g., time, skill, knowledge, support)

3. Assess the strength of the drivers and resisters

Step 3 in the process is mapping these by size onto a map of the forces (see Resources section for the map). The length of the line can be used as a measure of the size of the force.

4. Manage the forces

Suggest to the client what they can do to manage, mitigate or magnify these forces to help achieve their outcome. Take each force in turn.

The output from the process is a plan of action for each of the forces identified through the process. A blank form to create this process is available in Chapter 35: Resources, or can be downloaded from www.pavpub.com/becoming-a-coach-resources.

Systemic Coaching and the ICF Core Competency Model

The ICF Core Competency model outlines competencies that are relevant and applicable to any approach to coaching, however the systemic considerations are quite explicitly referenced in the model in several places:

Foundation Domain:
- Competency 1: Demonstrates Ethical Practice: *Is sensitive to client's identity, environment, experiences, values and beliefs.*
- Competency 2: Embodies a Coaching Mindset: *Remains aware of and open to the influence of context and culture on self and others.*

Co-Creating the Relationship Domain:
- Competency 4: Cultivates Trust and Safety: *Seeks to understand the client within their context, which may include their identity, environment, experiences, valuers and beliefs.*

Communicating Effectively Domain:
- Competency 6: Listens Actively: *Considers the client's context, identity, environment, experiences, values and beliefs to enhance understanding of what the client is communicating.*
- Competency 7: *Evokes Awareness: Helps the client identify factors that influence current and future patterns of behaviour, thinking or emotion.*

Conclusion

For clients who work within an organization, systemic coaching approaches allow them to better understand their place within the system, how they relate to others, and how they can manage these relationships to achieve their goals. Some systemic themes and challenges are explicit and some less so, and the role of the coach is to help the client look at their goals and their situation through a systemic lens. This helps to bring what was unconscious into more conscious awareness so that the client can recognize that some of their challenges are based on systemic considerations. Change can at times be limited to what the system will allow, and the systemic approach helps the client to focus on what they can and can't control, what is an area they can work on for themselves, and what is a product of the system within which they are operating. In this way, coaching can be more easily focused and targeted on developing resourceful strategies that not only support the individual, but which can also have a positive impact on the system at the same time. This is what is sometimes known as the 'ripple effect' of coaching and is closely linked to the rise in popularity and success of coaching teams and groups, as well as individuals (O' Connor & Cavenagh, 2013).

Chapter 21: Psychodynamic Coaching and Transference

Psychoanalytical consulting maintains the position that "the presenting problem may at best be a symptom and often is an issue that services to protect the real problem" (Czander, 1993).

Psychodynamic psychology has its roots in the therapeutic setting and is an approach that focuses on the psychological forces that underlie human behaviour, feelings and emotions. It particularly focuses on the dynamic relationship between conscious and unconscious motivation.

This chapter explores what 'psychodynamic' means and how this approach can be applied to the field of coaching. We look at some practical psychodynamic tools and concepts and see how the ICF Core Competency Model invites coaches to explore, uncover and work with the 'real issue' with their clients.

What Does 'Psychodynamic' Mean?

It is surprisingly difficult to find a succinct answer that does not mislead or obscure. Czander (1993) and Shedler (2010) offer definitions that approach an answer: "The essence of psychodynamic therapy is exploring those aspects of self that are not fully known, especially as they are manifested and potentially influenced in the therapy relationship."

This way of thinking about the human mind began with Freud at the end of the 19th century and has since evolved into the range of therapies known collectively as 'psychodynamic'.

The Evidence Base for a Psychodynamic Approach to Coaching

In one methodological review of research (Shedler, 2010), considerable evidence is presented that supports the effectiveness of psychodynamic approaches. Psychodynamic psychotherapy is also particularly effective in the longer term, after the therapy itself has finished. In similar ways, executive coaching aims not to resolve short-term symptoms but to build long-term, sustainable capability and promote independence, as opposed to reliance and dependency on the coaching process. Shedler's review outlines several key principles that can be usefully applied to the context of coaching.

The Containing Relationship

A psychodynamic coach prioritizes the psychological safety of the relationship between themselves and their clients. This includes such contracting aspects as clarity about confidentiality, frequency and regularity of meetings, and privacy of the encounters. It goes further than these important but rather practical matters, however. The relationship between client and coach needs to become one in which the client feels it is safe to discuss the 'undiscussable', that they will not be judged, and that their vulnerability will not be exploited. The relationship needs, in short, to function as a reliable container into which they can pour half-formed thoughts and shameful feelings with no fear of the coach's reaction.

Emphasis on Self-Awareness and Self-Determination

In psychodynamic coaching, it is the client who leads the way. It is their insights and resolve that determine what will happen. Not only that, but if they develop self-awareness and self-determination, then these gains can remain long after the programme of coaching has ended (Sandler, 2016).

Respect for the Unfathomable Complexity of Mental Life

The psychodynamic coach knows that the enterprise they and their client are engaged in is one of understanding more of what is currently unknown in the client's inner world. The coach may catch glimpses of this inner world, but they can never know for certain. They may offer hypotheses, but always tentatively and always ready to hear the client's response. They may say, "I wonder if…" or "I'm thinking perhaps…" By exploring and remaining open to all sorts of fantasies, daydreams and apparent tangents in the client's thinking, the coach can enable the client to begin to appreciate much more of their inner world.

Exploring Emotion and Intellect

Much of the emotional life of executives is kept private, through habit, fear, shame and a multiplicity of other cultural and individual factors that seek to deny the importance and prevalence of feelings. The psychodynamic coach will spend at least as much time encouraging exploration of feelings as thoughts, knowing that it is the experience of emotion that enables change. Freud is reported to have once said: "Unexpressed emotions will never die. They are buried alive and will come forth later in uglier ways". As a client becomes more aware of the feelings that are causing their behaviour, they also may begin to feel differently, and to see possibilities for responding differently.

Exploring Attempts to Avoid Painful Thoughts and Feelings

As part of expanding the client's awareness of what is currently outside their awareness, the psychodynamic coach is interested in the habits they have for avoiding painful thoughts and feelings. If the coach can encourage the client to recognize the thoughts and feelings they have been avoiding, they may well arrive at a point of emotional insight that produces change.

Focus on the Here and Now

Psychodynamic coaches are interested in the pattern of relationship that develops between them and their clients (transference and countertransference). These patterns have the potential to shed a great clarifying light on some of the most intractable relationships in the client's professional life. For example, if the client is always late for sessions when the coach is always on time, that pattern may serve some function for the client in their life generally. Perhaps the client fears rejection, and so positions themselves as the one who is doing the rejecting? Perhaps they are concerned that they will not be given sufficient attention, and so they make people wait for them? Exploring this behaviour with a safe and trusted relationship can make it possible for the client to appreciate more of the unknown in themselves.

Emphasis on Relationships

Through this kind of work, the psychodynamic coach creates the possibility for greater flexibility in interpersonal relationships generally. Not only does the client become aware of their motives for – and the impact of – their current choices, but they have the opportunity to develop new ways of relating within the context of a safe relationship with the coach. Since the vast majority of issues that the executive brings to coaching are at least partially to do with their interpersonal relationships, this is a great strength of the psychodynamic approach.

Fancy Dress Party Question

The fancy dress party is ideal for exploring relationships, and particularly unpacking aspects that are outside the conscious awareness of the client.

> **Box 21.1: The Fancy Dress Party Question**
>
> The coach invites the client to imagine they are going to a fancy dress party with the other person. Who would they go as? This can be followed by a question to explore what might happen at the party and why the client selected the characters and events shared.
>
> In reflecting on their choice and telling the story, interesting insights can emerge about how they view another person, how they view themselves in relation to that other person, and the story that is unfolding.
>
> A coaching conversation session can unpack these insights and the aspects of the relationship(s), and implications for how they might choose to reimagine the relationship(s), or how they can adapt their behaviour to achieve better outcomes.

Identification of Recurring Patterns and Themes

Psychodynamic coaches work to identify and explore recurring patterns and themes in the client's thoughts, feelings, self-concept, relationships, behaviours and experiences. In some cases, the client may be acutely aware of these patterns and yet feel unable to avoid them (e.g., the client knows that timekeeping is a critical aspect to building a good relationship with their manager and yet, try as they might, they seem unable to arrive on time). In this case, the coach might invite the client to explore what is underneath that pattern of behaviour, what does being late represent for the client, and their relationship with their manager? In other cases, the client may be unaware of the patterns and the coach helps them to recognize and understand them.

Exploration of Fantasy Life

With the psychodynamic approach, part of the coaching process might include an exploration of the client's hopes, desires, dreams and visions. The client shares freely and fully, leading to the exploration of options and possibilities. This approach can be likened to the coaching 'miracle' question ("What if anything were possible?") and also has resonance with Boyatzis's Intentional Change Theory (2008) and the discovery of the 'Ideal Self'.

By way of bringing these principles together, if we consider that a person who presents themselves for coaching may feel puzzled or challenged. They want change. But then again, they do not. They may seem, to an external observer, to resist change. Even when the coaching begins well, and all has been progressing for some time along a smooth and beneficial path, suddenly they resist and seem to sabotage their own intent. It is precisely at that point that the insights from psychodynamic thinking can be most useful to client. By becoming clearer about all of their thoughts and feelings, including those outside their immediate awareness, the client can begin to remove the barriers to change that have held them back.

The psychodynamic approach in coaching therefore offers clients great scope for self-discovery, using their insights in that process to enable understanding and change. Sandler (2016) proposes that psychodynamic coaching can support coaches to:

- understand their clients in depth, including those thoughts and emotions that lie 'below the surface'
- forge strong working relationships with their clients that rapidly engage them in the coaching process
- promote significant, observable improvement in their clients' behaviour and performance at work
- help clients to remain effective and skillful even when under pressure.

Psychodynamic Concepts Useful in Coaching

There are four particular concepts in psychodynamic theory that we feel are noteworthy and have relevance and use in the context of coaching.

Projection

Projection can be defined as our tendency to 'act out' our feelings, unintentionally, in a way that 'infects' others with the feelings we (often unconsciously) have. This act of projection is often a defense mechanism in which our ego defends itself against those unconscious qualities or impulses (positive or negative) by denying their existence in ourselves while attributing them to others. For example, a leader may feel uncertain and vulnerable in their role. They deny these feelings in themselves and 'project' them onto their line report, chastising and confronting them for their lack of confidence, decision-making and assertiveness. What this means for us as coaches is that our own feelings in our client's presence may give us useful information about our client's inner world. The question "What is mine and what is theirs?" comes to mind.

Transference

This is our tendency to 'transfer' feelings we have for a significant person in our past and/or present onto others who remind us of them. So, for example, if our mother disappointed us, we may anticipate being disappointed by women in general. In coaching, we might remind our client of their brother, sister, an old boss or a friend and this resonance can lead them to respond to us as though we were that person, as if they are "putting someone else's face" onto us. Naturally, this process can have positive and negative implications for the coaching relationship and can, of course, occur in either direction. It can also occur for the client with other individuals within their system, thereby having implications for their relationships with people in their network.

Countertransference

Countertransference is our tendency to respond to transference, not by noticing it consciously, but by having feelings of our own. So, for example, if someone anticipates being disappointed by us, what we feel is an unusual anxiety to do everything perfectly for them. This can be considered emotional entanglement with our client. What this means for us as coaches is that we must pay attention to our feelings. Countertransference can be another source of useful information, or it can get in the way of the work we need to do with our clients. In the example we have developed here, the coach's countertransference might lead the coach to try to meet all of their client's demands, rather than challenge them on their habit of making unreasonable demands.

Parallel Process

Countertransference and the concept of unconscious emotional entanglement and identification between two parties are also linked to the idea of parallel process. First described by Searle in 1955, it describes how the client can (unconsciously) recreate or 'parallel' their issue in the way they relate to their coach. In this way, the work that the client brings into the coaching session 'acts out' in the moment, in that session. For example, the client is working on how they can be less directive and more empowering with their team, and the coach (potentially unconsciously) finds themselves leading or directing the client more than is helpful in the coaching process.

The role of the coach when working with a psychodynamic approach is to support the client to make known the unknown. Looking at the Johari Window model (Luft & Ingham, 1955) can be a useful way to describe this. In the psychodynamic approach we may be working with the side that is unknown by the self. The coach invites the client to uncover thoughts and feelings that help to reach the source of the work they are doing together in the coaching relationship. Part of the coach's role might be to observe what they notice in the client regarding patterns or themes, etc., in order to reduce the blind spot, thereby increasing what is 'open' and known information. Indeed, information that is already known to the client but hidden from others can also be explored if the coach builds sufficient trust and psychological safety so that the client feels comfortable.

Figure 21.1: Johari Window

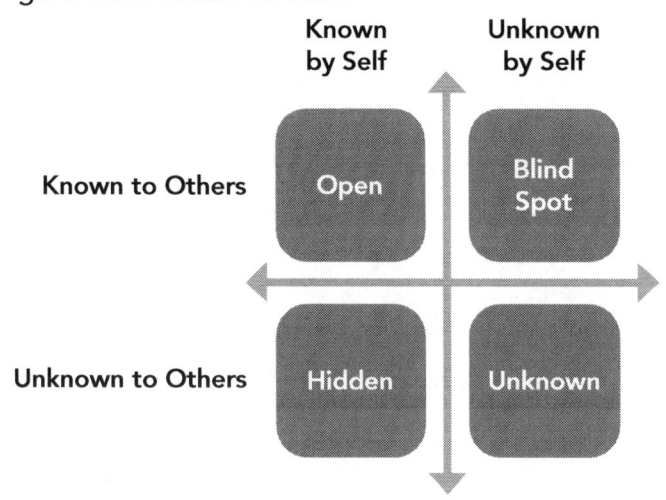

	Known by Self	Unknown by Self
Known to Others	Open	Blind Spot
Unknown to Others	Hidden	Unknown

Another way of looking at this is to consider the 'presenting issue' and the 'real issue'. When a client says that they want to work on their time management because they are staying late at work every evening, is that simply a case for better organization, delegation and prioritization throughout the day? Or could it be that they feel insecure and lacking in confidence in their role and are staying late to learn or achieve more because they feel like the 'weak link' in the team? Taking a psychodynamic approach in coaching can help us to uncover what is really going on and what is the real work that we should be doing.

On the flip side, we also need to take care that we do not slip into what is known as 'confirmation bias', which is the tendency to search for, interpret, favour, and recall information in a way that confirms or strengthens our own personal beliefs or hypotheses. In this way, self-awareness and self-regulation are important qualities for the coach to develop and to continuously check in and challenge ourselves on.

Psychodynamic Principles and the ICF Core Competency Model

Many of the principles of the psychodynamic approach can be found within the ICF Core Competency Model. For example, these include:

Competency 2: Embodies a Coaching Mindset

- Acknowledges that clients are responsible for their own choices
- Remains aware of and open to the influence of context and culture on self and others
- Uses awareness of self and one's intuition to benefit clients
- Develops and maintains the ability to regulate one's emotions
- Mentally and emotionally prepares for sessions
- Seeks help from outside sources when necessary

Competency 3: Establishes and Maintain Agreements

- Partners with the client to identify or reconfirm what they want to accomplish in the session

Competency 4: Cultivates Trust and Safety

- Seeks to understand the client within their context, which may include their identity, environment, experiences, values and beliefs
- Show support and empathy for the client
- Acknowledges and supports the client's expression of feelings, perceptions, concerns, beliefs and suggestions

Competency 5: Maintains Presence

- Remains focused, observant, empathetic and responsive to the client
- Demonstrates curiosity during the coaching process
- Is comfortable in a space of not knowing
- Creates or allows space for silence, pause and reflection

Competency 6: Listens Actively

- Recognizes and inquires when there is more to what the client is communicating
- Notices, acknowledges and explores the client's emotions, energy shifts, non-verbal cues, or other behaviours
- Integrates the client's words, tone of voice and body language to determine the full meaning of what is being communicated
- Notices trends in the client's behaviours and emotions across sessions to discern themes and patterns

Competency 7: Evokes Awareness

- Challenges the client as a way to evoke awareness or insight
- Asks questions about the client such as their way of thinking, values, needs, wants and beliefs
- Asks questions that help the client explore beyond current thinking
- Invites the client to share more about their experience in the moment
- Helps the client to identify factors that influence current and future patterns of behaviour, thinking and emotions
- Shares observations, insights and feelings, without attachment, that have the potential to create new learning for the client

Competency 8: Facilitates Client Growth

- Works with the client to integrate new awareness, insight, or learning into their worldview and behaviours

Conclusion

In this chapter we have explored how psychodynamic psychology can be applied usefully to the coaching process. Although its roots are in the therapeutic setting, the principles and concepts are relevant when working with clients to help them uncover and explore the information about themselves that is useful and necessary for them to more effectively work toward and achieve their goals. We have described what the psychodynamic approach is and shared its principles through the lens of the coaching relationship. We have also looked at some of the core concepts of psychodynamics and how this approach can also be found and is reflected in some of the competencies within the ICF Core Competency Model.

We also want to offer a 'handle with care' tag here. As coaches we can use our understanding of psychodynamic concepts to be a more effective and resourceful coach. However, we are not therapists. As one anonymous psychotherapy patient said: "Psychoanalysis was probably the most interesting thing that I've ever done. I learnt an enormous amount about myself. Only problem is, I was more depressed than when I started." This approach is to help uncover useful information that is in service of the client's forward movement toward their coaching goals. It is not our role as the coach to psychoanalyze them.

Chapter 22: Integration

Coaching has grown dramatically in the past two decades, with a proliferation of different models. Although a number of coaching schools and coaches still adopt a one-size-fits-all approach, we have consistently argued that coaches are best placed with their clients when they draw from different approaches and use a wide suite of tools and techniques. Most coaches recognize how important it is to adapt their coaching to suit each individual client and the different topic they bring. This has led to most coaches developing an integrated approach. In this chapter we will look at how coaches can best make choices about which model to select in which situation and develop an integrated approach to their practice.

What is Integration?

Humanity is diverse. We are different not only in our gender, ethnicity, nationality, physical ability and looks, but also in personalities, preferences and experiences. It's fair to say that no two people are identically alike, not even monozygotic twins.

If that's the case, why would we treat everyone the same in our coaching, using the same model or framework with every client? Not every DIY job at home requires a hammer. But when the only tool we have is a hammer, every problem tends to look like a nail.

We believe in an eclectic approach in which coaches learn a diverse range of models. This may start with learning two or three frameworks during ACC training, then adding one or two models as they progress toward their PCC status. Although there is no ideal number of frameworks that a coach must use, drawing on five to eight models will give coaches the flexibility to be able to meet their clients wherever they are, as opposed to forcing clients to adapt to their one style.

But having a diverse range of approaches is only the start. Coaches need to make choices about which model to use and when, and understand how and when they should deploy these different approaches. This is what is meant by integration.

Integration involves bringing together the different approaches to create a coherent way of working, while still having the flexibility to adapt to different clients and their different issues. Integration involves synthesizing our mass of learning, multiple models, ideas about change, and different tools and techniques, to create a unified whole that is consistent with our values and beliefs.

An Integrated Model for Coaching Practice

There are many ways to bring together different approaches or models within coaching. You will have your own way of making sense of what you do, which draws on your own experiences, training and practice. One of the challenges for a new coach is to describe their approach, so they have a sophisticated answer to the question from a potential client: "So how do you coach?" A response should go beyond simply "Oh, I am a Time to Think coach" – even if they are trained in Time to Think, and they use this as part of their overall practice.

This framework is based on a series of streams that the coach can swim, or work within, moving between streams as required. The framework emerged from practice during the early 2000s (Passmore, 2007) and has continued to develop over time.

The overall model consists of a pair of streams reflecting the developing and maintaining aspects of the coaching partnership. Within this pair of streams are a series of four streams that the coach can explore, working with the different facets of their client – behavioural, cognitive, emotional and physiological. All of this work takes place within a systemic context.

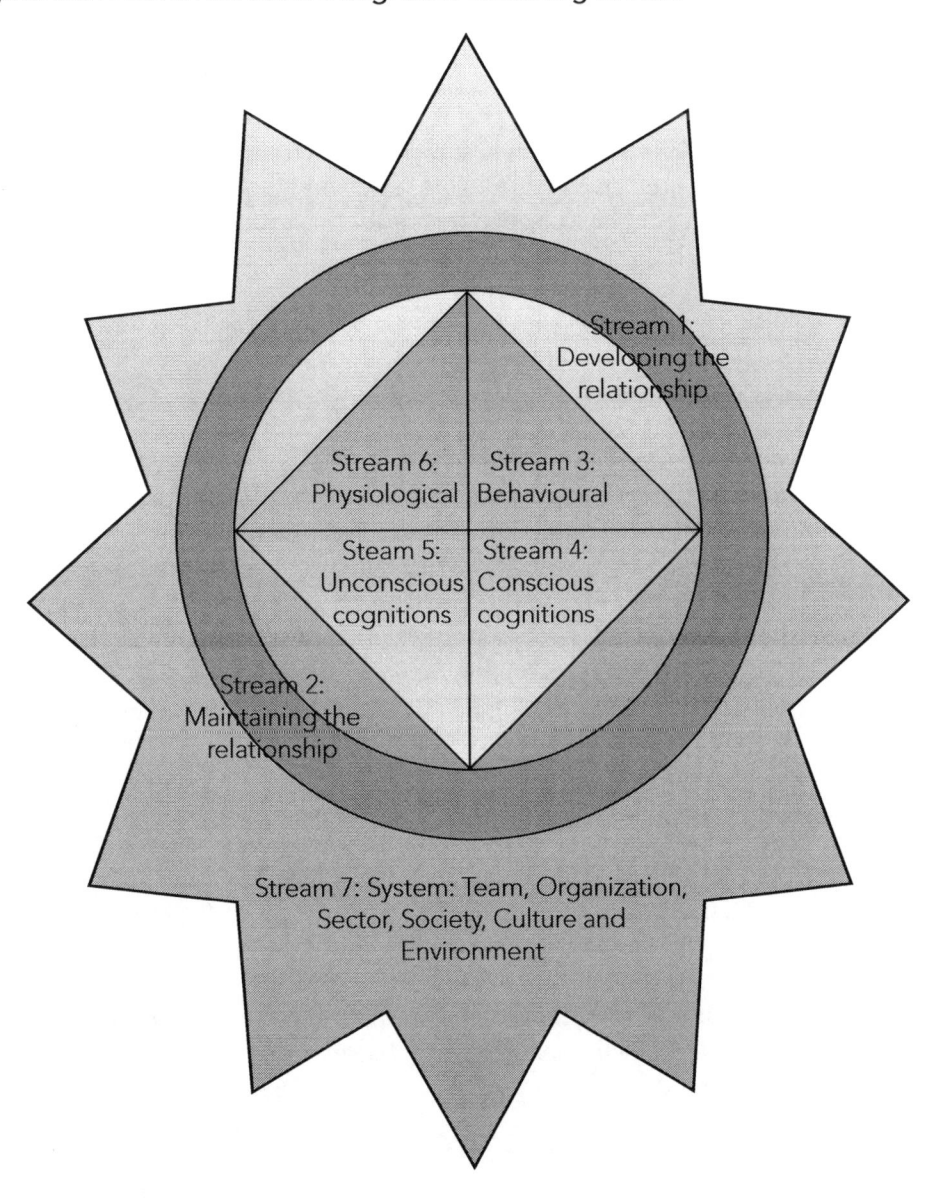

Figure 22.1: Seven Streams Integrated Coaching Model

Stream 1: Developing the relationship
Stream 6: Physiological
Stream 3: Behavioural
Steam 5: Unconscious cognitions
Stream 4: Conscious cognitions
Stream 2: Maintaining the relationship
Stream 7: System: Team, Organization, Sector, Society, Culture and Environment

People sometimes ask why we use the term 'stream', as opposed to box, category, or level. We prefer the term stream as this reflects the fluid nature of the concept we have in mind, and the ability of the coach to be able to move easily from one stream to another (and back), as required. Second, the concept requires that the water in which we work is flowing, moving, changing, which allows us to change and adapt even if we stay within a single stream. We will review each stream in turn.

The Coaching Partnership

Before any coaching can begin, the coach needs to build a working relationship with the client and maintain this relationship throughout the course of the coaching assignment. The coaching partnership emphasizes the collaborative and equal nature of the relationship. If either party is overly dominant, the coach is likely to feel restricted in their ability to act. Alternatively, if the client feels threatened, they are likely to be less open and willing to talk about intimate issues or may even terminate the relationship.

The first of these two streams (Stream 1) involves the coach working with the client to develop a relationship of mutual trust and respect. To create the right conditions for coaching, the coach needs to invest in the relationship. This starts at the first contact.

Psychological research tells us that our impressions of people are often formed in the first few minutes of an encounter. For the client this might involve reading the coach's bio or reviewing their website. What image would you want these documents to present of you? Getting the tone and message right is as important as your physical first meeting. These messages can build your credibility, offer reassurance, and provide a platform for the first conversation – be it by email, phone or face-to-face.

For many coaching assignments the first enquiry is likely to be by phone or email. Taking the time to listen to the client, provide reassurance, clarifications and guidance will further help the relationship. Finally, when you meet – either online or face-to-face – taking time to invest in the relationship before moving to action provides the platform for future work.

The relationship-building stream is likely to continue during the contracting phrase and into the story phrase in which clients talk about their current situation and what they want to focus on. During this phrase the coach works hard on three aspects – (a) being non-judgmental toward the client, (b) expressing empathy, and (c) being non-possessive (Rogers, 1957).

However, once established this work on the relationship cannot stop. The coach needs to continue to invest in this relationship. The focus, though, can shift into beginning to undertake the work required in the coaching assignment.

The coach thus seeks to create and maintain a safe container for the coaching work. If that container breaks, or is not created in the first place, the coach will be unable to progress the work the client needs to undertake.

Working with Behavioural Issues

The third stream in which the coach works is the behavioural stream. This is a useful place to start, as it helps clients to understand and gain confidence in the coaching process. In this stream the coach encourages clients to use simple problem-solving approaches; to set clear and measurable objectives; to think about their current issue and develop action plans (usually things to do) that enable the person to move closer to their goals. Models such as GROW (Whitmore, 2004) are well suited to this space because they are primarily behaviourally focused, which directs clients to think of actions they can take and use mechanisms for accountability to help them track their progress toward their stated goals.

Working with Conscious Cognitions and Emotions

The fourth stream is centered around the client's thoughts and beliefs. How do these help or hinder the client in their journey toward their goal? In this stream the coach will typically draw upon cognitive-behavioural techniques, such as those developed by Beck (1976), Ellis (1998), Gilbert (2009), and Hayes (2004), which have been refined by coaches to make them more suitable for coaching work (Neenan & Dryden, 2001; Edgerton & Palmer, 2005; Anstiss & Blonna, 2014; Anstiss & Gilbert, 2014).

The aim of the coach is to help clients recognize the relationship between their thoughts, feelings, sensations and their behaviour. Through this, the coach can help the client develop more helpful, supportive or evidenced-based beliefs – or simply become more compassionate toward themselves and, through this, change their thinking to improve their performance or reduce their anxiety.

Working with the Unconscious

The fifth stream is the work with unconscious cognitions. In Stream 4 the client may quite easily bring up the beliefs they hold and the words used by their inner critic that inhibit their performance or are a trigger for their anxiety. In Stream 5 the thoughts, beliefs and attitudes – and their relationship to their current situation – are not part of the client's conscious awareness. Often what has brought them to coaching can be something completely different. The aim of the coach in this space, which they work in sometimes for many sessions, is to help the client to explore the topic from multiple perspectives. Through this a greater self-awareness may emerge and ultimately a desire to address the issue. Approaches such as psychodynamic coaching or motivational interviewing can be particularly useful in this stream, as they help clients connect with often unspoken and unconsidered drivers and – where appropriate – challenge them to develop behaviours that are consistent with the core beliefs and values they hold most dear.

Work in this stream can be a slow and winding journey, during which the coach's understanding of themselves (as well as an understanding of others) can help the client to uncover layer by layer those deeper aspects of themselves that have been hidden or lay undiscovered.

Working with the Body

The sixth stream to work with is the body. For some clients and some coaches, work in this stream is uncomfortable and beyond the boundaries of coaching. Antonio Damasio's work in 2006 demonstrated that Descartes was wrong to suggest a separation of mind and body. He argued we are one – an integrated whole; mind and body. Understanding our bodies and using them to enhance our performance is therefore important if, as coaches, we are working with clients to help them be their best selves.

In this stream the coach works with the client to help them become more aware of their body and its physiological sensations. These sensations may be signals for current emotions, butterflies in the stomach in advance of a presentation, or sweaty palms before a job interview. Or they may be signs of deeper and longer-term issues; a shoulder or neck pain, a sign of stress. For example, one client we have worked with continuously complained of shoulder pain. Although we did not know what the issue was, we suggested he visit his doctor. A referral to the hospital led him to a triple heart bypass operation within the week. He was lucky that the body gave him a signal before he suffered a massive heart attack, which could well have cost him his life.

Work in this stream may involve somatic coaching or activities like the mindfulness body scan, which can help clients make the connection between mind and body and therefore better able to understand the messages their body may be communicating.

Working Within a System

The final stream, which surrounds and influences all of the others, is the Systemic Stream: Stream 7. This stream includes:

■ The work team (but also other teams such as our family and friendship circle)

- The organization (including the wider network of stakeholders around the organization, from shareholders to suppliers)
- The sector (including professional bodies)
- National society (which may set national laws or ways of working)
- Culture (including the modes of thinking and what is valued)
- The environment (the physical world, which imposes its own rules, from gravity to death).

These aspects become increasingly invisible to the client as one moves from team to environment. But these systemic influences inform, and sometimes drive, how we do the things we do at this point in human history – in our national society, in our regional culture, in our city, in our sector, in our organization, in our team and in our family. The aim of the coach is to bring these unspoken forces into the clients' awareness and recognize that systemic forces are powerful and influence both them and others. In short, the aim of the coach is to 'make the invisible visible'. Writers in this space, such as Oshry (2007), have provided fascinating insights into how organizational forces can impact on individuals and what individuals can do to both accept and manage these forces.

In this space the coach's role is to encourage the client to see their actions in the context of other stakeholders:

- "How would you feel if this appeared on the front page of a national newspaper?"
- "What would your grandchildren think of your actions if they look back when they are sharing these stories with their children?"

These questions allow the coach to bring wider perspectives, which encourages greater openness, transparency and accountability. We are sure that some of the actions Enron or Lehman Brothers would not have happened if the spotlight of openness was shone on these behaviours. Equally, we might reconsider some of our behaviours in the use of the earth's finite resources if we thought we had to explain them to our great-grandchildren.

How Can Coaches Develop Their Own Integrated Approach?

Using a diverse range of approaches can help coaches adapt to meet the different needs of individual client, but how should the coach go about developing their own integrated approach? The answer lies in what values and beliefs hold together the different approaches that the coach uses.

A starting point for this model is equality, i.e., a core belief that the coach and client are equals. Second, the coach is working in the best interests of their client. There are two riders to this. A recognition that the client does not always know what they want all of the time, and that sometimes the coach needs to encourage the client to explore more challenging spaces or confront unpleasant emotions to create a change. Also, the coach needs to balance the needs of multiple clients. In many coaching assignments the organization may be paying for the coaching while the individual client may be in the room. This requires the coach to act transparently, encouraging both parties to be open about their agendas and negotiating a shared agenda and review process. (We discuss this more in Chapter 24 on Contracting.)

The third belief underpinning the framework is that change is difficult. It can require failing and recovering several times before the change is successfully made. In essence, coaches need to equip clients to be able to cope with lapses and relapses, and to stay focused on the goal. This is best achieved through a positive and encouraging outlook, where the coach is willing to journey with their client, allowing them to fail and inviting them to reflect on the experience and learn what to do differently during their next attempt.

The final core belief is that coaching is a brief affair. Each assignment is working toward a clear objective and starts with the end in mind. It is not an indefinite ongoing relationship.

New coaches may wish to consider three questions when reflecting on how they will integrate their own approaches and develop a single coherent explanation of their approach to coaching.

Box: 22.2: Questions for Reflection

What beliefs underpin your work with clients?

Which models have you been trained in?

Which approaches do you feel confident to use and have you found helpful with your clients and their issues?

For some coaches, writing answers to these questions is the best way to think through and develop their own approach. For others, drawing their model works best. Either way, as integrated coaches, we should be able to describe what we do and how we work with clients in our own personal philosophy of coaching.

Conclusion

In this chapter we have considered one integrated framework that draws together different approaches to provide a single coherent model, underpinned by a series of core principles. This is just one way. Each coach needs to discover for themselves how they make sense of their practice, and how they can best describe their own personal approach to coaching.

Section 4: Coaching Practice

This section focuses on the practice of coaching. The first of the four chapters in this section is dedicated to ethics. Ethical conduct, integrity and professionalism are high on the agenda for good coaching practice. Ethical codes guide coaching practice and the behaviours of a coach. They also provide a framework that coaches commit to in order to fulfil their ethical and legal obligations in their coaching practice. Chapter 23 looks at what ethics are and introduces the notion of ethical 'dilemmas'. We also offer an overview of the ICF Code of Ethics, along with a useful model called APPEAR, to navigate and explore ethical dilemmas. The ICF Code of Ethics can be found in the appendices section of this book and is the focal point of Competency 1: Demonstrates Ethical Practice, which is covered in Chapter 6.

Closely linked to ethics and professionalism is the process of contracting in coaching. Chapter 24 looks at what a coaching contract is and also positions the idea of frames as a way of outlining the different levels of expectation of and from different stakeholders within the coaching process. A useful model of contracting frames is covered to ensure that all relevant aspects are considered. We also look at multiparty contracting and share thoughts on what should or could be contained within a coaching contract.

Another practical aspect of coaching is that of note-taking. In Chapter 25 we look at the pros and cons of taking notes, as well as important issues in managing those notes – particularly in terms of confidentially and data privacy and data protection. Our general recommendation is that note-taking is best kept to a minimum, for several reasons outlined in this chapter. However, we also offer some hints and tips on note-taking and also offer a simple model called PIPS to help coaches consider what notes to take.

The final chapter in this section focuses on presence as a central feature of good coaching practice. Coaching presence has already been positioned in Chapters 7 and 10 as an integral part of the ICF Core Coaching Competency Model. In Chapter 26, we look specifically at how our coaching presence can be established, maintained and enabled through the practice of mindfulness. We share some mindfulness approaches and techniques and highlight their direct positive impact on the qualities a coach is expected to bring into coaching, both in terms of their *being* as well as their *doing*.

Chapter 23: Ethical Practice

All coaches come across ethical dilemmas in their practice. This may be whether they can work with two different members of the same team in an organization, or whether to report illegal practices to regulators. Ethics mean making choices about what we consider 'right' or 'wrong' and are an essential component of good coaching, as well as good leadership.

Most professional bodies, including the ICF, publish ethical codes of practice. These codes provide advice on what the professional body considers to be acceptable conduct. They also provide a standard of practice that members of the public can expect from their ICF coach. The implication for coaches is that a failure to comply could result in removal from membership or removal of a credential.

In this chapter we briefly explore what ethics are, and what types of ethical dilemmas can arise in coaching. Second, we will consider the ICF Code of Ethics (ICF, 2019a) and ways coaches can become more familiar with the code and its application. Third, we will explore the limitations of professional codes of conduct, recognizing that any attempt to codify ethics risks treating situations as black and white cases. However, in reality coaches need to navigate ethical compliance in a complex world of ambiguity, half-facts and multiple perspectives.

What are Ethics?

Simply put, ethics are about deciding what is right and wrong. But really what we mean is 'morally right' or 'morally wrong', as opposed to financially, commercially or strategically right or wrong. Morality itself is concerned with the norms, values and beliefs embedded within society. Such norms, values and beliefs are often unspoken. They vary across time, culture and organizations. What might be considered acceptable 50 years ago at work would be considered sexual harassment today. What might be considered just banter between colleagues in one sector would be considered bullying in another sector. Coaches need to learn to navigate the challenges of their professional code, their personal values, and the environments in which they work (Turner & Passmore, 2018).

What are Ethical Dilemmas?

Ethical dilemmas are choices that occur when the answer about a future course of action is unclear: "Should I do A, or should I do B?" In coaching, these choices may involve issues about managing or even breaking confidentiality. In what circumstances would it be acceptable to whistleblow on a client who has revealed illegal activity within their organization? It may involve maintaining appropriate relationships with clients. In what circumstances would it be appropriate to go back to a client's flat? In what circumstances would it be appropriate to go for a drink with a client after a session? It involves conflicts between the needs of the individual client and the organizational client who is paying for the coaching. In what circumstances would it be acceptable to protect a client who is using their employer's resources to run their own business? In what circumstances would it be appropriate to break confidentiality to protect organizational intellectual property from being stolen?

ICF Code of Ethics

The ICF publishes a Code of Ethics, which relate to individual coaches, and a Code of Conduct, which relates to accredited programmes.

The Code of Ethics is divided into five parts, with Part 4 itself divided into four sections which contain the real detail. The first part is an Introduction that explains the code and its position within ICF coach practice.

Part 2 defines coaching and sets out the context for practice of ICF coaches within a professional relationship with clients. It helpfully differentiates between the individual client and the sponsor, who is the person responsible for commissioning the coaching. We have summarized these in Box 23.1.

Box 23.1: Definitions

- "Client" – the individual or team/group being coached, the coach being mentored or supervised, or the coach or the student coach being trained.
- "Coaching" – partnering with clients in a thought-provoking and creative process that inspires them to maximize their personal and professional potential.
- "Coaching Relationship" – a relationship that is established by the ICF professional and the client(s)/sponsor(s) under an agreement or a contract that defines the responsibilities and expectations of each party.
- "Code" – ICF Code of Ethics.   →

- "Confidentiality"—protection of any information obtained around the coaching engagement unless consent to release is given.
- "Conflict of Interest"— a situation in which an ICF professional is involved in multiple interests where serving one interest could work against or be in conflict with another. This could be financial, personal, or otherwise.
- "Equality"— a situation in which all people experience inclusion, access to resources and opportunity, regardless of their race, ethnicity, national origin, colour, gender, sexual orientation, gender identity, age, religion, immigration status, mental or physical disability, and other areas of human difference.
- "ICF professional"— individuals who represent themselves as an ICF member or ICF credential-holder, in roles including but not limited to coach, coach supervisor, mentor coach, coach trainer and student of coaching.
- "ICF staff"— the ICF support personnel who are contracted by the managing company that provides professional management and administrative services on behalf of ICF.
- "Internal Coach"— an individual who is employed within an organization and coaches either part-time or full-time the employees of that organization.
- "Sponsor"— the entity (including its representatives) paying for and/or arranging or defining the coaching services to be provided.
- "Support Personnel"— the people who work for ICF professionals in support of their clients.
- "Systemic equality"— gender equality, race equality and other forms of equality that are institutionalized in the ethics, core values, policies, structures, and cultures of communities, organizations, nations and society.

Part 3 of the ICF code sets out the ICF Values and Ethical Principles, while Part 4 sets out expectations for coach conduct under four headings. We have included the full code at the end of this book in the appendices. However, we would encourage you to check the ICF website as the code is updated from time to time. The Code of Ethics and ethical practice is also the focus of ICF Core Competency 1, which we explored in depth in Chapter 6.

It may be helpful to look at the following examples: conflicts of interest, confidentiality, and making public statements and claims.

A common challenge many coaches face is managing conflicts of interest. A guiding principle that coaches can use is transparency. This involves the coach making clear at the start who they are working with, such as coaching a manager or coaching several directors from the same board. It can also relate to conflicts between multiple stakeholders — i.e., the coach may be commissioned by the organization to deliver one agenda, while the client believes there is a second hidden agenda. By encouraging transparency from all parties, potential conflicts can be minimized.

Research into coaching practices suggest there remains widespread misunderstanding about what is acceptable and what is unacceptable practice (Passmore *et al*, 2018; Passmore *et al*, 2019). Confidentiality is often a source of confusion in coaching. Many coaches still refer to coaching as completely confidential, as though the coach is the client's priest and the coaching session confession. Although confidentiality is important, there is a danger that coaches prioritize this over other obligations, such as their contractual obligations to the sponsor and to wider society. Confidentiality does not mean protecting clients from the law or ignoring danger signs when there are serious risks to the client or to others. We suggest coaches make clear during contracting both the confidential nature of coaching but also the limits of confidentiality. Three key limits are serious criminality, risk of harm by clients to themselves, and risk of harm to others.

Judging the nature of a criminal offense is difficult for those who are not involved in the criminal justice system. One potential test of whether a crime is 'serious' is: "If I reported this matter to my local police station would the police actively investigate the crime?" A second test is: "Does the offense carry a potential custodial sentence?" This may be best illustrated by an example. Driving a car above the speed limit is a criminal offense in most countries. However, reporting an individual to the police whom we have seen speeding is unlikely to be investigated, unless the speed was significantly above the limit and an accident had occurred. In contrast, importing and selling hard drugs such as cocaine is a criminal offense and if reported to the police would result in an active investigation. Second, in most countries prosecution for this offense is likely to lead to a custodial sentence.

In contracting with sponsors, coaches need to agree when contracting some general principles about what is confidential and what the coach may be obliged to disclose. This is a difficult path to tread. The coach needs to be careful not to collude with their clients against the organization or wider society, while also not being overly influenced by the sponsor to share the details of each session. Some of these aspects have been expanded and further articulated in the updated ICF Core Competency Model, particularly in Competency 3. Established and Maintain Agreements (see Chapter 8).

The third example relates to making public statements. This is one of the areas in which the ICF receives the most complaints. A coach claims they are qualified in a psychometric tool or makes a similar claim to a client or on their website, which is not completely true. We therefore encourage coaches to read and think carefully about public statements, and only make statements that are true or can be proved.

The final Part of the ICF ethical code relates to Pledge, which summarizes the coach's commitment to the code and to behave in an ethical way. Further information on the ICF Code of Ethics and how it forms part of the ICF Core Competencies are outlined in Chapter 6.

Continuing your Ethical Learning

Having completed your training, you may believe you know all you need to about ethics. This would be wrong. Like the development of coaching competencies, ethical understanding and practice is a continual journey of development.

One helpful step after completing your ACC is to continue to engage through the Complimentary Ethics course available on the ICF website. The ICF online course involves a short video and quiz. The course offers CCE credits and is a useful stepping stone in the journey toward PCC status.

Working with Ethical Dilemmas in your Coaching Practice

Although codes are vital for setting out general principles, they cannot cover every situation, circumstance or eventuality that might arise between the coach and the client, or the coach and the client organization. Instead coaches need to be aware of the code and its contents. They need to be trained in how the code relates to them and their practice and they need to develop internal guides or processes for working with ethical dilemmas to guide themselves to the appropriate response in the situations they encounter.

A heuristic is a rule of thumb or an internal framework that helps us makes decisions. Heuristics can be valuable tools for coaches, guiding their thinking and improving the quality and consistency of the decisions they make in their practice.

The APPEAR ethical model is one such framework that can help in guiding ethical decision-making (Passmore & Turner, 2018). The APPEAR ethical model offers a step-by-step process from encouraging coaches to develop their ethical antenna to recognizing that making ethical choices brings with it consequences that we and others must live with.

> **BOX 23.2: APPEAR Six Stages**
>
> The model has six stages:
> - Awareness
> - Practice
> - Possibilities
> - Extending the field
> - Acting on reflections
> - Reflecting on learning

The model is non-linear and thus the coach can step back to consider or engage with elements more than once. The first stage of the process is Awareness. For high-quality ethical decision-making, coaches need to be sensitive to identify potential risks or challenges to their practice that may carry with them a choice or an ethical component. Having one's antenna continually scanning the environment, the relationship, and ourselves is the starting point. Without this, potential ethical issues can be missed, and the coach can act without consciously considering their decision or the implications of their action or inaction.

We also include in this stage an awareness of the relevant codes of conduct, of best practice, one's own values and of the cultural and societal norms, i.e., what's acceptable and what is unacceptable, at this moment in time and in this cultural, national or organizational context.

We have already emphasized codes of conduct and how some coaches may be members of more than one body and thus be bound by more than one code. Coaches, of course, also need to be aware of these codes and how to apply them. Second, self-awareness is also important. What are your values, and how do you maintain these? Third, sometimes best – or accepted — practice can change very quickly, and the published code takes a time to catch up. For example, the #Metoo movement in the US focused attention in a new way on the power dynamic that can exist in some relationships and the need for greater sensitivity in recognizing the role played by gender and age.

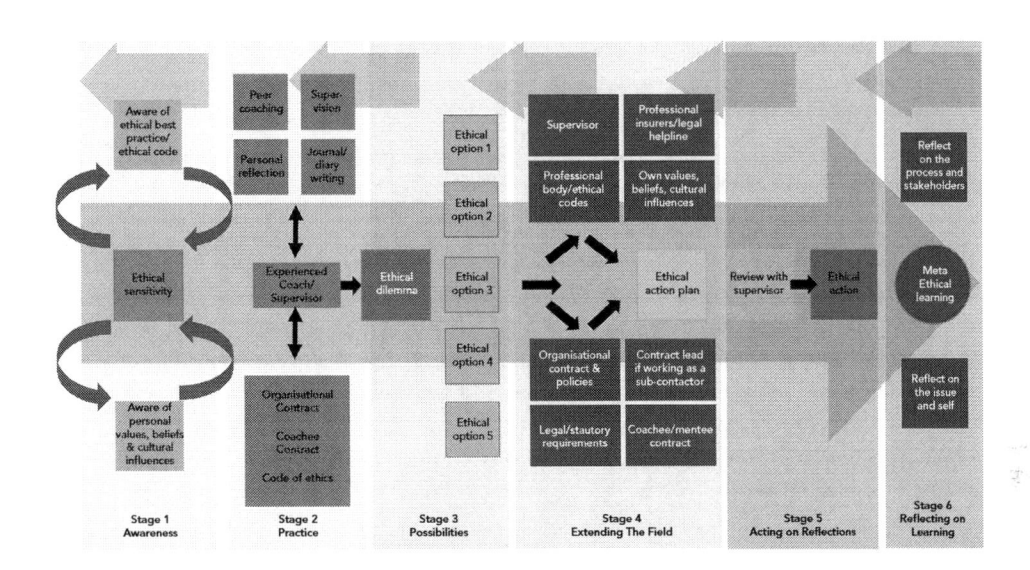

Figure 23.1: APPEAR Ethical Model

Values are also situated within a historical context. What may have been common practice 50 years ago may lead to dismissal in the modern workplace. Ethics also vary between countries. What is acceptable in the US may be different to practices in the Middle East, such as a male coach offering to shake hands with a female commissioning manager. The sector will also have an impact, with higher expectations of public sector bodies than the private sector, and of regulated sectors than non-regulated sectors. Finally, organizations may set different standards for what they consider to be acceptable – whether that's how they report their profits or the ethical standards they expect of their suppliers. There are likely to be vast differences in ways of working in a small family start-up in San Francisco to working for government in Washington DC.

The second stage is Practice. While coaches engage in their roles, regular reflection through supervision, journaling, or personal reflection can help develop and maintain situational and self-awareness. Although supervision has an important role to play in coaching as a means of reflective practice, coaches can and should reflect on their practice in multiple ways.

Stage 3 of the decision-making framework is the emergence of a dilemma and considering the possibilities of how to act. In some coaching roles, dilemmas can happen every week. In others, dilemmas may only emerge every few months, or once a year. Of course, the more sensitive we are to possible dilemmas, the more likely we are to spot them. The coach who never has any ethical dilemmas is most likely a coach who lacks awareness.

The key action for the coach at this stage is to generate alternative courses of action in response to the emergence of the dilemma. This may start with a dichotomy – "I can do A, or I can do B" – but as reflection deepens, and through conversations with others such as a mentor or supervisor, multiple options are likely to emerge.

At Stage 4 (Extending the Field) the individual should aim to work through the options. This involves scenario development – "If I do X, what may follow would be Y" – and this can lead to A and B outcomes. This exploration of the consequences, both positive and negative, will help the coach better understand the options available, discounting less attractive options and selecting the most ethical and practical option given the circumstances.

The fifth stage (Acting on Reflection) is about implementing the appropriate course of action. This takes courage and can come with unpleasant consequences – not just for others, but the coach and their organization, too. For example, whistleblowing about an illegal action can carry severe consequences. The coach may be criticized by the individual or threatened; the organization may prefer to manage the situation internally. The coach may be ostracized, lose their employment or the contract, or suffer damage to their reputation. Sometimes it's right to let the coach manage disclosure; other times it's appropriate for the organization to manage the issue internally. On other occasions, public disclosure is the only right course of action. In coming to this decision, deep reflection and discussion with a supervisor or a trusted colleague can help.

The final stage is for the individual to reflect on the learning that has arisen from the events. This reflection should be at two levels. First, a reflection on the process and the various stakeholders: what have they learnt as a coach from thinking through and implementing this ethical action? Second, reflection on the issue and themselves: what have they learnt about themselves as they encountered and worked through this situation?

Conclusion

Coaching is a journey of development and developing ethical maturity is part of that process. The ICF Ethical Code is a starting point. The next step is the ICF CCE course. Alongside this, thinking about, reflecting on, journaling and discussion in supervision will raise your ethical sensitivity and using a framework such as APPEAR in addition to the ICF code can help you navigate the challenges of coaching practice.

Chapter 24: Contracting with Clients

Contracts are an essential element in the work we do with clients. They enable a shared understanding between the main parties; the organizational clients who are paying for the coaching, as well as individual clients. Research evidence (Passmore *et al*, 2017) confirms that a reasonable proportion of coaches don't use written contracts in their practice. Although this varies between different forms of coaching and different countries, we believe that written contracts and agreements are an essential ingredient for successful coaching. A failure to use a written contract or an agreement leads to the potential risk of misunderstanding about the nature of coaching, how the coach will work and what the organization and the individual client can expect, and what the coach can expect. More importantly, it also fails to provide a means for clients to hold their coach to account, what ethical standards the client can expect the coach to follow, and how the client can complain about their coach if they are unhappy. In this chapter we will explore the role of contracts, think about the different forms of contract that exist, and what should be included or excluded.

What is a Coaching Contract?

A contract is a legal agreement setting out the terms between two parties. In coaching this might take the form of a contract for services between the commissioning organization and the organization supplying the coaching service. In other coaching projects, it may be as simple as a written agreement between the individual coach and the individual client.

In most projects it is likely there will be a number of contracts working simultaneously. There is likely to be a contract between the coaching or consulting company and the commissioning organization. This is the legal agreement for the service and is likely to cover issues such as indemnity requirements, payment terms and compliance. Many organizations also issue Purchase Orders for work, which set out the specifics of an individual task or series of tasks, such as "Undertaking six coaching sessions with Eva Gray between January and June".

Aside from the legal agreement, the coach is likely to discuss and explicitly agree some key points about the coaching with both the sponsor (the person who has commissioned the coaching) and the individual client. These discussions may be held separately or together. Each of these 'agreements' will contain references to coaching and its expected outcomes. However, alongside these, all parties are also following many unspoken 'agreements' about how to interact and work together.

Contracts as 'Frames'

One way of viewing this series of contracts is as a series of frames. These frames reflect the expectations the different stakeholders bring to coaching. Some may be written, some spoken, whereas others are unspoken and may even be outside the conscious awareness of the parties involved, while still influencing how they interact.

These frames operate at multiple levels. In the Eight Contracting Frames model we suggest contracts operate from a moment-to-moment basis to across the lifetime of the stakeholders (Figure 24.1). Let's look at each of the frames in turn.

Frame 1 covers the interactions, moment to moment, in the coaching session. Coaching is a social process. The coach and individual client are continually re-contracting; renegotiating the coaching contract in the moment-to-moment interactions. This contract relates to what is happening between them and what each party considers 'desirable', 'acceptable' and 'unacceptable' in the behaviours they display and how they communicate with each other. As an example, the level of challenge the coach brings into a coaching conversation can grow in proportion to the level of trust that exists between the two parties. When there is no trust, high challenge can rupture the relationship. When there is high trust and high respect, challenge can be seen as stimulating and cathartic. Although few, if any, of these elements will be explicitly covered in a written contract, they will affect the relationship and the work the parties can do together.

Figure 24.1: Eight Contracting Frames

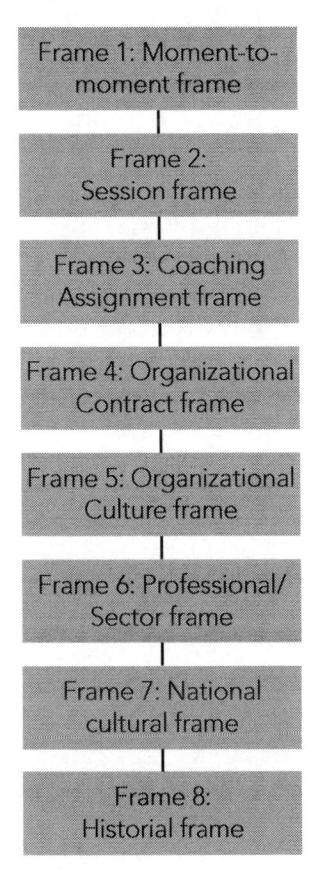

- Frame 1: Moment-to-moment frame
- Frame 2: Session frame
- Frame 3: Coaching Assignment frame
- Frame 4: Organizational Contract frame
- Frame 5: Organizational Culture frame
- Frame 6: Professional/Sector frame
- Frame 7: National cultural frame
- Frame 8: Historial frame

Frame 2 relates to the 'session contract'. A short contracting conversation at the start of each session allows both parties to agree a shared view on the agenda for the session. For example, does the individual client want to build on what was discussed last time, or deal with a pressing issue that has arisen since they last met? It can also be helpful for the coach to refer briefly to the key terms of the contract, and check nothing has changed. This 'contracting' conversation may take 60 seconds but provides a useful platform for each session. We see this an as essential agreement and good practice for the coach to start the session using this checking-in process.

Frames 3 and 4 are more likely to be written. Frame 3 covers the agreement between the coach and individual client. Frame 4 refers to the agreement with the organization (assuming someone else is paying for the coaching). Many organizations now have formal coaching contracts that the coach is required to sign.

If not, the coach should offer a written agreement, setting out the terms for the assignment. We suggest that, when finalizing both, a tripartite meeting between coach, individual client and organizational client (or the sponsor) will help ensure there is clarity and transparency about the reasons for (and focus of) the coaching assignment. This also provides a platform for a review meeting between all parties at the end of the assignment.

We differentiate the formal written contract between the supplier of the coaching and the purchaser and the agreement between the coach and the individual client. The written contract is a legal agreement and could be upheld by the courts. In contrast, we see the agreement between the individual client and the coach as a working document to help clarify how they will work together. This document thus does not need to be signed, but it is helpful for the coach to talk the individual client through its contents and check they are happy with it before the coaching assignment begins. We also think it is useful for the individual client to be given a copy of the agreement for future reference.

We suggest that these formal 'contracts' are mediated through a series of other unspoken 'contracts', or ways of working. These 'contracts' influence how the coach and individual client interact.

Individual clients work for an organization. This is true for most coaches. All organizations, whether a one-person coaching company or a multinational, will have an organizational culture. This culture will influence how the organization makes sense of and responds to customers, colleagues, its regulators, the government, and its competitors. These are unwritten rules and reflect day-to-day working practice. In summary, organizational culture is 'the way things are done around here' (Deal & Kennedy, 1988).

The organization is also likely to operate within a specific sector, a national or cultural setting, and within a historical context. These unspoken 'contracts' influence such issues from what people in the organization wear, how they greet each other, and what they can and cannot say to each other – for example, do they wear a tie, a T-shirt, or a sword? The latter might sound silly, but swords were standard issue 500 years ago, and the UK Members of Parliament still have an allocated space to hang their sword. Do they shake hands, dab, kiss cheeks, bow, or give high-fives? Different sectors, different countries, different races, and at different points in history (or generations) speak, behave and interact differently. Effective coaches are aware of cultural differences as they move from an Australian charity sector client to a French fashion house client, and from a US civil rights organization to a Swiss private bank.

Multiparty Contracting

We believe that a tripartite, or multiparty, meeting before coaching starts can be a benefit for all parties. The meeting might include the coach, the individual client, the sponsor (usually the line manager), and possibly the commissioning manager (HR manager).

The coach's role in this multiparty meeting is to facilitate the discussion. The aim is to secure a shared agreement about what the coaching will cover and what outcomes are expected from the process. Specifically, a list of goals, outcomes or themes to be agreed between the parties to ensure there are no surprises later in the process. A third useful element to discuss is confidentiality – for example, whether the sponsor is expecting a full written report at the end of each session or accepts that the coach will keep content confidential; and what information the coach will disclose to the organization or other authorities, such as the police or health professionals. This is certainly likely to be included where there is a risk of serious harm and issues where there is serious illegality, such as fraud, theft or bribery.

Most large organizations are experienced purchasers of coaching, and many now have bespoke contracts for coaching. However, if the organization is using a general consulting agreement, we believe there is value in a written agreement setting out the number of sessions, length of the sessions, contract value, payment terms and means of redress in cases of dissatisfaction, plus the high-level goals or focus for the work. This can be given to all parties at the end of the multiparty meeting.

With an initial shared understanding in place, the coaching work can begin. The meeting, however, does provide a platform for period reviews. On longer assignments, this may include a meeting with the stakeholders at the mid-point to discuss perceptions of progress and to refocus if needed. Whether there is a mid-point review or not, we advocate a final review meeting. The role of the coach in this meeting is to facilitate discussion between the parties, and their perception on what has been achieved. The coach in this meeting needs to take care not to be drawn into sharing confidential content of what was discussed or expressing an opinion on the individual client or organization. Instead, with skillful interventions the coach can draw out the views of each party, the individual client, the sponsor, and the commissioning manager, to help each to listen and accept each person's evaluation of the coaching assignment, and the next steps for each.

What Should be Included in a Contract?

Box 24.2: Elements in a Sponsor Agreement

- Professional indemnity
- Payment terms
- Termination clause
- Payment terms
- Cancellation terms

Box 24.3: Elements in a Tripartite Agreement

- What is coaching
- Roles of the coach, the sponsor and the client
- Tripartite meeting arrangements (commissioning, review, and end of assignment)
- A short description of the coach's way of working
- Logistics – frequency and length of sessions
- Statement on confidentially and its limitations
- Statement on supervision
- Focus of the coaching – High-level goal or focus
- Coach's professional members and ICF Code of Ethics
- How to complain about the coach

Box 24.4: What to Include in the Agreement with the Individual Client

- Session plan and goals
- Logistics (frequency, length of meeting)
- Contact details (including arrangements for contacting between sessions)
- How both parties can end the relationship (such as referral arrangements and no-fault divorce clause)
- Notice requirements for cancellation

You can read more about how these levels of agreement form part of the ICF Core Competencies in Chapter 8.

Conclusion

Contracting is an essential but often neglected aspect of coaching work. Get it wrong and the coach is vulnerable to complaints from the client or the sponsor, or at least failing to meet client expectations. Get it right, and it provides the bedrock for the subsequent coaching relationship during the coming four, six or 12 months of working together.

Chapter 25: Taking and Managing Coaching Notes

Many coaches ask what best practice is when taking notes during a coaching session. The ICF does not offer any specific guidance on note-taking. Advice is limited to maintaining the confidentially of information and expecting coaches to be in compliance with national legislation, such as data protection. In this chapter we explore ideas around note-taking and make some suggestions about when to take notes, how much information to collect, and how to store, manage and delete this data.

Should you Take Notes?

There is little specific guidance or advice from professional bodies or from thought leaders as to whether, or what about, to make notes within a coaching session or afterwards. The main reason for this is that practices vary. There are few definite right and wrong answers when it comes to note-taking.

Most coaches only make brief notes during a session. There are several reasons for this. The first is that taking detailed notes during a session can be a distraction. The coach spends more of their time looking down writing, instead of making eye contact and listening to their client's full communication. As a result, it can appear the coach is more interested in gathering evidence than engaging in the conversation. Such behaviours can damage trust and intimacy and reduce client disclosure.

Second, our definition of coaching centres on facilitating client insight not evaluating clients based on the information we have gathered. This is different from the many other activities the coach may have undertaken in the past, such as interviewing, performance appraisals or disciplinary hearings. In these situations, the interviewer's objective is to gather as much evidence as possible. The evidence must be accurate and comprehensive. In coaching it's all about the client and helping the client to discover insights and great awareness, and through this to become more aware of choices.

Some coaches do take detailed notes that run to several pages. The coach may have been asked by the coach to take notes for them; for example, if they have a disability or the coach may have been asked to write a report for the sponsor. However, as a general rule we caution against it, and instead encourage our client to take responsibility for themselves and gather their own notes, for example by making an audio recording if they have a disability. In terms of sponsors, we encourage the use of tripartite meetings as the mechanism for review and reporting back – in which the client reports back to the sponsor instead of the coach – with the coach facilitating this conversation as opposed to providing any input. In this way, the workplace manager – line report relationship is intact and maintained and the coaching process sits outside that relationship rather than in any way replacing or replicating it.

What Should We Make Notes About?

To guide our thinking about what information to capture we use the 'PIPS framework':

- Personal
- Ideas
- Plans
- Suggestions

'Personal' issues are non-sensitive, personal details. For example, if the client mentions the name of her partner, Sam, we would make a note. Or if their daughter Florence is playing in a netball tournament the following week, we will make a note. In this way we are able to ask about these aspects during the initial informal conversation at the start of the next session. As an example, our notes might simply read "Daughter: Florence – netball tournament at the end of month" and we might ask: "How did Florence get on in her netball tournament?" This helps build the relationship and demonstrates the coach's personal interest in the wider life of their client.

The second area is 'Ideas'. These may be passing remarks that are worth capturing and may be worthy of exploration at a later time. For example, while focusing on one issue, a client may talk about the challenge of balancing work – home priorities. Our notes may simply record "Future topic: Balancing work – home priorities?" In this area we would ensure we are careful not to use a label or a diagnosis to describe client behaviours, such as 'workaholic' or 'narcissist'. There are a number of reasons for this. First, we need to be careful not to issue clinical diagnoses that we are not qualified to use. Second, what evidence is there to confirm such a diagnosis? We probably only have limited information and the client is unlikely to have completed a standardized assessment questionnaire for such a diagnosis. The final and most compelling argument, however, is regarding client access to the notes. What would be the implications if the client asked to see the notes? In many countries there is a legal right to see all personal data and the coach may have to release such information to the client if asked to do so. We would therefore suggest keeping in mind when making notes that the client is going to read the notes after the session. This encourages the coach to focus on the essentials and avoid straying into areas of speculation.

The third area for notes is 'Plans'. At the end of a session we typically ask the client to summarize their insights or plans for action. We encourage them to make a note of this and, at the same time the client is writing, we make a note of these for review after the session. These plans likely include not just what the client aims to do between now and the next session, but also what barriers and hurdles they need to manage, who will support them, and who will hold them to account. If you have a large client list (maybe 30 or 40 clients), this information can be helpful for the coach to recall at the start of the next meeting the actions the client had agreed to explore as the starting point for the next conversation.

The fourth and final area is 'Suggestions'. These may be comments, feedback or ideas from the client for the coach to action. There may have been a request for a book to read, website, or other material to help the client explore their topic in more depth. It may be feedback from the client, behaviours to continue doing, or things to change for the next session. It might also include referrals or actions that the coach needs to implement, such as contacting the organization, sponsor, or connecting the client with someone else in their network, such as referral to a therapist or to another coach. If the coach does not write it down it's easier to forget and let these requests slip.

What Notes Should We Make After a Session?

This depends on your personal style. We suggest elsewhere in this book the use of a personal learning journal. The coach may use this to write reflections at the end of each session or the end of each week. We believe that reflection is an important component in the coach's developmental journey and that a journal can be a useful aid for noting down thoughts, feelings and insights after each session.

If the coach is able to gather information from each session, this provides several benefits. First, it's a source of material for the coach to take to supervision. What patterns do they observe over weeks or months or with specific clients or types of clients? Second, it provides an opportunity to think through issues while writing.

Finally, for many people the act of writing is a cathartic process allowing them to let go of the feelings or thoughts that are provoked during a session or a day of coaching, allowing them to move on to the next part of their day and leave these feelings behind.

The journal may be short or long, running to 100 words or 1,000, depending on your style and the issues the session or week provokes.

We have described in detail elsewhere in this book one tool for this reflection, known as the Henley8. The Henley8 is a series of questions that provide a useful framework to guide the reflective process.

Box 25.1: The Henley8 Questions for Self-Reflection

1. What I noticed was:

This sentence allows you to explore your observation. What did you notice in your client, the situation, your relationship, the environment?

2. My response was:

The focus here is on how you responded. This could include your behaviour, emotion or cognition. It might also include physiological responses such as blushing or a change in your heart rate.

3. What that tells me about me is:

You may seek to explore the meaning of this for you as a human being.

4. What this might mean for me as a coach is:

You can consider its meaning for you as a coach.

5. The strengths this offers me as a coach are:

All responses have potential benefits and pitfalls. What are the benefits of this response?

6. The potential pitfalls for me are:

What are the pitfalls or the potential things to watch out for?

7. My learning from reflecting on this topic is:

What did you learn from this situation? It could be a desire to adapt your behaviour or an insight about your automatic responses.

8. I will apply this new insight in the future by:

This is your action plan to consider for the future.

What Should You do if Your Client or Sponsor Asks for Your Notes?

This issue is best managed before it arises through the contract with the organization, sponsor and the individual client.

As a general rule, using tripartite contracting can reduce the risk of a sponsor asking for a feedback report. Tripartite contracting involves the coach holding a pre-coaching meeting with the individual client, line manager, or sponsor to discuss the nature of coaching and the expectations of each party. The coach documents the coaching priorities from each party that is used throughout the assignment to guide the coaching. At the end of the coaching assignment a second meeting is held to review the coaching programme. The coach facilitates this conversation, ensuring both the views of the sponsor/line manager, and the individual client are heard, while not expressing a personal opinion or judgment. In some cases, a mid-point review meeting can also be useful. This might happen after the fourth or sixth sessions in an eight- or 12-session assignment to check in with both parties for their views on progress and to realign priorities if needed.

With a tripartite meeting in place most sponsors don't ask the coach for a report or their notes. If this does happen, we would refer back to the initial meeting, saying the details inside the session are confidential.

It is useful to keep in mind any legislative requirements for disclosure of notes. In many parts of the world, such as the European Union (EU), individuals have a right to view any personal data held about them by an individual or organization, such as a coach (Passmore & Rogers, 2018). This would include any notes, files or records with the individual's name, address or other personal details. It is worth noting that even if the coach is not based in the EU, coaching someone based in that region via the internet or a conference call will also be covered by the legislation.

Given coaching has spread across the world – and the increasing use of the internet and conference call coaching – rules will vary across the globe, so bear this in mind when you are coaching.

The final issue to consider is the requirement to disclose notes to the police or civil authorities. Again, legislation varies widely. Notes may be required for employment law cases where the employer or employee is taking legal action. In most instances, the release of such notes needs to be ordered by a judge as opposed to a request by the police. It is best to understand how the law operates in your part of the world

(Turner & Passmore, 2017). Comments regarding coaching-related data can also be found in the ICF Code of Ethics.

Managing and Secure Deletion of Client Data

Once we have collected notes, we need to think about how we will store, manage and destroy these notes at the appropriate time. GDPR requires us to establish a policy for the management, storage, and destruction of personal data. This relates both to written and digital data.

In terms of management of notebooks, we need to think about what information we keep in them. We might, for example, only use initials in our notes. At home we might keep the files and notebooks in a locked office or a locked filing cabinet. For digital data you should ensure your computer is password protected and use anti-virus software that is regularly updated.

The policy should also make clear when and how you will delete your data. We would suggest approximately two or three years after completing the coaching relationship. We should make this an annual task to review our files and delete records that are more than two years old. For paper files this requires the use of a shredder. For digital files this requires deletion and emptying the Trash folder on our devices. It will also require appropriately disposing of computers and hard drives that contain data to prevent someone accessing the data after you have disposed of them.

Conclusion

In this chapter we explored briefly the issue of note taking. We suggested that, although it can be useful to take brief notes, coaches are best to spend more time and energy being fully present, rather than taking notes. When they do take notes, coaches might use the PIPS model as a guide to note-taking, focusing on Personal information, Ideas that arise in the session, client Plans and future Suggestions. We also discussed the need to be respectful to clients in our use of language, and to bear in mind that in many countries clients will have the right to ask to see our notes. Finally, we have talked about the importance of having methods of securely storing and destroying notes after a reasonable period.

Chapter 26: Maintaining Presence Through Mindfulness

A common challenge for many coaches is remaining present during a coaching session. We can often be distracted by events that have taken place before the session, or events during the coaching session, as our mind wanders from what the client has been saying, or as we start to think about the next session or client. In this chapter we consider one way that coaches can enhance their presence in a session through the development of mindfulness practice.

Maintaining Presence

In Chapter 10 we reviewed the ICF's Competence: Maintains Presence, specifically remaining conscious and present with the client, while employing a style that is open, flexible, grounded and confident. In Chapter 7 we also reviewed ICF Core Competency 2: Embodies a Coaching Mindset, which emphasizes the need for the coach to draw upon their own self-awareness and develop the ability to regulate their own emotions so as to be mentally and emotionally prepared for coaching sessions. These practices and qualities help to underpin our capacity to Maintain Presence with our clients and we will look at them further in this chapter.

One approach that we have found helpful in our own practice of establishing a coaching mindset and getting present is mindfulness. Mindfulness is a popular concept with growing evidence about its positive benefits for health and performance. However, mindfulness is also a useful coaching tool that coaches can use themselves, helping them to be fully present in the moment and being non-judgmental of themselves and clients.

What is Mindfulness?

The term mindfulness is derived from a translation of the Buddhist term sati. Sati combines aspects of awareness, attention and remembering that are conducted with non-judgment, acceptance, kindness and friendliness to oneself and others.

A number of writers have offered definitions of mindfulness during the 2,500 years of its history from its Buddhist roots. In the 21st century, one of the best-known writers on the subject, Jon Kabat-Zinn, suggests it is a way of paying attention – i.e., on purpose, in the present moment, non-judgmentally. For those who prefer a more formal definition:

> "Mindfulness is simply a practical way to be more in touch with the fullness of your being through a systematic process of self-observation, self-enquiry and mindful action. There is nothing cold, analytical, or unfeeling about it. The overall tenor of mindfulness practice is gentle, appreciative, and nurturing." (Kabat-Zinn, 1991, p. 13)

The Benefits of Mindfulness

During the past three decades, research has revealed that mindfulness offers significant benefits to practitioners. These findings result from an explosion of published papers examining mindfulness both in healthcare settings and the workplace (Passmore, 2019a; 2019b).

Research has shown that mindfulness has benefits that can be applied across a range of scenarios, from mental health and depression to cancer care, heart disease, pain management and reduction in blood pressure. Possibly less discussed, however, are the cognitive benefits that mindfulness practice confers. Research in this area has shown positive effects on general brain performance, including working memory and attention, control and brain efficiency (Neubauer & Fink, 2009; Ocasio, 2011; Smallwood & Schooler, 2015). It is in these areas that the regular practice of mindfulness can help coaches.

How can Mindfulness Help in Coaching?

We can think about this in three elements – first, the coach; second, the client; and finally the relationship. Effective coaching requires the coach to offer each client their full focused attention. This is not always easy when our personal and professional lives have blurred boundaries and the pressures of the two merge into a mix of worries and confusion. Mindfulness provides an answer; it helps us focus our attention exclusively to the moment that is here and now.

Clients are also likely to be caught in their own vortex of pressures and anxieties. Like the coach, they too carry unhelpful baggage from one event to the next, letting feelings and thoughts cascade from one event or relationship to the next. Mindfulness can provide them with the opportunity to focus their attention to the session and to their learning, too.

As both the coach and the client carry in with them past events and relationships, as well as fears and thoughts about the future, the coaching relationship can suffer. Writers like Carl Rogers and Fritz Perl recognized the importance of the relationship in one-to-one work.

As we noted, central to Carl Rogers' humanistic approach were the concepts of Congruence and Empathic Understanding (Rogers, 1961). Congruence is the way for the coach to be true to themselves. Rogers suggests that during this state the feelings the coach is experiencing are available to them, available to their awareness, and they are able to live these feelings, communicating them as appropriate. Through congruence the coach is best placed to facilitate awareness, providing curious enquiry, and helping clients identify insight.

Empathy can be described as the ability to 'put oneself into somebody else's shoes'. This implies that a person who is empathetic is able to 'step out' of their own reality and into their client's. Mindfulness can help us with this process too, enabling us to work with strong client emotions without becoming lost in these emotions. Being empathetic creates a support structure necessary for the client to feel the coach's presence, their support, and their understanding. Allowing the coach to be aware of the emotions they are experiencing and being able to contain these emotions helps the client to work with them to achieve insight and move forward.

Similarly, the work of Fritz Perl is centered on the empathetic, moment-by-moment exploration of the issues raised by the client. Key ideas are presence and working between the here and now and the next. Presence, in Gestalt, refers to the ability to focus attention on the client in order to respond as authentically as possible to their needs. The 'Here and Now' and 'Next' refer to the exploration of the present, helping the client integrate this learning for future action. We have explored Gestalt in detail in Chapter 18.

We believe there are four main ways mindfulness can be useful to coaching practice.

> **Box 26.1: Potential Benefits of Mindfulness in Coaching**
> - Helping the coach to prepare for coaching
> - Helping the coach maintain focus in a session
> - Helping the coach manage emotional responses
> - Available as a tool to share with clients

(Adapted from Passmore & Marianetti, (2007)

Developing Presence Before a Session

One challenge most coaches face is the challenge of the wandering mind. The coach may be moving from one client's premises to another, or from one conference call to the next. In these situations, the wandering mind can gravitate back to the previous call or drift off to consider the next issue. Mindfulness offers a practical way of putting such demands aside and focusing on the here and now. One way the coach can achieve this is by incorporating this tool into their practice. Allowing four minutes for a brief body scan before each session. Getting in the right mental space, just like an athlete before their next race, is important. A wide variety of body scans is available on the web and these can be downloaded as a digital file to play on a phone. Alternatively, we have included a guided body scan in Table 26.1.

Table 26.1: The Lobby Body Scan	
Step 1	Find somewhere comfortable to sit and create a posture of erectness and dignity.
Step 2	Start to observe the breath; the in-breath and the out-breath. Follow this for 8 or 9 cycles of slowly breathing in and out; filling the lungs and slowing exhaling, before starting the cycle again.
Step 3	Start to be aware of what's going on in the body: any pains, tensions, or sensations. Be open to these sensations, not judging them or seeking to explain them, but simply being aware of their existence.
Step 4	Direct the breath to any areas of tension or stress, and allow the breath to hold, caress and surround any uncomfortable sensations, letting these sensations dissolve or subside. Take each place of tension or stress in turn, and direct eight or nine breathes into each place, or as many as feel appropriate until each subdues.
Step 5	Start to broaden the breath and become aware of the sensation of the whole body as you close the mindful body scan, sitting erect and dignified in the chair.
Step 6	Take that closing sensation into the next part of the day.

Developing presence before a session is also part of embodying a coaching mindset which is addressed in ICF Competency 2 (see Chapter 7).

Maintain Presence During the Session

Mindfulness can also be useful for the coach in helping maintain presence in an individual session. With coaching sessions of an hour to two, the wandering mind can draw the coach away from full attention.

Being aware of this risk can help coaches to manage it better. This requires the coach to be attentive to what is happening to them in the present moment. Should they find themselves being distracted – for example, by noise from the street or thoughts about past or future sessions or other distractions – the coach can catch these thoughts and redirect their attention back to the client. Only when the coach is fully present can they act in service of the client with curiosity and emotional empathy. When out of step, the client risks missing both verbal content and meaning, and thus making the session about themselves rather than in service of their client. You can read more on maintaining presence in Chapter 10.

Managing Emotions During the Session

A third challenge faced by the coach is the relationship; specifically, managing the emotional content created from a personal and intimate conversation. Although supervision and peer mentoring can be helpful tools (depending on the topics that the coach works with), mindfulness is a useful tool to help clients in the moment.

Coaching can create strong feelings of attraction or revulsion toward the client, or their behaviour. This leads to a risk of collusion, where the coach becomes an ally of the client against the big bad organization or other stakeholders who are not present. It can also lead to physical attractions either from the client toward the coach or vice versa.

Mindfulness provides a resource to help the coach become more aware of themselves, their natural human emotional responses, and with this awareness better able to manage them appropriately. The coach's ability to manage their emotions is also explored in Chapter 7.

Techniques to Develop Presence

There are a wide number of mindfulness techniques which, when practiced regularly in coaching sessions or during other tasks, can contribute to improving our longer-term presence within sessions (Passmore & Amit, 2017).

Table 26.2: Three Practices for Mindfulness	
Awareness of environmental distractions	This exercise is about being aware of what is happening around us. A buzzing insect, noise in the street or the tap, tap, tap of the client's pen. Being aware of and accepting these as neither good or bad but simply noises in our environments and returning our focus to the client.
STOP	This exercise is a suggestion to help us become more proactive by stopping and choosing mindfully how we want to continue with our day. It's something we can do that does not require much time.
Being the observer	Rumination is a common human trait. It can happen especially when the client is upset about something that has happened or a conversation that did not go as they wished or planned. The client may over-identify with their thinking, leading them to become anxious, stressed or upset. In these circumstances the coach can simply notice their client's response, remind themselves they are not their thoughts, and these thoughts are not the truth but rather a perception. In this way the coach can avoid being drawn into the emotional turmoil that the client can be experiencing.

(Passmore, 2017a, 2017b, 2018)

Conclusion

Maintaining presence is an important task within coaching and mindfulness practice can be a useful tool for coaches to use when preparing for their coaching practice. The tool is useful in the present moment, but through regular practice also strengthens the coach's focus over time.

Section 5: Developing Your Practice

Section 5 is a series of chapters that offer a variety of ways for coaches to embrace the idea of lifelong learning and development. As highlighted in Chapter 1, when engaging in the process of becoming a coach there is an embedded philosophy and value of a long-term commitment to our own growth, self-awareness and maturity over time.

We begin Chapter 27 by looking at Continuous Professional Development (CPD). We continue in Chapter 28 by exploring one way to bring this into our practice through personal development plans (PDP's) We outline many reasons why your ongoing professional development is not only important but is also of great benefit to how you position yourselves in a growing market sector. We provide you with the ICF's perspectives and expectations of ICF-credentialed coaches regarding their professional development, along with an overview of the development process for credential renewal.

Chapter 29 introduces coaching supervision as a useful and powerful form of ongoing professional development for coaches. We define what supervision is within the context of coaching and share a simple model of supervision that describes the function and scope of this valuable activity. We also cover how supervision works in practice, as well as several examples of how it can benefit the coach on both a personal and professional level. Finally, we offer some hints and tips for helping you find a suitable supervisor and some thoughts on how to get the best out of this kind of development practice.

We continue with an exploration of reflective practice in Chapter 30. We begin by describing what reflective practice is and its benefits for the coach and their coaching practice. We also offer and describe different tools and approaches for you to engage in reflection.

Chapters 31 and 32 explore two aspects of the ICF's credentialing and ongoing development process – mentor coaching and the Coach Knowledge Assessment (CKA). In Chapter 31 we describe and define mentor coaching, specifically from a coaching credentialing perspective and how this differs from other definitions of mentoring. We give an overview of when and how mentor coaching is relevant and required by ICF for credentialing and credential renewal. Mentor coaching can be addressed in several ways; however, we share how it works in practice. We also offer guidance on finding a suitable mentor coach and how to get the best out of this really valuable development process.

Continuing in Chapter 32, we describe what the CKA is, including what its purpose and place is in the ICF credential application process. We share some examples of questions from the CKA and some guidance on how to prepare for this knowledge assessment exercise.

We bring this section to a close with Chapter 33, which explores how you can continue to develop your coaching skills over time. The concepts of coach maturity and lifelong learning return and we offer guidance on how a coach can continue their development within the ICF credentialing system. We look at what PCC is and what is needed to achieve that next level of credential along with some of the key differences between ACC and PCC level coaching. We also share aspects of coaching that differentiate PCC and MCC level and offer a model of professional development that describes the transition from science to art in terms of how we develop and grow in our coaching practice.

Chapter 27: Continuing Professional Development

Continuing Professional Development (CPD) is an important aspect of professional coaching and is integral to the embodiment of a coaching mindset. This chapter looks at how CPD is defined, as well as the many benefits it offers to coaches – not just in terms of their professional growth and development, but also its positive impact on the development of their coaching business and practice as a whole. We also outline the ICF's stance and requirements regarding CPD for coaches to maintain and renew their ICF credential.

What is Continuing Professional Development?

Continuing Professional Development is defined by The CPD Certification Service as the "holistic commitment of professionals toward the enhancement of personal skills and proficiency throughout their careers" (CPD, 2020). This commitment usually includes learning to gain and maintain professional credentials through academic degrees or professionally accredited courses of study. It also embraces informal learning and practice opportunities and usually involves some kind of periodic evaluation. What is also noteworthy is the term 'throughout their careers', which emphasizes the continuity of development over time.

From an ICF perspective, the coach progresses toward and earns their professional credential (ACC, PCC or MCC). The ICF's position on CPD states that: "As part of a self-regulating industry, ICF is committed to coaches providing consistent value to their clients. In order to maintain these professional standards, ICF's position on CPD keeps pace with industry expectations and emerging standards" (ICF, 2020b). The concept of being a lifelong learner is also one that is commonplace among the coaching community and this is actively expected via the process of the periodic renewal of an ICF credential every three years.

The benefits of Continuing Professional Development

The benefits of continuing professional development are many and varied. Apart from enabling us to meet the expectations of professional credentialing bodies and the demands of the coaching marketplace, CPD also offers us rich opportunities for variety, interest and growth.

Reasons for investing in your continuing professional development include:

- Renewing credentials – as already noted, an ICF credential expires after three years and the coach is required to demonstrate they have completed at least 40 hours of CPD during that period.

- Enhancing your offering – as coaching becomes more widespread, the marketplace is also becoming more competitive. Investing in your own CPD will enable you to enhance the depth and breadth of your offering, enabling you to articulate more clearly your unique selling points and skills, and what your clients can expect when they hire you as their coach.

- Staying fit for practice – not only does CPD enhance our skill set and professional offering, it also helps us to avoid stagnation. As with any profession – and indeed any activity – if we stop learning and developing after our initial qualification is secured, it can be easy to slip into bad habits, become complacent, and even begin to cut corners.

- Credibility and reputation – the marketplace of coaching, especially within organizations, is now increasingly aware of what coaching is and organizations are much more informed about coaching when making their buying decisions. This is part of the increasing competition and therefore distinction between good and not-so-good coaches is characteristic of a self-regulating industry. Coaching is also a profession that in many cases still relies heavily on referrals and so our credibility and reputation within the community of coaches and the buyers of coaching is important for our ongoing employment.

- More client work – proactively investing in our CPD plan of activities is going to help us to secure more client work and coaching engagements. Moreover, in many organizations, professional credentials are a requirement for eligibility to work as part of their coaching community. Coaching supervision, which is explored in Chapter 29, is a useful form of CPD and also something that informed organizations are increasingly expecting of coaches as a prerequisite for client engagements.

- Sharpening your saw – we previously noted the concept of the 'lifelong learner' and one of the more personal benefits of CPD is taking pride over the course of our careers to continuously sharpen our own saw so that our craft is the best it can be.

- Community – although coaches are working with people all the time, their professional relationships and connections often have a transitory nature. In this way, coaches are alone in their work and might even feel a degree of isolation. Continuing professional development offers a great opportunity to be part of a community, to experience a sense of belonging, and to engage in stimulating conversations and experiences with other professional colleagues. These coaching communities not only offer connection but are also useful places for networking, which could lead to other client opportunities.

- Growth vs. fixed mindset – Carol Dweck (2017) describes the many benefits of encouraging our brains to develop a love for learning as a basis for accomplishment. This also links to the Four Stages of Competence and how, even though we may aspire to reach 'unconscious competence' when our craft becomes second nature, there is also a danger of complacency and stagnation that can make us 'unconsciously incompetent' once more without realizing it. Continuing professional development helps us to avoid this through staying conscious about our learning and development.

What are CCEs?

The ICF's minimum requirement of 40 hours of CPD every three years is sought by the coach accumulating Continuing Coach Education (CCE) units toward their credential renewal. Typically, one hour of CPD equates to one CCE unit and these units can be earned in various ways. The CCEs are also split into two different types: Core Competency (CC) CCEs and Resource Development (RD) CCEs. For a credential renewal, the coach must complete at least 24 CCEs that are categorized as Core Competency (CC), at least three hours of which are in coaching ethics. The remaining 16 hours can be in Resource Development (RD) CCEs.

One easy way to earn these units is through participating in events that have received an official CCE accreditation from the ICF. Coach training schools and training providers can apply to the ICF to gain CCE accreditation for the CPD events they offer. Additionally ICF local chapters around the world, as well as the ICF Professional Coaches Global organization, offer CPD activities with CCEs and these are often either free of charge or at a reduced rate for members of the ICF. Examples of activities that offer CCEs include webinars, communities of practice (COP), training programmes, conferences, mentor coaching, supervision, and special ICF-approved projects. More details of eligible sources of CCEs can be found on the ICF Global website. The ICF Professional Coaches Global organization also have a calendar where events (both in person and virtual) all over the world are advertised, many of which carry CCEs. Local ICF Chapters often also advertise local events via their websites. The ICF Global organization also has a learning portal where members can access a wide range of learning and development opportunities.

In Chapter 29 we note that up to 10 hours of supervision can be counted toward a coach's 40 hours of CC CCEs every three years. Also, in Chapter 31 we explore mentor coaching and coaches can work with a mentor coach and allocate up to 10 hours of CC CCEs every three years toward their credential renewal. This is a requirement for those seeking to renew their ACC credential and optional for coaches renewing their PCC or MCC credentials.

Apart from these examples of ICF-approved CCE sources, there are other non-approved activities that can be counted as RD CCEs. Up to a maximum of 16 hours of this kind of development can be allocated toward the 40 hours required every three years. Examples of these activities include non-coach-specific training, reading, writing, and research. Once again, details of eligible activities can be found on the ICF Global website.

Table 27.1: A Summary of ICF Continuing Coach Education (CCEs) Units

Type	Core Competency (CC)	Resource Development (RD)	Total
Amount required	A minimum of 24 units every three years	A maximum of 16 units every three years	40 CCE units every three years
Examples	Webinars, programmes, conferences, COPs, mentor coaching, supervision, approved projects	Non-coach-specific training, reading, writing, research	
Resources	ICF Global website: ■ Professional development ■ Global events calendar ■ Learning portal ■ Mentor coaching ■ Supervision ICF local chapter websites		

Professional or Personal Development?

The concept of professional development is probably familiar to us. We may apply this to ourselves and also our work as coaches may relate directly to the professional development of our clients. Having explored what professional development is, its benefits and how we can engage in it, now let's look at this idea of professional development within the context of today's environment.

Terms like 'digital revolution', 'fourth industrial revolution' and 'VUCA (volatile, uncertain, complex and ambiguous)' have entered daily business language. We may find ourselves immersed in conversations around climate change, economic and political turbulence, mental health, and matters of social progress. In light of the characteristics and challenges this type of environment presents, the World Economic Forum has shared the following Top 10 most-needed skills from leaders in 2020 and beyond:

1. Complex problem-solving
2. Critical thinking
3. Creativity
4. People management
5. Co-ordinating with others
6. Emotional intelligence
7. Judgment and decision-making
8. Service orientation
9. Negotiation
10. Cognitive flexibility

One thing we think really stands out is that most, if not all, of these skills are as closely related to our personal development as they are to our professional development. We are struck by the distinct shift we see in the focus of our children's' education, which is now centered around equipping them with skills of the type noted above, as opposed to the more traditional approach of helping them develop subject matter expertise. We see the same concept applied to leaders in the workplace. One head teacher recently described their philosophy as 'future-proofing' leaders and we propose that actually the leaders we work with today need 'present-proofing' because the future is truly here…

At the ICF Converge19 event in Prague in 2019, one of the keynote speakers, Frans Johansson, said: "Today is the slowest day you will ever experience from now on."

Looking at the skills above, the ability to handle change and change at speed are crucial and these skills offer a foundation for that to be possible.

So, the first question that comes to mind is how can we as coaches support these leaders to be most effective in developing these skills? This is closely followed by a second question: How can we as coaches develop these skills and qualities so that we remain useful, relevant and fit for practice in our fast-changing world? Given that the business of coaching has change, growth, and development at its heart, how can we ensure that we too are role modeling the ability to change and grow alongside our clients?

One thing that comes to mind is that we consider the concept of 'first look within'. What is the personal development opportunity for us as coaches? For example:

- How are you with change?
- How are you with uncertainty and ambiguity?
- How are you with goal posts changing regularly and rapidly?
- How are you with the balance between perceiving something as an opportunity or a threat?
- Do you have the skills noted above?

By first looking within, the ripple effect of coaching actually starts with us… and perhaps this is one of the ways that we can make our biggest contribution.

Conclusion

In this chapter we have described what Continuing Professional Development (CPD) is and how it is defined by the ICF. We have also outlined several reasons why our CPD is important and why investing in this in a proactive way significantly benefits us. We have described the ICF's CPD approach using CCE units and shared examples of how to earn these units for credential renewal and general development purposes. Finally, we have also positioned the need for coaches to engage in personal as well as professional growth so that we can be the best we can be in our coaching practice throughout our careers.

Chapter 28: Personal Development Plans

In this chapter we focus on Personal Development Plans (PDP). PDPs are an important part of developing our coaching practice and are a way we can apply CPD in our daily practice. We begin with what is understood by the term personal development plan, along with the purpose and benefits of this as an ongoing process. We also look at some of the underlying theories in support of PDPs and the practicalities of creating them. Finally, we suggest that personal and professional development for coaches is intertwined and, as such, recommend reading Chapters 27 and 28 as a combined exercise.

What is a Personal Development Plan?

The Quality Assurance Agency for Higher Education (QAA), a UK body responsible for higher education, defines personal development planning as a "structured and supported process undertaken by an individual to reflect upon their own learning, performance and/or achievement, and to plan for their personal, educational and career development."

The QAA goes on to state that the primary purpose of PDPs is to "improve the capacity of individuals to review, plan and take responsibility for their own learning and to understand what and how they learn. PDPs help learners articulate their learning, achievements and outcomes more explicitly and support the concept that learning is a lifelong and life-wide activity."

As coaches, our personal and professional development may be intertwined, and this chapter links closely with Chapter 27: Continuing Professional Development, which outlines the ICF's stance and expectations of coaches regarding their ongoing professional growth. A clear commitment to our ongoing learning and development as a coach and our engagement in reflective practice are specifically noted within the ICF Core Competency Model in Competency 2: Embodies a Coaching Mindset, which is covered in Chapter 7.

We propose that an approach to PDP should embrace the following principles:

- Structured and proactively planned with intentionality and a commitment to being a lifelong learner
- Holistic in scope, covering academic, personal and professional development activities
- A process in which we feel supported and guided in some way (e.g., from a teacher, mentor coach, or supervisor) and also encourages self-sufficiency and a self-sustaining pattern over time
- An ongoing process involving goal setting, action planning, self-reflection and monitoring toward the achievement of those goals
- A process that enables us to share and demonstrate our incremental learning to others (e.g., with our clients, during learning events, and in coaching assessment activities such as credential applications and renewals).

The process of PDPs can be linked to learning theory and, in particular, to the four-stage cycle of effective learning based on the work of Kolb (Figure 28.1).

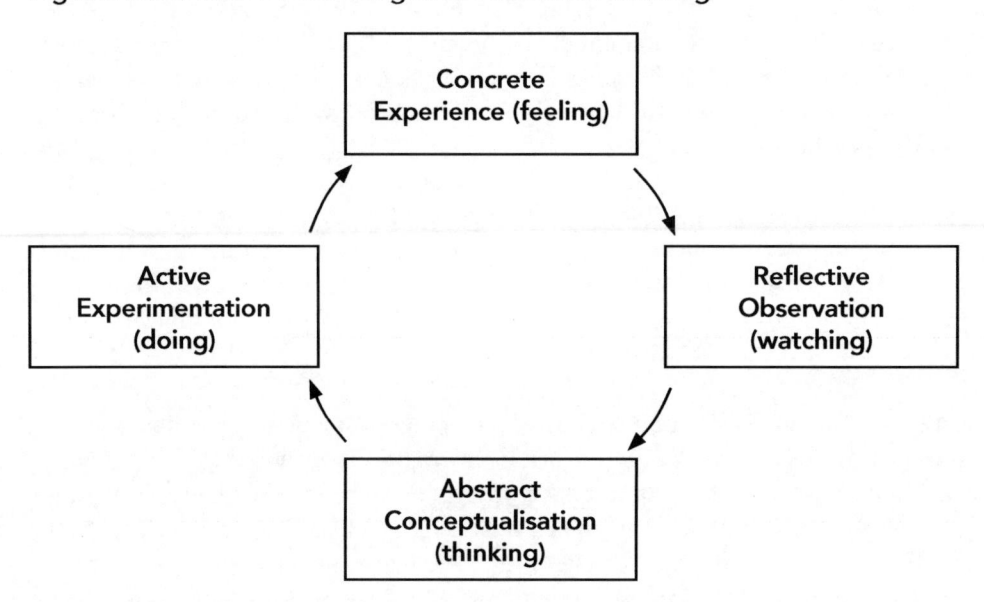

Figure: 28.1: Kolb's Four Stages of Effective Learning

```
          Concrete
       Experience (feeling)
         ↗         ↘
  Active              Reflective
  Experimentation     Observation
  (doing)             (watching)
         ↖         ↙
          Abstract
       Conceptualisation
          (thinking)
```

(Source: Kolb, 1984)

How can a Personal Development Plan help me?

The benefits of a PDP are in many ways similar to those of Continuing Professional Development (CPD). In particular, regular and sustained PDP activities help us to:

- recognize, value, acknowledge and evidence our learning and development in formal and informal ways
- take ownership for our growth
- become more aware of how we learn and what different learning strategies work well/less well for us, thereby expanding our own self-awareness on what is effective for us as learners and practitioners
- be more effective in planning, monitoring and reviewing our own progress
- develop our sense of identity as a learner and as a continuously developing coach
- identify and evaluate our strengths and development opportunities and make plans for enhancing the strengths and addressing our development needs
- be better prepared as coaches for individual sessions, overall engagements, and as a professional coach more broadly
- be able to maintain our alignment with current practices and expectations so that we can continue to thrive in our practice.

In order for these many benefits to be realized, the following characteristics underpin the most effective PDPs:

- Our PDP is a mainstream activity that overtly features in our annual calendar planning.
- Development activities are directly linked to development goals that we have set for ourselves.
- PDP activities are undertaken regularly and are valued by the coach.
- The coach feels supported and encouraged in their learning process.
- The PDP activities are recorded and reviewed to establish and acknowledge progress.

What Should I Include in My Personal Development Plan?

When creating your own PDP, make sure it accurately outlines your personal goals, why they are important to you, and how you plan to achieve them. To support the creation of your development goals, you might like to apply the mnemonic/acronym of SMART (specific, measurable, achievable, relevant and time-bound), which can help in fully considering what you will do, when, and how, etc.

Although all PDPs are specific to each coach, the plan will generally describe your ideal future based on your short, medium and long-term ambitions. Areas of development will be specific to you, and could be centred on further education, coaching practice or personal growth.

It is also recommended that you consider the potential obstacles you might face, and how you propose to overcome them – and if the barriers can't be tackled, include a contingency plan to help your development as a coach keep moving forward.

There are many ways to track our development activities and here is a simple template to illustrate how we might do this (Table 28.1).

Table 28.1: Personal Development Plan Example			
What do I need to learn?	How will I learn it?	When do I aim to complete my learning?	How will I know if I have been successful?
I would like to develop my understanding of Acceptance and Commitment coaching	I will aim to read a book and then attend a short two- or three-day course to develop my practical skills	I will aim to complete the learning by 30 December	I will be able to understand how ACT fits within coaching and my wider professional practice. I will be able to use five or six techniques from ACT in my coaching practice

I aim to complete 10 hours of CCEUs on competency rated topics	I will attend ICF or Henley Centre for Coaching webinars	I will aim to complete the learning by 30 December	I will have collected 10 CCEUs toward my accreditation renewal I will have a deeper understanding of the competencies, which will be reflected in my progress toward my PCC credential application
I will incorporate mindfulness into my coaching preparations as part of developing ICF Competency 2: Embodies a Coaching Mindset	I will research two or three mindfulness practices and start using one of them as a daily mindfulness meditation	I will start on 3 January	I will use this daily before I start work

When Should I Start My Personal Development Plan?

You can start your PDP at any point; in fact, we would propose the sooner the better. It may be that your attendance at your first coach-specific training marked the beginning of a new personal and professional journey for you; however, it may also be that your development up to that point was part of a plan that had you heading in the direction of coaching. Either way, it is never too early to start this valuable process.

In addition, a proactive approach and an attitude of intentionality when it comes to our ongoing development as coaches is something that is much valued and even expected within our profession. At the end of the day, we are the tool for our work and, regardless of where we are in our development journey, we can always continue to learn and grow so that we can be the best version of ourselves, for ourselves and for our clients.

Conclusion

In this chapter we have introduced the concept of personal development planning as a way to develop your coaching practice as part of your CPD. We have defined and described what is meant by PDPs, with their associated benefits and practical ways to create a plan that works for you.

Chapter 29: Supervision

Supervision has become an important element within coach continuing professional development, and although it's not the only way for coaches to reflect on their practice, the use of supervision as a mechanism is now widely accepted. Moreover, purchasers of coaching services want to know they are buying the best and knowing that a coach is in supervision can be a great way of demonstrating quality assurance, professionalism and integrity in one's coaching practice. Indeed, in some communities, being in coaching supervision is now a prerequisite for providing coaching services within certain organizations. In this chapter we explore what supervision is, its benefits and how it can form part of a wider portfolio of a coach's professional development and reflective practice.

What is Supervision?

The ICF defines supervision as "a collaborative learning practice to continually build the capacity of the coach through reflective dialogue for the benefit of both coaches and clients".

Coaching supervision focuses on the development of the coach's capacity through offering a richer and broader opportunity for support and development. Coaching supervision creates a safe environment for the coach to share their successes and failures in becoming masterful in the way they work with their clients.

Some writers prefer the term 'super-vision' (Passmore & McGoldrick, 2009), recognizing that the aim is not hierarchical but rather a collaborative process designed to enhance insight and understanding. When framing this as 'super-vision' we describe it as a process whereby the coach and the supervisor reflect together upon the coach's coaching practice and have over (super)-sight (vision) – i.e., they are reflecting upon the work to identify useful insights for ongoing learning and development. This reflection promotes enhanced professional practice by reviewing, questioning, considering, thinking, and critically assessing our work as coaches. This allows the coach to be the best they can be, which in turn maximizes the results for the client. Supervision is also an opportunity to think about the broader impact and changes our insights will have on our continuing professional practice as a coach, as well as to acknowledge and celebrate success. Supervision is an agreement between supervisor and supervisee that the highest function of the process is to protect and work in the best interests of the client.

Supervision is a shared learning partnership between equals and the learning is co-created and experiential. Therefore, by engaging in supervision, coaches are making an important commitment that will support them, their clients, their sponsors and wider society.

The Function and Scope of Supervision

Most coaching assignments require the coach to engage in challenging and intimate conversations that take place within complex systems. While doing this, the coach is managing the personal and professional boundaries, noticing the interpersonal dynamics in the relationship between them and their client, managing themselves in the moment, and being alert to the need for best practice and an ethically sound stance. This can be quite a juggling act.

Time spent in supervision gives them some breathing space. It is an opportunity to reflect on the things that affected them in a coaching exchange, other options that might have been explored, things that left them puzzled, where they felt at their most or least resourceful, and how their strengths and vulnerabilities might help and hinder them.

Supervision is there to help reflect on these processes and its function and scope cover three main areas:

Learning and Development

In this domain, the focus is on the continuous growth and development of the coach toward increasingly advanced competence. This aspect of the dialogue might focus on the ICF Core Competencies as well as other related theories, models and concepts that could be introduced into the discussion by either party. The focus is on the *coach as a coach* and their ongoing skill development as a practitioner. Mentor Coaching for Credentialing could sit somewhere within this domain with regards to the specific focus on the ICF Core Competencies; however, the roles of mentor coach and coach supervisor are not always the same and the focus and training for each discipline is different.

Support

Coaching supervision also provides support for the coach in terms of them feeling resourced, supported and nurtured. As such, the focus is on the person or the who of the coach; the *coach as a person*. In this domain, topics such as confidence, inner dialogue and helpful or limiting beliefs held by the coach might feature in the discussion.

Safety and Standards

This domain is centred on quality and professionalism. Here, the dialogue may reflect upon how the coach is managing their overall coaching practice, ethical considerations, and the safety of the coach and their client, as well as considering the system within which the coaching work is undertaken. Here, the ICF's gold standard and the core values of excellence, integrity, collaboration and respect are at the forefront of the reflective dialogue and the focus is on the *coach as a professional*.

Coaching supervision is sometimes described as working with 'where the personal intrudes on the professional', in that the focus is on making sure the coach does not get in the way of their client's learning and development but is instead an enabling vehicle for them.

This triangulated approach to supervision has evolved in the past few decades and many models of supervision have been imported into coaching from the fields of therapy, counselling, and management (Kadushin, 1976; Proctor, 2000; Hawkins, 2006; Newton, 2007) (Figure 29.1).

Figure 29.1: Scope of Supervision

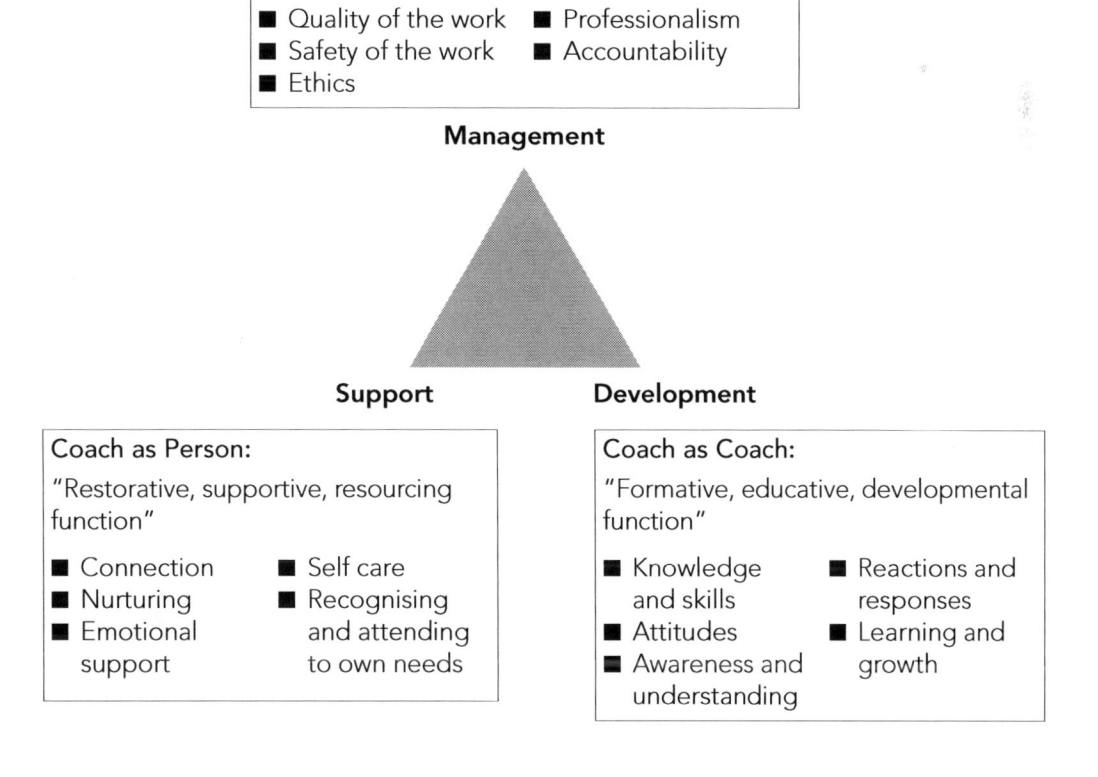

Coach as Professional:
"Normative, managerial, qualitative function"
- Quality of the work
- Professionalism
- Safety of the work
- Accountability
- Ethics

Management

Support   **Development**

Coach as Person:
"Restorative, supportive, resourcing function"
- Connection
- Self care
- Nurturing
- Recognising and attending to own needs
- Emotional support

Coach as Coach:
"Formative, educative, developmental function"
- Knowledge and skills
- Reactions and responses
- Attitudes
- Learning and growth
- Awareness and understanding

Table 29.1 The Functions of Supervision

Kadushin (1976)	Proctor (2000)	Hawkins (2006)	Newton (2007)
Managerial	Normative	Qualitative	Accounting
Supportive	Restorative	Resourcing	Nurturing
Educative	Formative	Developmental	Transformative

How does Supervision Work in Practice?

In practical terms, coaching supervision bears some resemblance to coaching in that the coach and supervisor need to establish rapport for them to work effectively together. They will contract with each other around how they will work, and similar boundaries of confidentiality are upheld. The focus of each supervision session will be clearly established and may be related to the above domains. For example:

- Case analysis (i.e., the coach's work with a particular client or a particular session with a client).
- Patterns and themes that the coach is noticing about their coaching practice across their client base.
- Observations that the coach is having about themselves within the context of their coaching practice.
- Review of the ICF Core Competencies or other coaching-related materials and how they are being demonstrated in the coach's practice.
- Exploration of the 'who' of the coach.

Sometimes it can be helpful to frame the supervision topic as a question that the coach and supervisor then work collectively to answer. Some examples of supervision questions might be:

- I have a lot going on personally at the moment. How can I be sure that I am fully present for my clients?
- My client has told me they are being bullied; what are my responsibilities as a coach and how can I be of best service to them?
- I find myself getting distracted and even impatient when coaching clients; what can I learn that will help me be the best coach I can be for them?

- I am usually confident as a coach. However, when coaching Client B, I find myself feeling intimidated and trying to impress them; what is it that is triggering this response in me?
- I get so engaged in coaching my clients that I lose track of time and our sessions seem to end abruptly, with no clear actions or forward movement. How can I manage the time for a better ending to the session?
- My client shared something that really goes against my values and I'm finding it difficult to coach them without feeling negatively toward them. How can I resolve this?
- I have noticed that I am more verbose when coaching clients who are younger than me. What is triggering this and what implications does this have for my coaching with them?

These are just a few of the questions that a coach might bring into supervision and the common feature is that the conversation aims to support the coach to be the best they can be in that situation and across their coaching practice.

Coaching supervision can be undertaken on a one-to-one basis or as part of a supervision group. The one-to-one arrangement is in many ways similar to individual coaching. A supervisor will be identified, perhaps based on recommendation and an exploratory conversation, and a contract will be put in place covering the commercial, practical and ethical conditions for the work. A group might be 'closed' and made up of a specified number of regular members who participate at each session. An 'open' group, by contrast, would accommodate a potentially different mix of attendees each time, while still having a limited number on each occasion. The contract for group work will acknowledge these variations and differences.

There are other ways of bringing supervision into coaching practice, which are perhaps best regarded as supplementary to or even by-products of the more formal options outlined already.

Peer supervision is a process whereby coaches supervise each other, without any one of them requiring a supervisor's qualification. This can be a vibrant, cost-effective, and readily accessible option, making it possible for coaches to work collaboratively one-to-one or in groups offering mutual support, insights and shared experience. For the purposes of meeting the supervision requirements of an organizational client, or accreditation bodies, this would generally be seen as a useful supplement to – not a substitute for – work with a qualified supervisor.

Finally, self-supervision – or the development of the internal supervisor – is an asset that all coaches should nurture as an integral part of their growth and attention to ethical practice. It is the capacity to bring a level of self-awareness and monitoring of oneself as a coach into the moment when working with clients, grounded in a habit of regular, private reflection. Self-supervision is a form of reflective practice, which is further described in Chapter 30. Once again, it is not a substitute for formal supervision; however, here are some self-supervision questions (Sinclair, 2016) that can offer a structure to your reflective practice after a coaching session. These questions are also available as a resource in Chapter 35, or can be downloaded at www.pavpub.com/becoming-a-coach-resources.

Box 29.1: A Tool for Self-Supervision

1. What went really well? (Reflect upon two or three areas of strength, using the coaching competency framework I was trained in [e.g., ICF])
2. Which competencies really showed up in my coaching?
3. Which competencies were less evident or could have been evidenced more?
4. What else could I have done more or less of?
5. Were there any missed opportunities on my part?
6. Deepening my reflection – how do I notice this piece of work through the lens of one or two models that I am familiar with? (e.g., PAC, Drama Triangle, Life Positions, Hogan or other profile, psychological distance, seven-eyed model, cycles of change, cycles of learning, and others)
7. What are any ethical considerations within the piece of work?
8. How was my doing/being balance and my coaching presence with my client – how was I being? Where was I personally in this piece of work?
9. What conscious bias do I notice or what unconscious bias might be outside of my awareness?
10. What might have been the parallel process and what did that mean for the work?
11. More generally in my coaching work, do I notice any patterns?
12. What are my own takeaways from my work? What am I learning about myself as a person, as a coach, about my work?
13. What difference does that learning make? What and how will I integrate this into my work?

How Can Supervision Help Me?

In the past the ICF was skeptical about the lack of evidence on coaching supervision and whether supervision was a useful tool for coaching reflective practice. However, in recent years, as further research has grown, the ICF has changed its position on supervision. It is now supportive of coaching supervision for full-time professional coach practitioners, as part of their portfolio of continuing professional development (CPD) activities designed to keep them fit for purpose. To that end, ICF credential holders may submit up to 10 hours of coaching supervision as Core Competency credits toward their credential renewal.

Further, the ICF recognizes that coaching supervision is different from coaching. As a result, specific training is needed for supervisors to provide the knowledge and opportunity to practice supervision skills. The ICF also recognizes that supervision is distinct from mentor coaching for an ICF credential, which we will address in Chapter 31.

Coaching supervision may include:

- Exploring the coach's internal process through reflective practice.
- Reviewing the coaching agreement and any other psychological or physical contacts, both implicit and explicit.
- Uncovering blind spots: For example, beyond the one-to-one, coach–client relationship, the coach needs to stay mindful of the bigger picture – the broader context of the client's circumstances, as well as information and perspectives that might be important yet outside their awareness. This aspect is also addressed in the ICF Core Competencies, which describe the need for a coach to hold an understanding of the client's identity, environment, experiences, values and beliefs.
- Ethical issues
- Ensuring the coach is 'fit for purpose' and perhaps offering accountability
- Looking at all aspects of the coach and client's environment for opportunities for growth in the system

There are an increasing number of books and academic articles (Hawkins *et al*, 2019; Tkach & DiGirolamo, 2017; Bachkirova *et al*., 2020) on the topic of coaching supervision that identify the benefits for coaches who receive supervision. The benefits include:

- Increased self-awareness
- Greater confidence
- Increased objectivity

- Heightened sense of belonging
- Reduced feelings of isolation
- Increased resourcefulness

In our own practice as supervisors and supervisees, we have also noticed the following benefits:

- Managing the quality, professionalism and integrity of the coaching work completed with clients
- Due diligence and governance (through underpinning quality and also via the thorough exploration and addressing of any relevant ethical issues or considerations)
- Coach continues to learn, develop and grow their skills through the reflective practice of supervision
- The organization underpins their return on investment in coaching and coaching supervision through the continued professional development of the coach and the subsequent benefit of the coaching work they complete for their clients and the organization at large

Coaching Supervisors

Coaching supervisors will usually be experienced coaches who have undergone additional training to gain a qualification in supervision skills. Many continue to practice as coaches alongside their supervision work and will have supervisors of their own.

Like coaches, supervisors will vary in their style, stance, and the approaches they bring to their work. As with coaching, there are many models and frameworks available in the field of supervision (see Passmore, 2011). Some supervisors will work with preferred approaches; others will adopt a more eclectic stance, drawing from a range of thinking and sources.

This discipline requires specific training, which will most likely cover at least one or more fields of (coaching) psychology, as well as specific supervision models. A coaching supervisor is likely to be an experienced coach and also self-aware and mindful of their own part in the coach–supervisor relationship. For supervisors working with groups, an understanding of group dynamics and group development is needed as well as knowledge of group supervision processes and practices.

How Can I Find a Suitable Supervisor?

Choosing the right coaching supervisor or supervisors is in some ways similar to the process the client might go through when selecting a coach. It is important that the coach knows what they want from supervision, and what specific experience and skills they want their supervisor to demonstrate.

It can be helpful to consider a blend of one-to-one and group supervision, perhaps with two or more supervisors who may be particularly well suited to different aspects of their work, their needs, and the contexts in which they are coaching.

In Box 29.2 we have included seven key questions to keep in mind when selecting a supervisor.

Box 29.2: Questions to Ask Potential Supervisors

1. What are your qualifications, accreditations and experience in coaching?
2. What are your qualifications, accreditations and experience in coaching supervision?
3. What experience do you have in the contexts in which I coach?
4. What experience do you have as a coach?
5. What are your own supervision arrangements for their work as a supervisor?
6. What approach do you use in supervision?
7. Are you familiar with the ICF Code of Ethics and ICF practice?

Roles and Responsibilities

It is important that the supervisor–coach relationship is one that is contracted for, thus modeling professional coaching practice. Part of that process will be to explore and clarify roles and responsibilities, which might include:

The supervisor will be responsible for:

- Time-keeping
- Managing the overall agenda of session
- Monitoring ethical issues of coaching and supervision that may occur
- Minimal note-taking
- Reporting any malpractice to the relevant governing body

- Co-creating a positive learning relationship, encompassing respect, encouraging autonomy and enhancing the supervisory experience
- Ensuring a high level of professionalism in all interactions

The supervisee(s) will be responsible for:

- Preparation for supervision – giving consideration to what is the 'Supervision Question'
- Learning objectives
- Keeping notes for their own learning
- Letting the supervisor know what is/isn't working in the supervision partnership
- Ensuring they are in an appropriate location for their supervision session
- Co-creating a positive learning relationship, encompassing respect, encouraging autonomy and enhancing the supervisory experience

Getting the Best from Supervision

Getting the best out of supervision is similar to getting the best out of coaching. Planning and preparation play an important part in this and we recommend the following as guidance for how you can engage in supervision and maximize your learning and development experience:

- ***Find a suitable supervisor(s):*** Apart from the qualifications and experiences aspects of a good supervisor, ensure that you have good chemistry with them. Supervision is an intimate working space. You will share your pride, achievement and success in a way that is hopefully fully and abundantly owned and celebrated. You will also share your fears, concerns, and vulnerabilities as a coach, as a professional and as a person. Who is the right supervisor for you to do that with in a safe, supportive and developmental environment?
- ***Frequency:*** Some supervisors have views on this and there are also no hard and fast rules on how frequently a coach needs to be in supervision. Logic might indicate that the more client work you have, the greater the need for supervision... and supervision is also useful to reflect upon just one single coaching conversation. What is the right frequency for you, which will offer you meaningful development and professional over-sight of your coaching practice and be something that is achievable for you from a time and cost perspective?
- ***Contract:*** With your supervisor so that you can quickly develop a strong working connection and relationship.

- ***Prepare:*** The process of reflective practice starts before the supervision session takes place. This preparation could take on many forms according to your preference; however, considering some of the self-supervision questions previously noted will certainly help to generate thought.
- ***Co-Create:*** Work in partnership with your supervisor to co-create your working relationship and how you engage with your supervision topics and questions.
- ***Reflect (again!):*** After your supervision session, take some time to reflect once again on what it is that you are noticing and learning about yourself and your coaching practice. How will you integrate that learning for your ongoing professional development?

Conclusion

In this chapter we have positioned coaching supervision as a powerful reflective practice for professional development. We have explored definitions, function and scope of supervision and what it means in practice to engage with this process. Finally, we have also described some of the benefits of working with a supervisor and how to get the best out of your investment in this form of professional development.

Chapter 30: Reflective Practice

Learning to reflect in order to improve one's own practice is seen as increasingly important across a range of professions, from teaching to counselling, and from management to clinical work. We have argued in Chapter 1 that knowing the self and managing the self are key skills for every coach. The ICF competencies also draw our attention to reflective practice, encouraging coaches to develop an ongoing reflective practice. This self-awareness enables us to be in best service of our clients. In this chapter we consider what reflective practice is, why it may be helpful, and how we can incorporate this into our coaching practice.

What is Reflective Practice?

The ICF competencies encourage coaches as part of the coaching mindset to develop an ongoing reflective practice. However, they do not provide a definition or description of what reflective practice is and how one might go about this process. Some work has been undertaken by members of the ICF team (Hullinger *et al*, 2019), who have reviewed the literature and offered a model for coaches and clients.

Reflective practice may be defined as the ability to reflect on one's actions so as to engage in a process of continuous learning. We believe reflective practice is the foundation of all professional development. It enables the coach to transform experience (coaching hours) into practical insights for personal growth and impact, learning new ways of being and doing that can be applied in the coach. Without reflection, collecting coaching hours can be just collecting stones; we may have a whole pile of them, but they add little to who we are. Reflection allows us to carve statues of insight and meaning from the rubble of coaching conversations.

Reflective practice involves integrating regular activities into our routine that raise awareness, prompt critical analysis and aid self-management and decision-making. It involves:

- Learning to pay attention – listening to ourselves
- Exploring our assumptions
- Observing patterns

We can assume learning is a discrete activity that is restricted to the coaching classroom, where we listen and learn from a tutor or read a coaching book. But we have the potential to learn all the time; from everything we do, every conversation we have, every strand of information that comes our way. Reflective practice is a way of recognizing and articulating this learning, squeezing every insight from every hour of coaching practice. However, to make best use of our coaching practice we need to integrate reflective practice into our daily routine.

Why Reflective Practice is Important

As a new coach it can be tempting to think at the end of the 65, 125, or 200 hours of coach training that you know everything you need to know about coaching – after all, you have completed the course. You can now get on with applying what you have learnt. But learning to coach might be compared with learning to drive. The classroom sessions are no more than the driving lessons, and the ICF ACC or PCC assessment is the driving test. What we all know is that, during our first few years on the road, we really start to learn how to apply what we have learnt in the complexity and chaos of sharing roads with other road users, in multiple weather conditions, and sometimes in different countries, where road signs have different meanings and even which side of the road you drive changes. If we stopped learning in these situations we could be in for a nasty accident. Good drivers, and good coaches, continue to learn.

For the experienced PCC and MCC coach, maybe they have driven thousands of hours and in multiple weathers, in multiple countries, and over multiple terrains. But we know that nothing stands still – if anything, the pace of change is accelerating, and new technologies are impacting on driving as they are on coaching. Experienced coaches need to engage in reflective practice as much as new coaches.

In summary, reflective practice encourages us to continue learning from our coaching practice, and to hold ourselves as eternal students or holding a Beginner's Mind. This allows us to remain open, curious, flexible and client-centered.

How to Develop Reflective Practice

Understanding what reflective practice is and how to do it are two different things. The first step is to develop the skills needed for the reflective process. Only once these skills have been identified can the coach start to find ways to incorporate these into their routine.

A host of writers have offered different strategies for reflective practice and, as in many areas, we suggest there are several approaches. Here are few examples for consideration.

Schön (1983) suggested the following stages:

- Puzzlement: 'What the heck just happened? Or, what the heck is happening?'
- Comparison: 'How have I really been doing this until now?'
- Opportunity to experiment: 'What can I gain/learn/get/know from this?'

Bain *et al*, (1999) identify five levels of reflection:

1. Reporting
2. Responding
3. Relating
4. Reasoning
5. Reconstructing

Moon (2004) refers to four levels:

Level 0: Description of what happened (reporting).

Level 1: Descriptive writing with some reflective potential. Reference to impact of events and indication of points where reflection could occur.

Level 2: Reflective writing (1). Reference to the value of exploring motives or reasons for behaviour. Some self-awareness/criticism or possibly reflection on motives of others. This stage is sometimes described as relating or reasoning.

Level 3: Reflective writing (2). There is clear evidence here of the learner standing back from an event, of mulling it over, and holding an internal dialogue. There is awareness of the learning involved and how it will be used in the future direction. This phase is sometimes described as reconstructing.

Henley8 Model for Self-Reflection

In our coach training we encourage our coaches and leaders to use eight practical questions. These eight questions are a handrail to guide the reflective process. They provide one way to structure our thinking (see Box 30.1).

In the Henley8 model the starting point is to notice: What did I observe? This requires situation awareness, being fully present and noticing changes in events around us. The observation may be a change in the situation – for example, a fire bell rings during the team meeting. It may be observing a behaviour of an individual who is the client or the sponsor, or an event.

The second step is to identify our response: What was my response? This may be behavioural, but is likely to also be cognitive (What was I thinking and why?) and also: What was I feeling? Our thoughts and feelings often drive our behaviour and recognizing the relationship between these is helpful, and how these are associated with the trigger event (what we have observed).

Behind these initial feelings and thoughts are likely to be beliefs and values. Being conscious of these, and bringing these core beliefs to mind, will help us make more sense of our own response.

The third and fourth quesions involve considering what these behaviours, thoughts, feelings, and possibly our beliefs and values say about us as individuals, and what they say about us as leaders, reflective practitioners or coaches within the context we are working. Meanings can vary widely depending on the organizational and national culture and taking these into account needs to be part of our reflection.

The fifth and sixth questions explore the pros and cons of these beliefs. How do these beliefs or attitudes help or hinder us in our role? Do they make us more effective? Do they contribute to our happiness and well-being? Do they contribute positively to our team or others? What do we need to be aware of in terms of how we can build on these positives and what we should guard against?

The seventh and eighth questions are what we learn and may take away from the reflection. They set the stage for future development. Reflection without action is meaningless. The purpose of reflection is to understand ourselves and others more deeply and, through this, learn and adapt in the future to enhance our own effectiveness and that of others.

A checklist of Henley8 questions can be found in Chapter 35, or can be downloaded from www.pavpub.com/becoming-a-coach-resources.

> **Box 30.1: Henley8 Questions**
>
> 1. What did I observe?
> 2. What was my response?
> 3. What does this tell me about me?
> 4. What does this tell me about myself as a coach or leader?
> 5. What strengths does this offer?
> 6. What are the potential pitfalls?
> 7. What did I learn?
> 8. What might I do differently next time?

We have suggested in Chapter 1 that the coach creates a personal learning journal and starts the practice of regularly using this for their reflections. This may be after each coaching session, when the coach spends 10–15 minutes reflecting on the session using the Henley8 questions, or it may be at the end of each day or week, reflecting back over the sessions in that day or that week. The frequency will depend on how much coaching you are doing and your own schedule. What is important is finding a pattern that works for you. If you find you are not regularly writing in your journal, we suggest you review your routine and find a time which will enable you to make this part of your practice.

Of course, there are several aspects to consider when writing your learning journal. The first is to avoid the use of client names (use initials which you can recognize, but others can't) and avoid the use of organizational names or facts that identify the organization. By excluding personal data, you can be more relaxed about the security of your learning journal. The second issue is about reviewing what you have reflected on. There are several ways of doing this; first, taking issues from the learning journal to your supervision. If for whatever reason you have decided not to use supervision, we suggest finding a way to review and reflect on patterns or themes that may be arising each quarter, and scheduling time in your diary. Without a formal pattern of supervision, it is easy for this to be missed, which is why allowing an hour or two in your diary ensures that the learning can be incorporated into new behaviours, or into your personal development plan.

> **Box 30.2: Example of Reflective Writing Using the Henley8**
>
> I noticed that Kate was late for the meeting. She came in and apologized.
>
> I observed that my response to this lateness was that I had been clicking my pen while I was waiting and that my heart rate had risen. I was conscious that I was irritated by her lateness. I was thinking she is wasting my time when I am so busy at present and could have done with that extra 15 minutes.
>
> This tells me that time-keeping is important to me. A commitment is a commitment, and my interpretation of her lateness was that she was being rude. This tells me that I can be intolerant to others in certain circumstances and that breaking these unwritten rules leads me to be judgmental.
>
> As a coach, it tells me that certain behaviours can lead me to starting sessions in a judgmental mindframe, and that this may interrupt my client mindset of being open, curious, flexible and client-centered.
>
> The strengths of being highly sensitive to time-keeping are that I am never likely to be late for a meeting. I always leave sufficient time and extra for client meetings. →
>
> The pitfall is if I am or others are late, this can be a significant hurdle to recovering the relationship and getting started on the coaching process. The irritation does not quickly pass and can pervade the whole session.
>
> What I learned about myself was that it would be helpful to change my belief: this is their time and thus how they choose to use it is their responsibility and choice, not mine; I will still finish at the agreed upon time.
>
> What I might do differently next time is to be clear with client that we have an hour, with a starting time at point A and a finishing time at point B, 60 minutes later. It is then their responsibility to make choices about how the hour is used. I will bring something to do, so I can make the best use of any down time should this happen in future coaching meetings.

Conclusion

In this chapter we have reviewed the importance of reflective practice. We have argued that it is central to coach development, but also to an essential for all coaches, and helps us to retain a Beginner's Mindset, which allows us to remain open, curious, flexible and client-centred, whether we have 50 hours of practice or 5,000 hours. We also suggested that using several frameworks, including the Henley8, as ways for the coach to structure and capture their reflections and develop new insights for their practice.

Chapter 31: Mentor Coaching

As part of a self-regulating industry, coaches can provide consistent value to their clients by actively engaging in CPD activities to ensure that their skills are still active, current, relevant and of a high standard. Such professional development can come in many different forms and is covered in more detail in Chapter 28. This chapter focuses on a specific form of professional development: mentor coaching.

What is Mentor Coaching?

There is sometimes confusion around what mentor coaching is when it comes to its definition and scope of activity. From personal experience in this field, it is proposed that mentor coaching tends to fall into two different categories of: General Coach Mentoring and Mentor Coaching for International Coaching Federation (ICF) Credentialing purposes.

General Coach Mentoring

General coach mentoring is quite closely aligned with what we probably understand by mentoring as a discipline. It is typically a relationship in which a more experienced or more knowledgeable person helps to guide a less experienced or less knowledgeable person. The mentor may be older or younger than the person being mentored, but she or he must have a certain area of expertise. It is a learning and development partnership between someone with considerable experience and someone who wants to learn.

Given this definition, the scope of this kind of mentoring could be very broad and could cover a range of areas from competency development to building and maintaining a coaching practice or business. Within this broad range, some of the topics the mentee might bring into the conversation with their mentor could even be considered as supervision enquiries, and so we now see a crossover with yet another way of working.

Supervision is a very specific form of professional development, as explored in Chapter 29, and also requires the supervisor to have undertaken specialist training in this field. Mentor coaching for ICF Credentialing is also a very specific form of professional development, again requiring particular skills and attributes. To that end, it is important that the coach seeking any of these services gains clarity about what is being offered, along with ensuring the person they are thinking of working with has the appropriate skills, qualifications and experience to provide that service. It is therefore proposed that, in practice, there are three different services that in some ways cross over: general mentoring, mentor coaching for credentialing, and supervision. Furthermore, with mentor coaching for credentialing and supervision being so much more clearly defined and scoped, it is proposed that general coach mentoring services need to be carefully contracted for in order for the coach to understand exactly what is the service they will be receiving and how will that be of value to their professional development.

A final note on this is that these services may be provided by different individuals or the same person, thereby once again implying the need for clarity of what is being offered and in which modality you are working.

Mentor Coaching for ICF Credentialing

This form of professional development is recognized by the ICF and its purpose is to provide professional assistance in achieving and demonstrating the levels of coaching competency demanded by the desired credential level sought by a coach-applicant (mentee). This way of working is defined and consists of coaching and feedback in a collaborative, appreciative and dialogued process based on observed or recorded coaching session(s) to increase the coach's capability in coaching, in alignment with the ICF Core Competencies.

Mentor coaching should take place over an extended time (for a minimum of three months) in a cycle that allows for listening and feedback from the mentor coach while also allowing reflection and practice on the part of the individual being mentored. Furthermore, mentor coaching means an applicant (mentee) being coached on their coaching skills rather than coaching on practice-building, life balance, or other topics unrelated to the development of an applicant's coaching skill.

When do I Need Mentor Coaching?

Mentor coaching is a useful and valuable way of working and developing our coaching competence and is undertaken at various points in a coach's development as follows:

1. Mentor coaching as part of an initial ICF credential application
2. Mentor coaching as part of an ICF credential renewal

3. Mentor coaching as part of a coach's general professional development

1. Mentor coaching as part of an initial ICF credential application

As noted in Section 2, part of the application process for all three levels of ICF credential (ACC, PCC and MCC) requires the applicant to complete 10 hours of mentor coaching as defined and outlined above. Some coach training schools offer mentor coaching as part of their programming and others do not. As such, mentor coaching is also a service that is offered by certain coaches within the ICF-credentialed community as well as by ICF-accredited schools.

2. Mentor coaching as part of an ICF Credential renewal

The ICF credentialing system is based on the credential being renewed every three years. When a coach holding an ACC credential seeks to renew their credential at that same level, they need to complete an additional 10 hours of mentor coaching as part of their renewal process. The rationale for this is that if, in the previous three-year period, they have not built up enough coaching client hours to take them from the 100 hours required for ACC to the 500 hours required for PCC, this additional checkpoint is put in place via the mentor coaching process. This is to ensure that the coach is in fact still current in their coaching skills and is still consistently offering coaching in alignment with the required ACC standard of coaching as per the ICF Core Competencies. The 10 hours of mentor coaching completed also counts toward the 40 hours of professional development and CCE across that three-year period required for the renewal process.

Coaches who are renewing their credentials at the levels of PCC or MCC are not required to do this extra 10 hours of mentor coaching. However, mentor coaching is considered to be a very valuable form of professional development. As such, PCC- and MCC-credentialed coaches can complete and apply up to 10 hours of mentor coaching as part of the 40 hours of CPD required for their credential renewal.

3. Mentor coaching as part of a coach's general professional development

As noted above, mentor coaching offers a great form of professional development for any coach and is a highly recommended practice for ICF-credentialed coaches to engage in periodically with a mentor.

How Does Mentor Coaching Work?

The purpose of mentor coaching is to support the coach (mentee) to develop their coaching skills against the ICF Core Competency framework. Such development is pitched at whatever is the relevant credential level for that mentee and comprises a full and in-depth review of the ICF Core Competency framework, the ICF Code of Ethics, and how the mentee is or is not demonstrating the competencies in their coaching practice. The coach's demonstration of coaching competence could be explored and worked with in several ways:

- Using recordings of client sessions (these need to be real client examples for which the client has given their permission for their session to be used for mentoring purposes)
- Coaches coaching each other in live group webinar sessions
- The coach (mentee) coaching the mentor

The ICF partnered with the Association of Coach Training Organizations (ACTO) to produce a set of duties and competencies of mentor coaches. The duties of the mentor are described in Box 31.1.

Box 31.1: Duties of a Mentor Coach

1. Model effective initiation and contracting of client relationship
2. Explore fully with a potential mentee what they are looking to achieve
3. Ensure both are clear about the purpose of the mentoring
4. Establish measures of success in partnership with the mentee
5. Fully discuss fees, time frame and other aspects of a mentor coaching relationship
6. Inform the mentee regarding all aspects of the ICF Code of Ethics
7. Inform the mentee of the availability of the Ethical Conduct Review Board
8. Support mentee self-confidence by encouraging potential mentees to interview more than one mentor coach candidate in order to find the best match
9. Make no guarantee to the mentee that as a result of the mentoring the mentee will obtain the credential level they are seeking
10. Focus on core competency development by reviewing and providing oral and written feedback on a series of the mentee's coaching sessions. These sessions are to be conducted one at a time, with a feedback session between each one, giving enough time between sessions to allow for incorporation of the mentee's learning and development.
11. Provide specific verbal and/or written feedback, using targeted examples from the sessions so that:
    a. The mentee will know exactly what they are doing well.
    b. The mentee understands what needs to be done to develop a deeper level of mastery in coaching. →

> 12. Demonstrate that they are learning about the mentee at many levels at once and are able to hold all of that in the context of:
>   a. Who the mentee is
>   b. What the mentee is seeking
>   c. Honouring the mentee's unique style

This list of duties provides a good overview of what one can expect to be covered across a series of mentor coaching sessions.

In practice, these sessions can be designed in many different ways and part of the initial contracting process with the mentor would be to discuss and decide upon a mentor coaching plan based upon the specific needs and development goals of the mentee.

The 10 hours of mentor coaching can be undertaken on a completely one-to-one basis or as a blend of one-to-one and group mentoring work. The ICF requires that a maximum of seven hours of mentoring can be undertaken in a group setting (with a maximum of 10 mentees in a group). There is no 'right or wrong' way to approach this and it is down to personal preference, timing, and budgeting as to which way might be preferable for the mentee. Accredited schools offering mentoring and individual mentors who offer group work may provide this as part of a structured programme, whereas fully one-to-one mentoring is down to the mentee and mentor to schedule themselves.

Mentor coaching could be undertaken on a face-to-face basis; however, most mentoring nowadays tends to be done via a virtual platform of some kind, thereby benefiting from the associated time and cost savings. The 10 hours are typically completed in one- or two-hour sessions using the examples of client work noted above. These sessions are to be 'conducted one at a time, with a feedback session between each one, giving enough time between sessions to allow for incorporation of the mentee's learning and development'. This means that the 10 hours are a blend of reviewing, discussing and sharing feedback on a series of recordings (or live coaching sessions) ensuring that all aspects of the ICF Core Competencies and the ICF Code of Ethics are covered across the period of time taken for this work.

The ICF's requirement that the 10 hours of mentor coaching is completed across a minimum of a three-month period is so that there is evidence of the mentee integrating their learning into their coaching practice. This means that, although the minimum period for completion is three months, in practice the 10 hours may take longer to undertake. This might depend upon how much client work the mentee currently has (in order to integrate their learning and also to secure additional recorded examples), the availability of the mentee and mentor, and the mentee's chosen timeline for this exercise. Personal experience as a mentor has shown that, typically, mentor coaching packages can easily take anything up to six or even nine months to complete.

Planning your Mentor Coaching Sessions

There are several aspects to consider when planning your mentor coaching package including *when*, *how* and *with whom*. The first aspect of planning your mentor coaching sessions is to consider when to start this process.

As for *when*, this is partly personal choice; however, in the case of an ACC credential renewal, the timing will be indicated by the renewal cycle. For first-time credential applications, it is recommended that two factors are taken into consideration:

1. The purpose of the mentoring is to help mentee demonstrate their coaching competence in relation to the level of credential they are going to apply for (or renew in the case of ACC). To that end, apart from being a highly developmental process, mentoring is also an assessment preparation process. This means that, wherever possible, it is useful to time the mentoring activity so that there is a minimal time gap between its completion and the mentee applying for their credential and undertaking the assessment process for that purpose. This way the mentee's knowledge of the Core Competencies and the Code of Ethics are fresh and current, which is helpful for their completion of the Coach Knowledge Assessment (CKA). In addition, the mentee needs to find one (for an ACC credential application) or two (for PCC and MCC credential applications) recordings of them demonstrating their coaching skills and evidencing the competencies. The process of mentoring, which works with recordings of coaching sessions, is a great opportunity to find those recordings for submission, especially during the latter part of the mentoring process when the mentee's skills are hopefully most developed.

2. Mentoring has a practical aspect to it, in that the mentee and mentor are actively reviewing and working with real examples of coaching. It is ideal, then, that the mentee engages in this work at a time when they are coaching a variety of clients. They can use the opportunity to integrate their learning and keep building their coaching 'muscles' while at the same time reviewing, reflecting and receiving feedback from the mentor.

Regarding *how* to complete a mentor coaching package, once again personal choice will prevail. There are several factors to consider:

- One-on-one mentoring can offer the most flexibility in terms of diary planning and the mentee also gets personal, in-depth, one-on-one attention and focus across the whole 10 hours.
- However, it could also take longer, possibly be more expensive, and the benefit of working with other coaches, exchanging ideas, and learning from each other is not available.
- Group mentoring sessions need to be scheduled for a whole group and are often therefore fixed as part of a programme.
- However, some mentees prefer the structure a programme offers, and the process can sometimes be completed more quickly and with the benefit or working with colleagues in a safe and collaborative environment.
- With group mentoring, the mentee also still has the opportunity of three hours of one-on-one work with their mentor.

Finally, and regarding with whom to work, the mentee does not have to complete all of their 10 hours of mentoring with the same mentor, although in practice many mentees do. We recommend that mentees who do choose to work with more than one mentor have an overarching mentoring package that ultimately covers the whole competency framework and code of ethics. Some level of co-ordination is required to ensure this is the case when working with multiple mentors.

This next section offers more guidance on how to find and choose a mentor.

Finding a Mentor Coach:

There are several ways to find a mentor coach, including via:

- ICF-accredited coach training schools, which will either offer mentoring services directly or can often put the mentee in touch with potential mentors known within their community.
- ICF Mentor Coach registry: Some mentors register their services on the ICF Global website so the mentee can choose to contact them for an exploratory discussion.
- ICF local chapters also either list or know of mentors within their area.
- Word of mouth is a common way for mentors and mentees to find each other.

Whichever way the mentee finds a mentor, it is important to note that working with a mentor does not guarantee a successful credential application. We recommend mentees undertake a proper selection process to ensure that they are working with someone who is appropriately skilled, qualified and experienced, and who is going to work with the mentee in a way that creates safety, support and useful developmental feedback. The guidelines set out by ICF and ACTO (ICF/ACTO, 2020) propose some of the personal traits and competencies a mentor coach should display.

> **Box 31.2: Personal Traits and Competencies of a Mentor Coach**
>
> **Personal Traits**
>
> The ICF mentor coach:
>
> 1. Is trustworthy and has the ability to connect with the mentee in terms of fit, chemistry and compatibility.
> 2. Is someone who encourages the mentee to reach beyond what the mentee initially feels is possible, assisting in broadening their creative process.
> 3. Demonstrates equal partnership by being open, vulnerable and willing to take appropriate risks –for example, in providing feedback that may make one or both individuals uncomfortable.
> 4. Understands the value of partnership and encourages the mentee to design areas to be worked on between sessions that will lead to more powerful, leveraged coaching.
> 5. Is supportive and authentic in celebrating who the mentee is, their achievements, and growth throughout the process.
> 6. Is secure in their own work and is able to demonstrate appreciation and respect for the unique style of each mentee.
> 7. Encourages the development of the mentee's own coaching style.
> 8. Is willing to hold both self and mentee accountable for performance and to periodically encourage mutual assessment of the effectiveness of the relationship.
>
> **Competencies**
>
> The ICF mentor coach:
>
> 1. Listens beyond content to discern application of the skills related to the Core Competencies (i.e., skill vs. direction, skill vs. style, or skill vs. outcome for the client).
> 2. Listens on all levels – physical, intellectual, emotional and intuitive.
> 3. Listens equally for strengths and areas for growth.
> 4. Is aware of and allows for differences in style, culture and language.
> 5. Has a working knowledge of the assessment tools used by the ICF in the evaluation of recorded coaching sessions used in the credentialing examination process.
> 6. Listens both for the presence of individual competencies and for the overall totality of skill level.
> 7. Has the ability to distinguish which critical underlying competency(-ies) may be giving rise to ineffective or limited coaching impact. →

8. Can discern and articulate the gap between levels of skill demonstrated and next skill level to attain. Identifies areas of growth, competency use, and skill level using competency-based language and specific behavioural examples from the coaching.
9. Creates a safe and trusting space for the delivery of feedback by using a respectful, clear, judgment-free tone.
10. Describes, with specific detail and examples, what is being observed and the particular development needed to move to the next skill level, and delivers this sensitively.
11. Offers feedback that is relevant to each specific coaching core competency, recognizing strengths as well as potential growth areas.
12. Demonstrates the ability to self-manage relative to any coaching model preferences and remain focused on the skill assessment relevant to the core coaching competencies.

It is worth noting finally that coaches can mentor for credentials up to the level of their own credential. In the case where a mentor holds an ACC credential, they must have held their credential for at least three years and renewed it at least once in order to be eligible to mentor others.

Getting the Best out of Your Mentor Coaching Experience

Although mentor coaching is a requirement for a credential application (and ACC credential renewals), it would be a wasted opportunity if this were treated as a 'tick-box' exercise. Mentor coaching can be a rich and rewarding developmental experience. In addition, through the process of mentoring, the mentee becomes much more deeply familiar with the ICF Core Competencies and the Code of Ethics and can thereby leave the mentoring process equipped with a powerful self-reflective tool. This enables them to self-reflect periodically by recording their coaching practice and listening back to the session, exploring when, if, and how the competencies are being evidenced.

Here are some tips for getting the best out of your mentor coaching package:

- Do your research and ensure that your mentor is appropriately skilled, qualified, and experienced to work with you.
- Check that you have a good rapport and chemistry to work well together in a safe, collaborative and developmental environment.

- Contract with your mentor around your goals for mentoring and all other aspects of how you will work together (in this way you are also both role modeling and mirroring the process of contracting and establishing agreements in good coaching practice).
- Allow enough time and space for you to fully engage in the learning process.
- Plan ahead and consider which clients you will ask for their permission to record your work with them for this purpose.
- Consider how much coaching client work you currently have so that you have sufficient opportunity for ongoing practice and integration of your learning as the mentoring process evolves.
- Think about your preferred timeline. How long do you want to take for this important development activity? How will it fit alongside your other commitments?
- Listen to your own work! Your mentor will listen to your recorded client work and then discuss it with you and share feedback. However, listening to your own work is an incredibly powerful way to develop, and will most certainly enhance your learning experience. When listening to your work, consider when, if, and how you feel you are evidencing the competencies. When you then debrief the work with your mentor, you can explore your own accuracy in identifying the competencies, thus enhancing your own knowledge for future self-reflection.
- Consider your mindset for doing this work so that you can bring openness and a desire to learn and develop and receive useful – albeit at times challenging – feedback in service of your professional growth.
- Once your mentoring package is completed, take the process forward by keeping up your own reflective practice by periodically recording and reviewing your client work. This can also be a great activity for a peer group of coaches to undertake; coaching each other followed by review and debrief against the Core Competencies or by using examples from your shared client work (with the client's permission, of course).

Conclusion

In this chapter we have positioned mentor coaching as a powerful professional development tool for coaches, as well as outlining how it is a required part of the ICF credential application process. We have covered the *when*, *how* and *with whom* of mentoring, as well how to get the best out of this process.

Chapter 32: Coach Knowledge Assessment

This chapter introduces the ICF Coach Knowledge Assessment (CKA), explains its purpose, and describes the assessment process (ICF, 2020a). We also look at how you can best prepare for this assessment with a successful outcome.

What is the Coach Knowledge Assessment?

The Coach Knowledge Assessment (CKA) is an online assessment tool, which is used by the ICF to measure a coach's understanding of the knowledge and skills that are important in the practice of coaching. Specifically, it tests coaches on a body of knowledge including the ICF definition of coaching, the Core Competencies, and the Code of Ethics.

The CKA is a required element of ACC, PCC and MCC credential applications. The purpose of this assessment step is to offer a standardized and scientifically constructed test to underpin fairness and rigour in the credentialing process. It is created from the competency job analysis process, which is also described in Section 2. Although this test measures knowledge, the application of that knowledge is then assessed by the review of actual coaching sessions.

The CKA is periodically reviewed and updated; however, its typical format is that it comprises around 155 multiple-choice items. Each item contains a short statement or a question with four possible answers. For each item, there is one answer that the ICF has established as being the best response.

The test covers the four domains of the ICF Core Competency Model: Foundation, Co-Creating the Relationship, Communicating Effectively, and Cultivating Learning and Growth, as well as the eight competencies that sit underneath those domains. The test items are related to the ICF definition of coaching, the core competencies and the Code of Ethics and they vary in levels of difficulty. Some of the items are intended to assess the coach's awareness of a coaching concept or skill and others present a scenario that requires the coach to demonstrate a deeper understanding for the correct response to be identified.

> **Box 32.1: Examples From the Coach Knowledge Assessment**
>
> **Domain: Foundation**
>
> The client is a high-energy manager with a generally positive outlook. Just before coming to the coaching session, the client was told that their responsibilities are about to drastically change and they will no longer be doing the work they are passionate about. The client has come to the session in a particularly negative mood and has expressed the desire to address this situation in today's session. What is the best way for the coach to proceed?
>
> A. Ask the client about all the potential positive outcomes from this situation.
>
> B. Remind the client that the agenda for this session was set at the last session.
>
> C. Explore the outcomes for the session and ensure the client and coach are both clear on them.
>
> D. Point out to the client how important it is to be passionate about the work we do.
>
> **Domain: Communicating Effectively**
>
> When dealing with a client who brings many issues to the table, it is best for the coach pick the option:
>
> A. Where the coach has the most experience.
>
> B. Asking where the client would like to start
>
> C. That looks most likely to be handled in the time available.
>
> D. That the coach thinks can do the most good for the client.

In practical terms, the coach completes the CKA at some point during the credential application process. The exact timing of this will depend upon which type of credential application path the coach is following. These different paths are dependent upon which type of coach-specific training the coach has completed and details can be found on the ICF website. The test will be received via a link in an email to the coach and, upon receipt of the link, the coach has 60 days within which to complete the test.

Once the link is opened, the test needs to be completed in one sitting (there is not a 'save and continue later' option) and a total of three hours are given for this process before the online session expires. In most cases, coaches complete the test in less time (usually around two hours). Once completed, the results of the test will be available immediately and sent directly to the coach via email. The pass mark for the CKA can also change over time as the questions and test items are reviewed and updated periodically; however, the pass mark is typically around 70%.

The score is broken down into a score for each of the four domain test areas, and no feedback is given regarding any incorrect responses. However, feedback is given for the recorded coaching sessions that are also submitted as part of the assessment process for a credential application. If a coach does not pass the test first time, it can be taken again at an additional cost, with a maximum of the test being taken twice a quarter. However, if a coach is well trained, has completed their mentoring and prepared for the test, repeating this part of the process will hopefully not be necessary.

How can I Best Prepare for the Coach Knowledge Assessment?

Preparation for sitting the CKA actually starts when you enroll and begin your coach training. Coach training programmes that have been accredited by the ICF (ACTP and ACSTH programmes) are required to include the ICF definition of coaching, the Core Competencies and the Code of Ethics within their curriculum. You will have received instruction and feedback during your coaching practice sessions that is in alignment with that body of knowledge.

In addition, the mentor coaching process provides another opportunity to discuss, review and reflect upon these areas, thereby deepening the coach's knowledge and understanding.

Advice for Taking the Online Assessment

When it comes to taking the test, here are a few tips to help you:

- Once you receive the link to sit the exam, make sure that you look at your diary and plan ahead so that you can comfortably allocate some time to prepare for the test and also the time needed to take the test.
- As part of your final preparations, review and digest the following materials:
  - Your coach training manuals and notes
  - Your mentor coaching notes and feedback
  - The ICF Core Competency Model
  - The ICF Code of Ethics
  - Other ICF competency-related documentation as referenced in the Introduction to Section 2.
- Have the above materials to hand when you sit the test. The CKA is not intended to be a 'memory' test; it is more like an open-book exam and you can

have these materials around you, which will provide useful sources of reference when considering your responses to the questions.

- On the day, create a comfortable, quiet, distraction-free environment for yourself so that you can complete the test undisturbed.
- Finally, relax!

Conclusion

We have given an overview of the Coach Knowledge Assessment tool as part of the ICF credential application process, including the purpose and format of the test, along with some example questions. We have also shared some advice on how to prepare for this test with a most successful outcome. More details and resources for this test are available from the ICF website.

Chapter 33: Progressing Your Coaching Skills

The completion of the ACC accreditation is only the first step in your coaching journey. Most coaches aspire to become a PCC or an MCC. The journey toward these is based on reflective practice, during which the coach continues to apply their skills, builds their experience, and also engages in further coach training.

In this chapter we will explain the requirements for PCC and MCC and how you can plan to achieve these standards in the coming few years. If you are already an MCC, we will also look at coach maturity and invite you to think about your own personal journey for development to retain the Beginner's Mind in your practice.

What is a PCC?

The acronym PCC stands for Professional Certified Coach, which is intended to offer a benchmark for a gold standard of coaching. Some coaches progress toward their PCC credential having first successfully secured their ACC credential and other coaches apply for their PCC straight away, if they fulfill the relevant criteria and requirements. There is no right or wrong approach and it often hinges largely on the amount of coaching an individual is undertaking, which in turn influences the speed at which the coach can build their client hours and their experience.

Although the ACC is a highly reputable and globally recognized credential, many coaches choose to continue with their development in the field of coaching and aim for the PCC. Coaches who remain at the level of ACC are those who are probably using their coaching skills less and for whom coaching is perhaps a smaller part of their overarching role.

Individuals who practice coaching as a significant or complete part of their work are recommended to consider pursuing their PCC credential at some point. As coaching is now so widely recognized as a powerful developmental way of working, many organizations are increasingly aware of the credentialing levels and often require professional coaches to hold at least a PCC-level credential. On this note of organizational client expectations, there is also an increasing expectation in some organizations that coaches are engaged in regular supervision as part of their ongoing professional development and reflective practice.

What do I Need to do to Achieve PCC Status?

As outlined in the Introduction to Section 2, a PCC credential requires a greater amount of coach-specific training and coaching experience compared to an ACC credential (Table 33.1).

Table 33.1: Comparison of ACC and PCC Credential Requirements

Associate Certified Coach (ACC)	Professional Certified Coach (PCC)
■ 60+ hours of coach-specific training ■ 10 hours of mentor coaching ■ 100+ hours of coaching experience ■ Coach Knowledge Assessment (CKA) ■ Core Competence performance evaluation to ACC-level minimum requirements	■ 125+ hours of coach-specific training ■ 10 hours of mentor coaching ■ 500+ hours of coaching experience ■ Coach Knowledge Assessment (CKA) ■ Core Competence performance evaluation to PCC-level minimum requirements

The training hours and the coaching experience hours are incremental. For example, once a coach has completed at least 100 hours of coaching experience for their ACC application, they then continue to coach and build up at least another 400 hours, making a total of at least 500 hours to be eligible to apply for their PCC. The same principle applies to the coach-specific training hours. The other difference is that an ACC credential application requires one example of a client session, whereas for a PCC application two examples are required.

What Differentiates the PCC Coach from an ACC Coach?

In addition to completing more coach-specific training and undertaking more hours of client work, the PCC-level coach is expected to know, understand, and demonstrate the ICF Core Competencies to a greater level of depth.

The ICF Core Competency framework is a single body of work that is applicable to and relevant for all three levels of credential. It is therefore the depth of understanding and demonstration of that framework that typically differentiates coaching at the three credential levels. Here are some examples of how that might show up in practice. An important point to note when reading these differentiators is that they are reflections on ACC or PCC-level coaching, as per the Core Competency model, and are not an evaluation or judgment of the coach.

For example, a coach may currently hold an ACC credential; however, they may in practice be coaching more at the level of PCC.

Coaching Mindset

The PCC-level coach is likely to be fully committed to and invested in the practice of coaching and, as such, engages in ongoing learning, development and reflective practice in perhaps a more structured, consistent, focused and in-depth manner. This is in no way an indication that an ACC-level coach has less commitment to their work and their development; it is merely that, for a PCC-level coach, coaching and coaching development probably forms a greater part of their professional identity.

At PCC level, a coach is expected to be more skilled at using their own intuition for the benefit of their clients. Whereas at ACC level the coach is likely to be more focused on the technicality of the coaching process and competencies and, as such, may either not notice, access, or be comfortable using their intuition in their coaching practice.

Coaching Agreements

Although three key levels of coaching agreements are outlined in the Core Competency model, the extent to which these agreements are explored and established may vary significantly from ACC to PCC-level coaching. Part of what is evaluated in this competency is the depth of creation of the agreement(s) and the degree to which the coach demonstrates they are able to fully partner with their client in that creation.

At ACC level, the coach is expected to establish what the client wants to work on and then attend to that coaching agenda. In essence, the focus at ACC level is on the 'what' of the coaching topic. Whereas at PCC level, there is likely to be a much deeper, richer exploration of 'why' the topic is of significance and importance to the client and perhaps even 'why now'? Furthermore, at PCC level we may also see an exploration into the 'who' of the client that is bringing the topic. This deeper exploration can also include aspects of the following skills:

- Asks and explores with the client what they want to work on (this might include exploring what the topic really is, as opposed to what is initially presented by the client).
- Explores and confirms that the agenda is meaningful for the client and will move the client toward a desired outcome.
- Engages in some exploration of the measures of success for each outcome desired in the session.

- Engages in some exploration of the issues related to each outcome.
- Attends to that agenda, those measures, and those issues throughout the coaching.
- May raise unseen issues with the client, but will not change agendas, measures, or issues unless redirected by the client.
- Should also check with the client during the session to make sure that the client's goals for the session are being achieved and/or if the goals are evolving or changing.

Although all of the Core Competencies are important, the competency of Establishes and Maintains Agreements is critical to the successful foundation of a coaching conversation and a thorough review of Chapter 8, which describes this competency, is highly recommended.

Trust and Safety

At all levels, the coach is expected to demonstrate genuine concern and respect for their client and to create a safe, open environment in which to work, adapting their own style where necessary. However, at PCC level the coach is expected to be more comfortable and skilled at allowing space and support for full client expression, as well as being highly attuned to the client's style and way of being.

Presence

As the credential levels progress there is an expectation of increasing ability and confidence with being able to work with the client's expression of emotions (especially strong emotions) and to manage one's own emotions. This also applies to developing a level of comfort working with the unknown and maintaining an open curious mindset allowing space and silence for reflection (for both the client and the coach) as opposed to slipping into suggesting or 'fixing'. As such, coaching presence also speaks to the level of self-awareness and personal development of the coach and this should be increasingly evident for each credential level.

Active Listening and Evoking Awareness

At ACC level, the coach is expected to be fully engaged and to listen attentively to their client. This includes listening with the ears and noticing how the client's body language is also a form of communication. ACC-level coaching also expects the coach to bring a stance of enquiry vs. telling and to ask questions that attend to the client's agenda.

At PCC level, the depth of listening should include a curiosity about what is not being said, noticing and exploring subtle shifts in the client's energy, and exploring patterns or themes in the session or across the coaching engagement. PCC-level coaching also expects the coach to evoke awareness by asking questions that are less focused on the 'data' or 'content' of the coaching topic and more focused on the client who brought that topic and how they are processing their thinking and feelings in relation to their topic.

Client Growth

This aspect of the competencies can highlight significant differences between ACC- and PCC-level coaching. At ACC level, the coach is likely to ask the client about next steps after the coaching session and also to enquire what the client's key takeaways are from the conversation. This level of exploration often leads to this aspect of the coaching session being relatively brief and contained. Whereas at PCC level, there is an expectation of a much deeper and richer exploration, which includes inviting the client to summarize their insights from the session and how that learning will be integrated after the session. There will also be a more in-depth enquiry around next steps, including how those steps might be taken, what support or resources might be needed, what might get in the way and how committed or confident the client is about those steps being accomplished. As such, at PCC level this aspect of the coaching may be a longer, fuller enquiry.

What do I Need to do to Achieve MCC Status?

An MCC credential requires a greater amount of coach-specific training and coaching experience compared with an ACC or PCC credential (Box. 33.1).

Box 33.1: MCC Credential Requirements
Master Certified Coach (MCC)
■ 200+ hours of coach-specific training ■ 10 hours of mentor coaching ■ 2,500+ hours of coaching experience ■ Coach Knowledge Assessment (CKA) ■ Core Competence performance evaluation to MCC-level minimum requirements ■ Coaches are also required to hold a PCC credential before they can apply for the MCC credential

Once again, the training hours and the coaching experience hours are incremental. For example, once a coach has completed at least the 500 hours of coaching experience for their PCC application, they then continue to coach and build up at least another 2,000 hours, making a total of at least 2,500 hours to be eligible to apply for their MCC. The same principle applies to the coach-specific training hours.

Like a PCC application, two examples of a client session are required to be submitted for assessment and for an MCC application.

What Differentiates the MCC Coach from a PCC Coach?

In line with the transition from ACC- to PCC-level coaching, MCC-level coaching sees an even greater, deeper and more consistent application of the Core Competencies. As MCC applicant coaches need to pass and gain their credential at PCC level before they are eligible to apply for MCC, a significant level of depth of understanding and use of the competencies will have already been established. Therefore, MCC-level coaching is sometimes called coaching 'beyond the competencies' and the MCC-level coach will display some of the following traits, skills, and qualities over and above thorough attention to the Core Competency framework:

- Demonstrates and maintains full and complete partnership and a relationship of trust and equality with the client in all aspects of the coaching work.
- Thoroughly explores all aspects of the coaching agreement, any potential changes in direction for the coaching, and regularly checks in with the client to ensure alignment to all agreements.
- Demonstrates complete trust and confidence in the process of coaching, in their client and in themselves.
- Is at ease with silence and creates a spacious environment for the work, regardless of the length of the coaching session.
- A sense of ease and naturalness will be evident in the coaching conversation.
- Can hold an objective and emotional perspective simultaneously and take on the stance of 'observer' to the process (immersed and detached simultaneously).
- Works with the 'who' of the client, the whole person, and considers the client's context, environment, circumstances and background to be rich and relevant aspects of the coaching work.
- Is totally at ease with not knowing, working with client emotions, self-regulating and managing own emotions even when there are moments of discomfort.

- Is comfortable with being vulnerable and is willing to allow the client to teach the coach.
- Communicates in a way that is clear and aligned with their client's style.
- Notices and works with the full range of qualities and gifts the client displays, as well as their limiting beliefs and patterns.
- Is at ease with and skilled at balancing respect, mutuality, and partnership with challenge and provoking new thought, even if this will make either the coach or their client – or both – uncomfortable.
- Is able to share observations, intuitions and feedback freely and without attachment.
- Frequently invites the client's learning, insights and intuitions to come forward and be shared and explored.
- Supports the client to develop goals, actions and next steps that achieve more than just the presenting concerns of the client.
- Is able to appropriately hold the client to account or discussion if agreed-upon forward movement does not occur.

A Model of Professional Development

Although we talk about the 'art and science' of something, Michael Grinder (2007) suggests it is the science that usually comes first when we are learning a new skill. We are often drawn to the pursuit of mastery, actively seeking out the magic of the artistic coaching conversation. In reality our growth and development as coaches usually means that we go through learning the science of coaching first and then begin to develop the Art of Coaching. Grinder's model of professional development for communication can be easily overlaid onto the process of coaching, as effective and advanced communication are such a core part of a good coach's skill set.

Figure 33.1: Art and Science

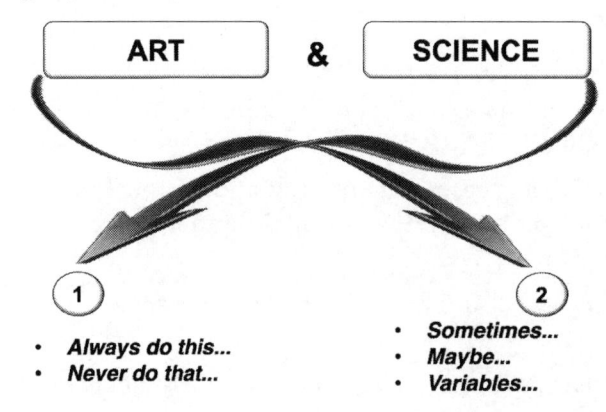

```
           ART          &         SCIENCE
            ↓                        ↓
           (1)                      (2)
   • Always do this...      • Sometimes...
   • Never do that...       • Maybe...
                            • Variables...
```

Within these two stages, first science and then art, sit four levels of development (Figure 33.2).

Figure 33.2: Science and Art

Science:
1. Content: the verbal level – the 'what'
2. Process: the non-verbal level – the 'how'

→

Art:
3. Perception: timing – the 'when'
4. Receptivity: permission – the 'if'

Science

When we first learn to coach, we can be focused on the content – i.e., **'what'** the client is saying to us and what we say in return. We may be concerned that we will forget what they have said, that the whole story is important, and that we need to understand the full detail of the situation in order to effectively coach our client. At this stage, we may be very grounded in trying to coach the topic the client has brought to our session. We may also feel that we need to bring some level of 'knowing' or expertise in order to be confident that we have added value for the client. As we develop in skill and confidence, we notice that there is more than simply the content or the words that the client is saying. We begin to realize that some of this content is not even needed for us to coach our client – in fact, the content could even get in the way.

There is also '**how**' they are saying it and, indeed, what they are **not** saying. We learn that there are more than simply the words and our listening becomes broader, deeper, and more holistic. We find ourselves expanding our attention to the person bringing the topic as well as the topic itself. We are more observant of body language, energy, emotion and tone, etc.

In summary, Grinder (2007) believes that in order to learn a new skill we first need to understand the science of that skill by establishing some clear guidelines so we know what to do or not do. For example:

- "Always ask questions; never give your opinion"
- "Always allow the client to fully express themselves; never interrupt"

Art

As our development continues, we expand our own sense of perception to increasingly sense 'when' to intervene, when to ask a question, when to stay silent and allow space and time for reflection, when to challenge, when to probe further and so on. We find ourselves increasingly more present and 'in the moment' with our clients. We work more fluidly and naturally as we sense our way through the conversation; the solid foundation is our understanding of the science of coaching, underpinning how we operate. Our ability to work in this way is also enabled by our growing level of trust – trust in ourselves as coaches, trust in clients, and trust in the process of coaching.

A high level of technical skill (science) allows us to accurately access our own intuition and, as all of these skills come together, we build higher levels of permission and rapport with our client. In this way, we also begin to know if now is the time to intervene and how receptive the client might be to what we offer.

At this stage, the somewhat rigid guidelines we needed to follow in the beginning can be relaxed, like taking the stabilizers from a bike, as we can now manoeuvre and navigate more fluidly and confidently. For example:

> "As a coach, I ask questions to evoke my client's awareness… and sometimes, depending on the circumstances, I might offer my perspective if I felt it would useful for them."

> "As a coach, I encourage my clients to fully express themselves… and possibly, if I feel it might be useful for them, I might interject and invite them to summarize what they feel is the key issue for them."

This process of navigating the science and art is in itself a dance, as these two aspects of great coaching interweave, rather than being a singular, linear learning process. As we transition into finding our 'art' as a coach, we do not leave the science behind. It is still there, embedded into the foundations of our knowledge, training, and experience – it is in fact built upon as we continue with our professional development over time.

Retaining the Beginner's Mind

You may have already become an MCC. It's tempting at this stage – particularly when much of your role is helping and supporting other coaches through mentor coaching, supervision and webinars – to think you have become an expert or guru. After all, you are at the top of the tree. We have known several well-respected coaches who publicly describe themselves as gurus. In our view this is a dangerous place to be. As soon as we start to think of ourselves as an expert or a guru, there is nothing else for us to learn and we all know what happens to species that stop learning and changing. Today's guru is tomorrow's dinosaur.

To manage this challenge, we suggest a three-step process. First, to acknowledge our expertise while simultaneously challenging it – for example: "I know a lot about the current ICF competencies and how these can be applied, but I am less skilled at [XYZ]. In the next two years I will focus my learning on thinking about this aspect of my practice."

Second, continuing to foster a Beginner's Mind. When you started out you were probably curious about everything ("How does this work?", "Why did they say that?", "I wonder what that means?", "What shall I do next?"). As we get more experienced and our knowledge grows, we understand more – or, at least, we think we do. In Buddhism, the Beginner's Mind is a term used to describe an empty mind. That is, one that holds no preconceived ideas or rules about what is or should be. It is open, eager, and receptive. The master coach needs to remain open and curious.

> **Box 33.2: A Zen Parable**
>
> A student comes to a famous Zen master and asks for instruction in the way of Zen Buddhism.
>
> The master begins to discuss several topics of Buddhism, such as emptiness and meditation. But the student interrupts the master in an attempt to impress him: "Oh, I already know all that."
>
> The master then invites the student to have some tea. When the tea is ready, the master pours it into a teacup, filling it to the brim, spilling over the sides of the cup and onto the table.
>
> The student exclaims: "Stop! You can't pour tea into a full cup."
>
> The master replies: "Return to me when your cup is empty."

Third, the master coach should have their own annual PDP and remain actively engaged in collecting CCEUs and reflective practice through supervision. The master coach, working with a fellow experienced coach whom they know, trust and respect, can be challenged and stimulated to continue their own personal quest toward maturity. Maturity, like infinity, is a quest; the pleasure and delight is in the journey, not the destination.

Conclusion

In this chapter we have looked at how to progress from ACC to PCC to MCC-level coaching and outlined the ICF requirements for each credential level. We have also described some of the differences between each level of coaching in terms of how the Core Competencies are demonstrated. Finally, we advocated the adoption of a Beginner's Mind; when the cup is empty, there is still space for it to be filled with more learning and growth. As are our clients, so are we…

Section 6: Tools and Techniques

This final section of the book looks at some tools and techniques that can form part of the coach's pool of resources, which are shared in Chapter 34. These offer many ideas for coaches to use in their ongoing growth and development on both a personal and professional level. These resources are also available to download at www.pavpub.com/becoming-a-coach-resources.

From the client perspective, we do not advocate that coaching is a tool-driven process by any means, but understand that some of the concepts and approaches contained within this section offer many ways to evoke new awareness, insight, and learning for our clients. When these tools are introduced – with permission and in partnership with our clients, in a way that is congruent and intuitively aligned with the work that the client is doing – they can become a great source of new perspective and creative thought.

Some of these tools have already featured in the book and they are summarized in this section for easy reference. We go on to include many other coaching tools and techniques with an introduction and overview of the tool or technique itself. We also provide a description of how they are used in practice, with examples and other useful and relevant references.

Chapter 34: Coaching Tools

In our experience, new coaches like to learn new techniques to try out. For this reason we have included a selection in this book. We have included techniques in the individual chapters and now add to these in this section.

We appreciate that different techniques suit different coaches, different clients, and different presenting issues. By having a wide range of techniques and tools to draw upon, we believe you are best placed to adapt your approach to meet your individual client's needs.

So far in this book you have come across the following tools and techniques, summarized in Table 34.1.

Table 34.1: Coaching Techniques in Chapters		
Chapter	Technique	When is this Tool Useful?
15	Time to Think	Providing space for clients to think
16	ABCDEF	Helping clients explore the connection between their thoughts, feelings and behaviour
17	Empty Chair	Exploring relationships and our thoughts and feelings about others
18	Miracle Question	Ideas generation
19	Force Field	Exploring the forces at work in supporting and resisting change
20	Desert Island	Exploring the hidden aspects of the relationship between individuals
25	PIPS	Note-taking
29	Self-Supervision	Reflective questions for reviewing your coaching practice
30	Henley8	Self-reflection or writing your learning journal

Using a new technique can be tricky. One way of trying out new ones is to ask the client if they are willing to do an experiment. You can explain that you are not sure it will work, but also say you know other people have found it helpful. In this way, if it fails, it was just an experiment and it is less likely to have a negative impact on your relationship with your client. Of course, if it works, the client may ask to use the tool themselves.

In this chapter we include techniques as listed in Table 34.2.

Table 34.2: Additional Coaching Techniques		
Technique	When Is This Tool Useful?	Resources
1. Mindfulness Meditation	Preparing for a coaching session/becoming present	
2. STOKERS	Goal setting	STOKERS Checklist
3. Typical Day	Reviewing the current situation/reality	
4. Developing Change Talk	Helping clients focus on building intrinsic motivation to change	
5. Walking and Talking	If clients are stuck	
6. Heaven and Hell	Exploring alternative futures	Cartoon template
7. Reflections	Building motivation for action	
8. VIP	Options/ideas generation	
9. Post-It	Options/ideas generation	
10. Desert Island	Exploring relationships between the client and a key stakeholder	
11. Vicious and Virtuous Flower	Exploring faulty thinking	Flower
12 Virtuous Flower	Exploring strengths thinking	Flower
13. Personal Board of Directors	Accountability and support	
14. Strengths Cards	Helping clients identify and talk about their strengths	

15. Jelly Baby Tree	Exploring mood, emotion and relationships	Jelly Baby Tree
16. Consequences Wheel	Option evaluation	Consequences chart
17. Legacy	Making values-based decisions	
18. Wheel of Life	Evaluating current reality	Wheel
19. Sphere of Influence	Reflecting on the stakeholders involved in the situation	
19. DOUSE	Closing the coaching relationship	DOUSE Checklist
20. Three Good Things	Refocusing on the positive	
21. Blessings	Cultivating compassion	

Technique 1: Mindfulness Meditation

Mindfulness has emerged into popular organizational practice. It has been written about widely as a useful tool for coaches to enhance presence during the session, as well as helping the coach to prepare for a session. We described its use for coaches in Chapter 26. Mindfulness can be an equally useful tool for clients.

Tool

There are a wealth of mindfulness podcasts, exercises and materials available on the web and in books that coaches can explore (Passmore & Amit, 2017; Chaskalson & McMordie, 2017). One technique that we find useful with clients, particularly those in highly pressurized roles with multiple completing prioritizes, is STOP (Passmore, 2017a).

STOP is useful when we observe a pattern of distraction or frenetic behaviour in our client, where stopping, reflecting and reprioritizing may be helpful. By using STOP, we may reflect back to the client what we are observing and invite them to clear their mind and notice the sensations they are experiencing in their body, the thoughts going through their mind, and whatever emotions they are feeling. We are not inviting the client to share these but just to be aware of them as an outside observer, not judging, evaluating or engaging with the thoughts or feelings.

We next invite the client to move their awareness to their breathing; to be aware whether it is fast or slow, deep or shallow, from the diaphragm or lungs. Spending maybe 30 seconds just observing the breath without judgment; observing the full in-breath and the full out-breath. Finally, we invite the client to consider – now with enhanced awareness of the present moment – what changes they want to make to best achieve their objectives for the day.

Conclusion

The short two-minute exercise can be useful to refocus in a coaching conversation. It is also useful for clients to incorporate the technique as part of their routine; to stop work every two hours, to step back from the whirlwind, and to bring their attention to the present moment – sensations, thoughts and feelings, and breath. Once they have reviewed their priorities, they can move forward with new focus.

Technique 2: STOKERS

The STOKERS framework was originally developed by Clare Pedrick for supporting clients during the goal-setting phase of a coaching conversation. In our work with clients we have developed STOKERS, offering seven steps for the coach to work through with their clients.

Tool

The STOKER is a person on a steam train who puts the fuel into the engine. They shovel coal while the driver makes decisions about when the train leaves the station, where it goes, and when and where it stops. This is a useful metaphor for coaching. The coach acts to add the fuel for the conversation, but it is the responsibility of the client to make choices about when and where the train goes. The coach explores each step with the client through a specific question and uses follow-up questions as required.

1. **Subject** – The conversation starts with the coach inviting their client to identify the subject they wish to discuss during the session.
2. **Time** – This subject is refined by a question that encourages the client to consider and agree to the amount of time for the session.
3. **Outcome** – The aim of the third question is to help the client think about the end point of the conversation. This may be a learning point, a new insight, or a series of actions to take away and implement.
4. **Know** – This question focuses on clarifying the goal with success criteria; making the goal measurable in SMART terms.
5. **Energy** – This is an additional question that encourages clients to consider whether and why this topic is a priority now, and how much energy or motivation there is to address the topic.
6. **Role** – This question explores the roles each party will play in the conversation and provides an opportunity for the two parties to agree how they will collaborate to achieve the client's goal. As the model makes no formal reference to confidentiality, the topic can be discussed at this stage as part of the working relationship.
7. **Start** – The final question invites the client to identify a starting point and begin.

The tool makes goal-setting a collaborative process, while also ensuring the key elements are included, thereby setting the coaching up for a successful outcome.

Figure 34.1: STOKERS for Goal-Setting

| 1. Subject | 2. Time | 3. Outcome | 4. Know | 5. Energy | 6. Role | 7. Start |

> **Box 34.1: STOKERS Useful Questions (Checklist)**
>
> 1. What do you need to think about today? (Subject question)
> 2. Given we have [X] time, which element should we focus on in our conversation? (Time question)
> 3. What would you like to be different by the end of our time together? (Outcome question)
> 4. How will you know when you have reached this point? (Know question)
> 5. How important is this issue for you right now? (Energy question)
> 6. How are we going to do this? (Role question)
> 7. Where shall we start? (Start question)

Conclusion

The STOKERS model is a shorthand way to help coaches cover the key elements during the contracting and goal-setting phase of the conversation. A STOKERS checklist is available in Chapter 35: Resources, or can be downloaded from www.pavpub.com/becoming-a-coach-resources.

Technique 3: Typical Day

The 'Typical Day' exercise is a good way to start a coaching session and follows on from the initial contracting and goal-setting segment of the session, which might form the first 10 minutes of the conversation. Typical Day is a technique drawn from Motivational Interviewing and originally developed by Bill Miller and Steve Rollnick (2002). More recently it has been adapted for use in coaching (Anstiss & Passmore, 2011).

Tool

The Typical Day question is a good way to get clients talking about the issue in a non-threatening way. The technique provides the opportunity for the coach to show a new client that coaching is about them. It provides a time when the coach can actively listen and demonstrate curiosity. The coach can use summaries and reflect back words, emotions and appropriate content about what is said. They can also offer insights into what they may not have said themselves while helping the client place their remarks into a wider cultural and systemic context. Overall, the technique builds empathy and rapport and increases the client's commitment to the process.

The coach may introduce the technique by saying: "Perhaps you could help me get a better understanding how your average day goes; starting from when you get up in the morning until you go to bed. How does your day start?"

In response to this question some clients will rush ahead and focus on the issue they wish to discuss – for example, work–life balance or relationships with their team. They may say: "Well, nothing really happens until…" We suggest inviting the client to slow down and to take each part of the day in turn, even if they think nothing significant happened. Other clients may spend several minutes telling you about their thoughts even before they get out of bed. The coach can manage the process by helping the client to explore their day with new eyes, with a specific focus on the issue the client wants to consider in the session.

A second part of this technique is using the content to build the 'change talk'. We will look at this in Technique 4.

> **Box 34.2: Typical Day Useful Questions**
> 1. "Perhaps you could help me get a better understanding of how your average day goes at work – starting from when you get up in the morning until when you go to bed? Would that be okay? How does your day start?"
> 2. "Can you tell me more about this?"
> 3. "Before you move on to the afternoon team meeting, tell me about the morning and what happens in the team?"

Conclusion

The technique helps coaches provide a space for clients to talk openly about an issue and for the coach to demonstrate active listening and empathy. Used well, the technique can also provide an opportunity for the coach to encourage the client to spend time developing change talk and a belief that the situation can be different.

Technique 4: Developing Change Talk – DARN CAT

During most coaching conversations, clients use language that signals their desire to make a change and also language that signals a reluctance to change. Helping clients explore this ambiguity and build their motivation for the change is the focus of DARN CAT as a coaching tool.

Tool

During a typical coaching conversation, the client may use both what Bill Miller and Steve Rollnick call 'sustain talk' and 'change talk' (Miller & Rollnick, 2002).

Sustain talk is speech that reinforces the client's view about a situation (e.g., "I just can't start stand working in this place; women are treated as second-class citizens"). 'Change talk' sounds more like "I used to work for a different tech firm and had an enjoyable time working there". These will spontaneously emerge during the session without coach direction. Such responses provide the opportunity to explore this language.

Miller and Rollnick (2002) suggest that change talk is like a hill. It comes in two parts; the uphill and downhill of change. The uphill side of the equation is the preparatory change talk, which is most likely to occur during the contemplation phase of the cycle of change. This happens when the person is thinking about change and weighing up whether change is really for them and, if so, how they might do it. In many cases the person is well aware of the advantages of making the change but balanced against this are a series of barriers that have blocked their path to successfully making the change. It is often these barriers that the coach is helping the client to overcome.

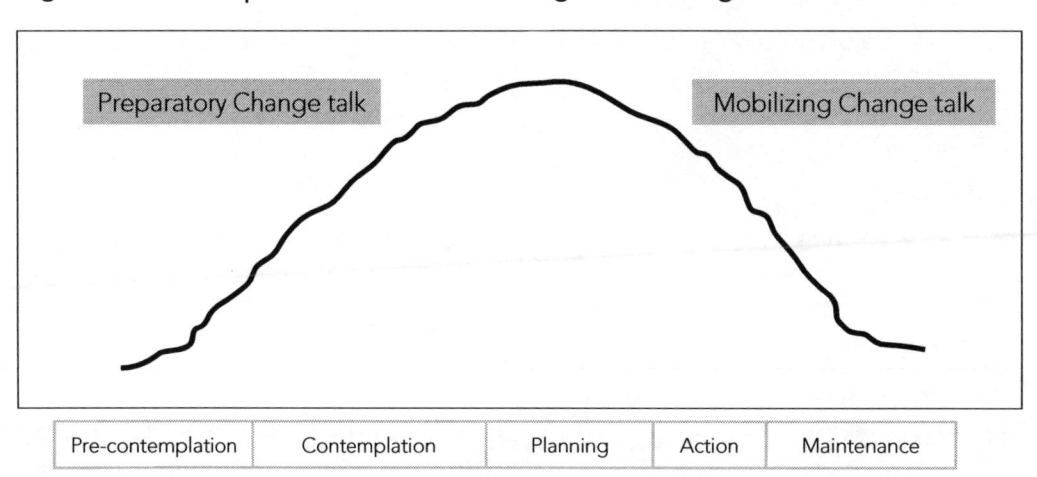

Figure 34.2: Transpersonal Model of Change and Change Talk Phases

During the contemplation phase the coach needs to listen for what Miller and Rollnick (2011) have labeled DARNs. These statements reveal an interest in, and consideration of, change; however, the client lacks a specific commitment to making the change. Such statements might express the individual's personal desires about making a change, the ability to make the change, their reasons for making the change, and the need to change. Examples of these are summarized in Box 34.3.

> **Box 34.3: Samples of DARN Statements**
>
> **Desire:** "I really want to do Y"
>
> **Ability:** "I think I could do Y if I really wanted to…"
>
> **Reason:** "If they did X, then I think that would be enough and I would then do Y"
>
> **Need:** "I really need to do Y, or… will happen"

In general terms, the coach should look out for statements that are conditional or hypothetical. These statements express desires ("I need to" or "I want to"), they may express ability ("I can" or "I could"), they express reasons for making the change, and they may also express the risks in their mind. However, although such statements reveal the client has shifted from the pre-contemplation to contemplation phase of the model (Prochaska & DiClemente, 1983), there is no expressed commitment to make the change. There is not a specific plan for how the change is going to be made – particularly how barriers and hurdles that have held the individual back will be overcome.

At this stage the role of the coach is to encourage the client to explore the situation and focus more on the values or beliefs that attracted them to this change. As this happens and the coach maintains effective listening and interventions, the client will grow in confidence and commitment language is likely to develop. In place of DARN statements, CAT statements will emerge (Miller & Rollnick, 2011). CAT statements are likely to reflect a change in the client from early commitment to mobilization; from "I want to" to "I will". Box 34.4 provides examples of the three types of CAT statements that the coach should be looking for.

> **Box 34.4: Examples of CAT Statements**
>
> **Commitment:** "Next week I will do Y."
>
> **Action:** "I am really keen this time to make a success of it. I have thought about what went wrong last time and it's going to be different on Tuesday."
>
> **Taking Steps:** "In advance of next Tuesday, I have already done X. This will mean that when the meeting comes on Tuesday Y should be much easier this time."

As Box 34.4 shows, the CAT statements are concerned with intentions and promises. The client makes an unambiguous statement expressing their plans for the future. Key words for the coach to listen for are 'will', 'promise', or 'guarantee'. Action statements reflect the individual's state of being willing, ready and prepared to act.

Conclusion

DARN CAT is a useful framework to help coaches to listen to the client's language, to understand where clients are within the cycle of change, to encourage clients to focus on values and their desires for change, and through these interventions to observe the client's language shift from DARN toward CAT.

Technique 5: Walking and Talking – Eco-Psychology Coaching

This technique can be useful for helping clients break out when they feel trapped or stuck. Changing the physical environment can help clients see issues from a fresh perspective, but more generally getting out into blue–green environments can have a positive impact of well-being and make for a welcome change from the office or meeting room.

Tool

Most coaching takes place in corporate meeting rooms or executive offices. These can be sterile environments, with few views or fresh perspectives to stimulate new thinking. Many of us in our 'normal' lives go for a walk to clear our heads. We find that a walk offers us a new insight or fresh perspective. Eco-coaching combines the psychological benefits of being outdoors with a change of environment to help a new perspective emerge. This may involve a stroll in a rose garden, a hike up a mountain, a walk along a riverbank or a beach. What seems to make a difference is the introduction of blue–green colours in the environment, combined with the physical movement of walking and a side-by-side conversation, as opposed to a face-to-face style of engagement.

From our experience, this may be a tool to introduce once you have got to know your client; however, for some clients it may be an appropriate tool to use from the start. We know some coaches who specialize in this type of approach and use it as part of the way they coach.

Conclusion

Eco-coaching or 'walking and talking' can be useful way to freshen up the coaching relationship and offer clients a different space where they can think in new ways about their issue.

Technique 6: Heaven and Hell

Goal-setting is a key task in most coaching conversations. Most novice coaches rush too quickly from identifying the topic and diving into the detail of the issue. We think it's important that the coach spends time exploring the topic, understanding its importance and relevance, unpicking what aspect to focus on during this particular conversation, and deciding what can realistically be achieved in the 20 minutes or two hours planned for the session. Heaven and Hell is a visual technique that can help the client clarify their outcome in more refined detail by considering both the perfect outcome (heaven) and its opposite (hell).

Tool

The tool aims to help the client explore the initial topic; to clarify and refine a vague goal toward a more specific and concrete goal. The first part of the process is similar to a normal goal-setting discussion, asking the client to set out their goal. Given the goal, what might this mean for them? Here the coach aims to ensure the goal is important and relevant.

The next step in the process is to invite the client to describe (or draw) what the perfect outcome would be ('heaven'). The more detailed the description, the better. The next step is to invite them to do the same for the worst possible – but realistic – outcome.

After the client has described or drawn 'hell', the coach invites them to consider what steps would lead to a hellish outcome. Now using a cartoon sketch book, the client is invited to draw pictures to represent the key steps that lead to each outcome, but working backwards. Table 34.3 illustrates the steps in sequential order, working backwards from hell. A blank version of this table for clients to complete can be found in Chapter 35: Resources, or can be downloaded from www.pavpub.com/becoming-a-coach-resources

Table 34.3: Heaven or Hell Cartoon Planning		
Step 9 Picture of now	Step 8	Step 7
Step 6	Step 5	Step 4
Step 3 ←	Step 2 Key factors starting here and working backwards from heaven to now	Step 1 Picture of heaven

Try to avoid clients becoming too extreme in their scenarios. Encourage them to focus on likely events, as opposed to rare events. Once the client has worked through hell, they can switch back to heaven.

Box 34.4: Heaven and Hell Useful Questions

1. What would you like to focus on during the session today?
2. Given we have X minutes, what aspect of this would you like to focus on?
3. Why is this important to you today?
4. What outcome would you want to achieve?
5. If this was the perfect outcome (heaven) what would it look like? Can you describe for me (draw for me) what it would be like?
6. Now for just a few moments, imagine the worst outcome (hell). Can you describe for me (draw for me) what it would be like?
7. Let's start with hell, working backwards through a series of stages. How could you have ended up here? (Draw or note some of the things that have happened along the way.)
8. Let's return to heaven, again working backwards through a series of stages. How can you increase the chances of ending up here? (Draw or note some of the things that have happened along the way).

It is important to make sure that at the end of the coaching session any notes on whiteboard, flipcharts or paper are removed from the room, or rubbed out from the boards.

Conclusion

This technique is really useful for encouraging clients to consider, describe and draw their perfect outcome (heaven) and its opposite (hell).

Technique 7: Using Reflections: Simple, Amplified and Muted

Reflections and summaries are useful tools that coaches should be using as part of active listening to ensure clarity and understanding. This technique offers ways these competencies can be used by providing different types of reflections, i.e., simple and amplified. The technique is drawn from Motivational Interviewing (Miller & Rollnick, 2002).

Tool

Reflective listening is a key coaching skill. In popular language, 'listening' often means just keeping quiet and waiting for our turn to talk. This Level 1 style of listening is unhelpful in even basic coaching, although it is a frequently used style in many everyday conversations. Competent coaches should be aiming to listen at Level 4, with professional coaches working at an interpretive level and sharing their insights where this is helpful to their client.

Box 34.5: Five Levels of Listening

Level 1: Waiting to speak – at this level we are simply waiting for our turn to talk.

Level 2: Basic listening – at this level the listener focuses on the words being said.

Level 3: Attentive listening – at this level the listener focuses on the words and tone of the communication to understand the true meaning.

Level 4: Active listening – at this level the listener focuses on the words, tone and body language of the speaker and is trying to understand what the speaker is intending to communicate.

Level 5: Interpretive listening – at this level the listener is seeking to move beyond the intended communication. They are interpreting meaning from the whole communication, which includes both intended meanings and unintended communications.

At Level 1 and at Level 2 the coach might be drawn into using an intervention that creates a roadblocks for their client. The roadblock acts to stop the client moving forward (Gordon, 1970). These responses might include agreeing, reassuring, cautioning, labelling, or even asking a question. For the client who is stuck in a dilemma and is seeking a way forward, but remains ambivalent about making a change, a roadblock intervention is likely to result in the person entering a holding pattern that maintains them in their current position.

Box 34.6: Example of Typical Coach Response

Client: "I am feeling fed up with my boss."

Coach: "Sounds really bad; what are they doing?"

In Box 34.6 the coach uses both an affirming statement ("sounds really bad"), as well as a question to explore further the nature of the behaviour that is creating the feelings. The outcome of this intervention is that the client will talk about what is causing the emotion, i.e., becoming stuck in the problem.

The coach could employ a different approach. They could encourage the client to focus on more change-related talk and thus help the client begin to move forward. Change talk is a statement from the client that focuses on their desires or plans for making a change. We explored this in Technique 4.

Simple Reflections

In using 'simple reflection', the coach tries to understand the meaning of the client and reflect this back, capturing their words, phrases and, critically, the meaning of the client's communication. Using a reflective statement is less likely to provoke resistance. For example, if the coach asked about the meaning of the statement, this directs the client to step back and reflect on whether they really do mean what they have said. To illustrate this point, the coach could say: "You're feeling unsure?" This is done through an inflection, with the tone rising toward the end of the sentence in Received Pronunciation English (sometimes called BBC English). In contrast, the coach could use reflective listening to reflect back: "You're feeling unsure." This involves using a neutral tone throughout the sentence. The reflective statement communicates understanding and becomes a statement of fact. Such statements are more likely to encourage the client to talk more about this emotional state. As the client talks, they think about this state and draw out for themselves the evidence of why they are feeling as they do. This deepens their insight and is more likely to lead into change talk.

Reflective statements can be quite simple and involve reflecting back a single word or a pair of key words from the client's story. The coach's skill is in listening and selecting the right word or words to reflect back that capture the heart of the message.

A more sophisticated series of options, however, are also available to the coach. These involve amplified (over-stating) or muted (under-stating) reflections. The use of these and the frequency of application will vary with the coach's skills, and the meaning they carry may vary in different national and cultural contexts. Inappropriate use, or over-frequent use, can leave the client believing their coach is not listening to them and can undermine the coaching relationship. As a result, we suggest coaches use these statements with caution, and certainly avoid using the technique more than once or twice in any session.

Muted (Understated) Reflection

This is best used when the coach wishes the client to continue exploring an issue and to confirm the strength of feeling they have about an issue. The coach may reflect back a lower level of emotion than that communicated by the client. For example, the client communicates 'anger', the coach may select to reflect back a lower intensity of 'anger', such as using the word 'irritation' or 'disappointed'. This works well where understatement is a feature of the culture. The effect is the client is likely to speak further about their true emotion, possibly correcting their coach about the strength of feeling and talking more honestly about their true feelings.

The key skill is to avoid understating to the extent that the client feels the coach has not listened to what has been said. This takes both a high level of listening to the whole communication and a high level of skill in selecting the right word to reflect back.

Amplified (Overstated) Reflection

If the coach chooses to amplify the emotional content and overstate the emotion compared with the client's original communication, it is likely the client will deny and minimize the emotion.

This is useful, for example, if the client was speaking about faults in their manager's working style. The coach may repeat an overstatement in this manner: "So you think your manager is totally incompetent" or "It must be hard working for your manager as it sounds as if you believe they are a walking disaster zone". The coach needs to make it clear the label is one the client is applying, not one they are applying. "You think" as opposed to "You are" is useful in this context to make the ownership of the views clearly placed with the client. This intervention will help the client to recognize some of the positive attributes of their manager and thus begin to build a more balanced and evidence-based perspective.

Once again, the danger is that the client may feel they have not been heard. The coach needs to be careful and limited in their use of overstatement if they wish to avoid damaging the coach–client relationship. There is also the risk the client will agree and, if poorly phrased, it can appear is as if the coach is colliding with the client.

Conclusion

Reflection, like coaching, is not a passive process. It is the coach who decides when to intervene, when to be silent, when to nod, and what to say. Making a choice is therefore important. The coach can direct the attention of the client and encourage them forward toward their goal, to dwell in the moment, or to reflect back to the past. Reflections can be a useful tool in the coach toolkit.

Technique 8: VIP

This technique is most useful during the ideas generation stage when the client needs to think beyond their current experiences and develop new perspectives. The technique invites the client to consider how others (Very Important People) might deal with the issue the client is exploring and thus provide new ideas to draw from. The technique can be kept serious, or made fun, depending on the characters the coach selects.

Tool

Very Important People (VIPs) can be inspirational for us and our clients. They often have an image that projects a distinct way of doing things, be they Donald Trump or Nelson Mandela.

The technique is most helpful when a client is stuck at the Options stage of the GROW model, and feels they have a limited range of options available to them. The VIP question invites the client to step out of their own style and way of working to consider alternative ways to solve the problem by imaging they are someone else.

The coach can select some commonsense suggestions, such as Warren Buffett or Greta Thunberg. Or they can draw on diverse figures from history or cartoon characters, such as Abraham Lincoln, Rosa Parks, Genghis Khan or Lisa Simpson. In most cases, we and the client will hold a shared stereotype about the character, which is used by the client to imagine their approach to resolving the problem.

> **Box 34.7: VIP: Useful Questions**
>
> 1. Would you be happy to do an experiment with me? Let's imagine that Margaret Thatcher was faced with this problem. What would she do?
> 2. Now let's imagine that Martin Luther King faced this problem. How would he work toward a solution?
> 3. What about Abraham Lincoln?
> 4. Finally, what about Greta Thunberg?

Offering four or five characters, which the client is familiar with, provides the opportunity to generate four or five different and creative new insights to move forward with the problem. Once these have been generated, the coach can invite the client to think about these ideas and how they may fit the client, their organization, and cultural context. In some cases, the ideas may need to be translated into a modern-day context. Massacring the finance department by sending in a crack commando squad may be both unrealistic and illegal. But taking the fight to them, by highlighting each and every error, may be a legitimate (albeit a highly confrontational) approach.

Conclusions

VIP is a fun technique that clients usually enjoy. The coach needs to take care in selecting VIPs within the client's frame of reference and ones that will not cause offense. Beyond this, diversity usually adds value in bringing creativity into the conversation.

Technique 9: Post-It

This technique is useful during the ideas generation stage. It works best with clients who prefer a visual representation of their ideas and who are better suited to internal processing. The technique involves inviting clients to write their ideas on Post-It notes, which they spread across the table and can take away at the end of the session.

Tool

The coach invites the client to think about new ways of addressing the problem, but to do this by writing them down instead of speaking about them. Research has shown that brain writing (Rohrbach, 1969) is a more powerful technique than brainstorming in group situations. Individuals are less likely to move from idea into evaluation, instead staying focused on generating ideas. This separates the two parts of the process more clearly, thereby making it more enjoyable and effective for people (Litcanu *et al.*, 2015).

This technique applies the same process to a one-to-one coaching conversation. The coach invites the client to write as many ideas as possible on Post-It notes. For some clients it can be fun to set a target for maybe 12 ideas in two minutes. Others prefer time with no target. During the writing period the coach will hold the silence. Once the ideas are generated, the coach invites the client to put the Post-It notes out on the desk as a collection. The notes can then be reviewed and discussed individually. It is possible to start to move the notes around – for example, it would be possible to use a whiteboard or flipchart to write some criteria with an X–Y axis to consider the Top 5 or 6 ideas against the criteria. Some clients at this stage like to score or rank the ideas against the criteria; others are less data driven and are happy simply to discuss idea each in turn.

Conclusions

The tool provides an opportunity to expand the number of ideas through an evidence-based approach.

Technique 10: Desert Island

The purpose of this technique is to encourage clients to think about the problem they are facing in a different dimension or location. The desert island is outside space and time and provides an opportunity to develop fresh perspectives on a problem.

Tool

The tool involves a single question, with follow-up and deeper exploration of the client's thinking. The question is: "Imagine you were shipwrecked on a desert island with the person, and this problem/situation occurred. What would happen on the desert island?"

Box 34.8: Desert Island Useful Questions

1. "Imagine you were shipwrecked on a desert island with the person, and this problem/situation occurred. What would happen on the desert island?
2. "What would happen next?"
3. "How might you survive (with them) if rescue was two months away?"
4. "What insights does this tell you about your relationship with X/the key stakeholders?"
5. "You are now rescued and are transported back to work. Given the discussion we have just had, how would you wish to resolve the issue?"

Conclusion

The Desert Island technique is a helpful technique to introduce when clients are seeking a fresh perspective or want to consider the issue beyond the confines of the organization's processes, systems and culture, which can sometimes stop solutions emerging.

Technique 11: Vicious Flower

The Vicious Flower is a simple tool that can help clients explore their faulty thinking. The tool sits within the CBC approach and works well alongside the ABC framework, as clients consider their Activating event (trigger), Beliefs and Consequences. The technique encourages clients to look at the maintenance cycles that (often unintentionally) prolong or sustain their faulty thinking pattern.

Tool

The coach might draw the flower (or use a pre-drawn image) and explain that the petals represent the thoughts the client has. Figure 34.3 is available for clients in Chapter 35: Resources, or can be downloaded from www.pavpub.com/becoming-a-coach-resources. At the centre of the flower is the core belief. The coach might help the client to explore the self-talk statements they are using – for example, "I am no good at presenting", "I always forget key parts of my message", "Colleagues will think I am stupid" and "I always lose my thread and start talking about irrelevant things". These thoughts might all be sustaining "I am not worthy to be a manager".

Having got the client to label the petals (thereby making these thoughts conscious), the coach can work with the client to challenge these thoughts, using questions such as "How helpful is it to think like this?", "What's the evidence for that statement?" and "Is it logical to think like this?"

Figure 34.3: The Flower

> **Box 34.9: Vicious Flower Useful Questions**
>
> 1. "I have drawn a flower. We call this the vicious flower as it is poisonous. The aim will be to label as many of the unhelpful thoughts you have and write them in the flower petals. Where would you like to start?"
> 2. "How helpful is it for you to have these thoughts?"
> 3. "How logical is this?"
> 4. "What's the evidence this 'always' happens?"

Conclusion

The technique is a useful tool to be used alongside ABC within a CBC session.

Technique 12: Virtuous Flower

The Virtuous Flower is the opposite of the Vicious Flower technique and can be used as a follow-up to it or as a self-standing tool. The tool sits within the positive psychology coaching approach but is also consistent with compassion-based approaches within third-wave cognitive-behavioural approaches. Instead of labeling and removing petals that are unhelpful negative self-talk statements, the aim is to develop or capture positive self-talk statements that are reinforcing and compassionate.

Tool

The coach uses the same flower drawing as in Technique 11. This time, however, they explain that the petals represent the client's strengths, virtues, or positive statements. The center of the flower represents the client's main virtue or strength. The coach might help the client to explore these virtues, possibly based on results from the VIA, or drawing on positive feedback the client has received. If the client does move into negative comments, the coach redirects the attention through an intervention, reminding the client that the agreed focus is on strengths, virtues, or positive statements.

Having got the client to label the petals, encourage them to reflect on in what situations they demonstrate these virtues and how they draw on these virtues more in different situations to achieve more effective outcomes.

> **Box 34.9: Virtuous Flower Useful Questions**
>
> 1. "I have drawn a flower. We call this the virtuous flower. What I would like you to do is think about yourself when you are at your best. What character words come to mind? Use these words to label the petals."
> 2. "What does it feel like when you draw on these qualities?"
> 3. "How could you use one or more of these in the recent challenge we were discussing?"
> 4. "How can you cultivate these virtues to use them more frequently?"

Conclusion

The Virtuous Flower is a useful tool for encouraging people to talk about their strengths or virtues and reflect on how they can use these character strengths to be at their best more often.

Technique 13: Personal Board of Directors

One element that many clients neglect is how they can leverage their personal network of clients, family and colleagues to help them achieve their goals. Personal Board of Directors is a metaphor that many clients can use to provide a support team outside coaching to help them progress toward their wider goals.

Tool

The technique, like most in this section, is fairly simple. It addresses the challenge of the time between the coach meeting the client once a week or once a month, during which the client needs to call upon their own resources to make progress. For every hour in a coaching conversation, there are a further 100 hours (or more) when the client has to find their own way forward.

The Personal Board of Directors is a way of the client creating their own support team, or The A-Team (a popular 1980s American TV show). The technique is most valuable while the client develops their plan. The coach can then invite the client to consider whom they would like to support them as they proceed with the plan.

> **Box 34.10: Personal Board of Directors Useful Questions**
>
> 1. "As you think about the plan, whose help or support would you like to draw on – a bit like a personal board of directors – to help you deliver the plan?"
> 2. "In what ways can each person best help?"
> 3. "How will you engage their support?"

Conclusion

This technique helps clients recognize they are not alone. If they call upon friends, family members, and colleagues to support them – by providing advice and encouragement, championing them when they slip back, as well as holding them to account – they are more likely to reach their goal than if they try to achieve behavioural change by themselves.

Technique 14: Jelly Baby Trees

The Jelly Baby Tree was originally developed for use in schools but has spread widely and there are now many versions available, including some for adults. The origin of the tool is hard to establish, and multiple people claim to be the originators. The picture allows people to project their feelings onto one of the characters in the drawing, thereby providing an opportunity to explore the character's feelings and what it might be like to be one of the other characters in the drawing.

Tool

The process starts by sharing the drawing with the client and asking them which character they most identify with today. They are asked to explore what they think the character is feeling and why. They are then asked to explore other thoughts, such as "What could the character do to change their feelings? Who could they join in with?" A larger version of the drawing is available in Chapter 35: Resources, or it can be downloaded from www.pavpub.com/becoming-a-coach-resources.

Box 34.11; Jelly Baby Useful Questions

- "Which character do you most identify with today?"
- "What might have happened to that character?"
- "What could you do to change these feelings?"
- "Which character would you most like to feel like?"
- "What could you do to move closer to feeling like this?"

Conclusion

The technique is great for starting conversations about feelings and provides a safe mechanism to do so. Only move into personal matters when you consider the client is ready.

Technique 15: The Consequences Wheel

This technique is focused on providing a structure to explore the advantages and disadvantages of each of the options identified. The tool offers a deceptively straightforward process to map short and long-term implications and, from this, helps clients plan how to mitigate risks and harvest the benefits.

Tool

The tool invites the client to think through the consequences in a formal way. As most decisions involve multiple consequences, it's best to focus on the three or four that are high-probability outcomes. We also consider the one or two low-probability outcomes that are carry high risks. The more important the decision, the more important it will be to consider a wider number of scenarios.

Most clients tend to focus on high probability, but if the action has a low probability of happening but contains a high risk then this risk is important to consider. In the example of drink-driving, being stopped by the police and breathalyzed is a medium probability. The consequences may be losing your license for a period, which could be inconvenient. Having an accident with another vehicle and skidding onto the pavement killing five preschool age children is a low probability. However, this event could have life-changing consequences, not only for the children and their families, but also for the driver, their career, and their whole family.

The coach invites the coach to complete a chain of events emanating from each possible consequence, containing short-term events and longer-term events, as well as an opportunity to think through both the desired, or intended, consequences, as well as the unintended consequences.

The output is a diagram (Figure 34.4) that can help the individual decide the appropriate course of action, and plan to mitigate or manage less desirable potential consequences, as well as thinking about how to harvest or amplify intended and positive consequences. A blank version of the Consequences Wheel can be found in Chapter 35: Resources, or can be downloaded from www.pavpub.com/becoming-a-coach-resources.

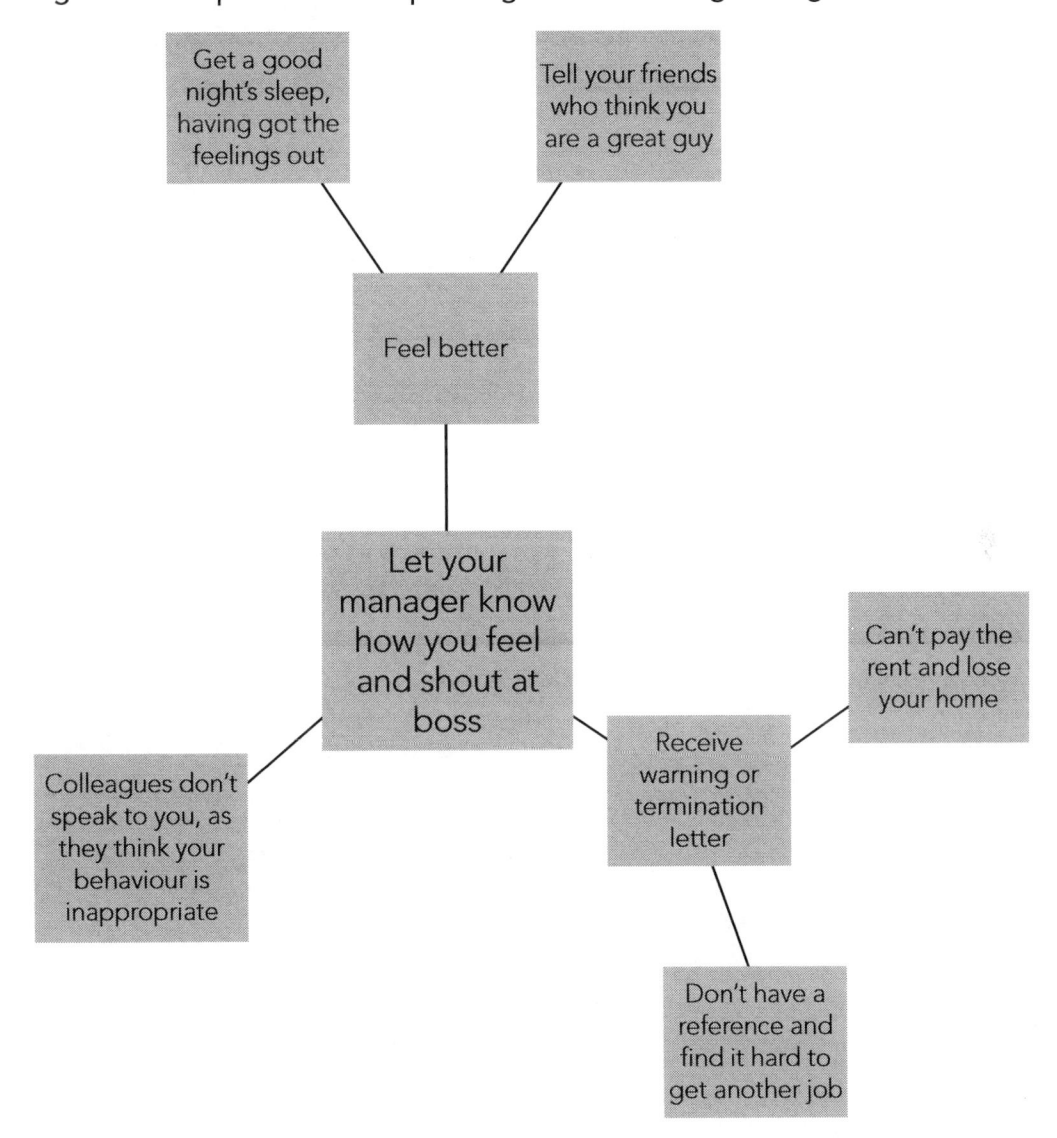

Figure 34.4: Option A for Responding to a Frustrating Manager at Work

- Get a good night's sleep, having got the feelings out
- Tell your friends who think you are a great guy
- Feel better
- Let your manager know how you feel and shout at boss
- Colleagues don't speak to you, as they think your behaviour is inappropriate
- Receive warning or termination letter
- Can't pay the rent and lose your home
- Don't have a reference and find it hard to get another job

Conclusion

The technique is simple to use and can be developed for as long as the client has the time or inclination, with short-term consequences that develop into longer-term and secondary consequences.

Technique 16: Legacy

In our world our focus is too often on the short term – this week, this month, this year. We have a tendency to neglect the longer-term implications of our actions. This technique flips this and invites the client to consider the genuine long-term impact of their plan or their desires.

Tool

The technique invites clients to think about their legacy. There are a variety of ways of asking the question, and judging which depends on the client and their situation. Our most popular ways of framing this are:

- "Imagine you are 80 and in a care home, telling fellow residents this story. What would you want to say looking back on these events about how you handled this?"
- "As you think about the long term impact of these events, what legacy do you want to leave behind?"
- "What would you like your fellow team members to say about you after you retire/move on to a new role?"

On most occasions, this question creates a reflective stance, an inhalation of breath, and a moment of much deeper thought than a simple, "So what's your next step?" question.

We can, of course, make the intervention even more challenging by introducing an emotional element via relationships. This works really well for very senior managers or individuals with a public profile: "As your grandchildren or great-grandchildren look back on this time in history/your stewardship of the company, what do you think they will say about how you should have handled these events?"

This later question invites people to consider their actions against their values and, from experience, encourages people to re-orientate their behaviours toward their values compass.

Conclusion

The technique can be helpful in encouraging clients to consider the long view of their actions, and how they may impact on them and future generations.

Technique 17: Wheel of Life

In a fast-paced world with multiple demands on our time, are we making the right choices about how we use our time? How do our current choices make us feel? The Wheel of Life enables the client to explore how they use their time and how happy they are with the balance between the different aspects of their lives.

Tool

The Wheel of Life is one of the coach's most versatile tools. It's an easy-to-use exercise that can help clients find out which areas of their lives are most satisfying and where they would like to focus attention on improving their quality of life. There are only two steps to this exercise.

The first is to identify six or eight categories for the segments of the wheel and think about what would represent a satisfying life in each area. Possible areas might include:

- Health
- Friends and family
- Significant other
- Personal growth
- Fun and leisure
- Home environment
- Career
- Money

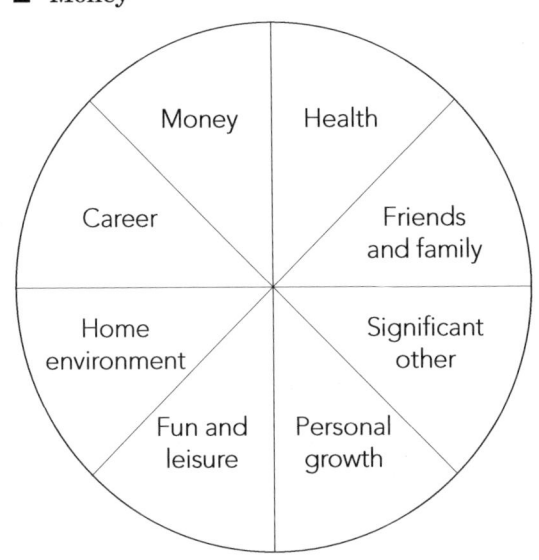

The second step is to draw a line across each segment that best represents the current level of satisfaction, with the center of the wheel equal to 0 and the edge of the wheel equal to 10, i.e., the maximum level of satisfaction.

The end result looks a bit like a spiderweb and can give your client a general idea of their overall life satisfaction in relation to their desired life satisfaction. A blank Wheel of Life can be found in Chapter 35: Resources, or can be downloaded from www.pavpub.com/becoming-a-coach-resources.

The results provide a useful platform to explore client ratings, followed by possible courses of action to address each area.

Conclusion

This technique provides a useful tool for exploring work–life balance priorities.

Technique 18: Spheres of Influence

Tool

One of the many ways that we tend to get off track or bogged down while striving toward our goals relates to our 'spheres of influence'. The idea behind the spheres of influence tool is that there are three distinct areas in our lives:

1. Things we can control
2. Things we can influence
3. Things we can't influence, either right now or at all times

Although we feel like there is nothing under our control, there is often at least one thing we have direct control over. These are our attitudes, thoughts and behaviour. Even when under enormous pressure or when we feel trapped, we always have the opportunity to reframe our thoughts.

We also have the ability to influence certain factors. We can influence these in our direction, even when we cannot completely change them. For instance, although we cannot control others' attitudes or behaviour, we can offer them advice and guidance, or provide evidence to help them reflect.

The final area is things that we have no control or influence over. This is for most people the largest area because the majority of what happens in life is not under our direct control. The coach will help clients recognize and accept that there is much we cannot control, and how to concentrate energy on what we can influence.

Conclusion

The framework provides a useful tool for enabling clients to focus their emotional and physical energy toward aspects of life they can control or influence, and to develop the ability to accept aspects they have no influence or control over.

Technique 19: DOUSE

DOUSE is a useful tool to help manage closing the relationship.

Tool

We use STOKER as a framework to manage the start of the coaching conversation. The STOKER shovels the fuel into the steam engine. It therefore seems appropriate to use a DOUSE, as a second train metaphor, for closing the relationship as we quell the fire of the conversation jointly with our client.

The coach explores each step with the client through a specific question and uses follow-up questions at each stage as required.

1. Double check – The coach starts to close by acknowledging the conversation is coming toward an end and inviting their client to review the initial goals or plan set by the conversation.
2. Obstacles – The coach invites the client to think about any obstacles that might occur to prevent them achieving their plan.
3. Uncovered – The aim of the third question is to reflect and enhance their learning and insight about themselves and their situation.
4. Support – This question explores what support or resources the individual might need to achieve their plan.
5. Ending – The coach invites the client to close the session.

Figure 34.5: DOUSE for Closing a Coaching Conversation

1. Double check → 2. Obstacle → 3. Uncovered → 4. Support → 5. Ending

> **Box 34.12: DOUSE Useful Questions**
>
> **1. Double-check:**
> What progress have you made during the conversation toward the goal you set at the start?
>
> **2. Obstacles:**
> What might stop you taking your next step?
> What allies can you invite to help progress?
> Who can you invite to hold you to account?
>
> **3. Uncovered:**
> What have you uncovered?
> What have you learnt about yourself?
> What have you learnt about this situation that you can apply going forward?
>
> **4. Support:**
> What support do you need from here?
>
> **5. Ending:**
> Is this a good place to end?

A checklist of the useful questions in Box 34.12 is available in Chapter 35: Resources, or it can be downloaded from www.pavpub.com/becoming-a-coach-resources.

Conclusion

The DOUSE model is a shorthand way to ensure coaches cover the key elements to close the coaching conversation appropriately.

Technique 20: Three Good Things

This technique involves a simple question and is a great one to share with clients as a takeaway task for them to use. It works well for clients who can overfocus on the negative, and for helping clients develop a more positive orientation

Tool

The tool is drawn from positive psychology, and the wider humanistic tradition, and a belief that in each of us there is a natural force for good, i.e., a self-righting reflex.

Our role as a coach is to help clients cultivate the right conditions for this growth and development.

The tool revolves around a single question. The coach can use this within a session and then invite client to use the question at the end of the day, as the last thing they do before they switch the light out: "Tell me about the three best things that have happened so far today."

It can be particularly useful if the client writes down the event and focuses on how the event made them feel. Different clients like to record different amounts of detail; some may like to write a short journal entry with all the details, others a single sentence with the emotions.

We have found that many clients, having experimented with the technique for a few weeks, start to incorporate the technique into their daily routine.

The effect, based on clients reporting back, is they find it easy to go to sleep.

Technique 21: Blessings: Cultivating a Compassionate Mind

This technique is useful for cultivating an empathetic or compassionate mindset, either as a tool for the coach or one to use with clients. The process is one to be used regularly because, like a muscle, the more compassion and empathy are used the more they develop within us (Passmore, 2019).

Tools

Like most people, we travel frequently on the underground, as well as on trains and planes. When sitting in a carriage we have a habit of looking at each of our fellow passengers and seeking to understand the challenges they face. One passenger may be struggling with a young child, another is looking in a worried way at his phone, a third may look annoyed. We try to empathize with any feelings shown, or simply offer them a blessing for their day: "May your day be blessed, and you carry with you joy and peace in your heart to the next people you meet."

Occasionally, just occasionally, someone looks up and makes eye contact. In these situations, we smile back warmly. Often the person smiles back or nods, while all around us our fellow travellers are trying hard to pretend there is no one else there, avoiding eye contact.

It's not clear whether this brightens another's day, but showing loving kindness toward each fellow passenger is a valuable reminder that there are eight billion people on this planet just like us – trying their best to earn a living for their family and live a peaceful, happy and fulfilled life.

Conclusion

Although this technique may not change the world, it may help to change you.

Chapter 35: Resources

We have developed this resources chapter that contains key information you need for your coaching resources kit. You can photocopy the pages in this chapter to use for yourself and/or with your clients, or direct clients to this book's website which has pages to download and print. These can be found at www.pavpub.com/becoming-a-coach-resources. You can also find out more about how and when to use some of these tools in Chapter 34.

Resources List

STOKERS Checklist – Contracting

ABC Framework

Cartoon template – Heaven and Hell

Vicious / Virtuous Flower

Forces field sheet

Jelly baby Tree

Consequences Wheel

Wheel of life

DOUSE Checklist – Closing

Henley8 – self reflection

Self-supervision

Contracting: STOKERS Checklist

Subject:
What do we need to think about today?
_____
_____

Time
Given we have *X* minutes, what about that do we need to focus on?
_____
_____

Outcome
What would you like to be different by the end of our time?
_____
_____

Know
How will you know you have got what you need out of this time?
_____
_____

Energy
Why is this goal important to me now?
_____
_____

Role
How are we going to do this?
_____
_____

Start
Where shall we start?
_____
_____

ABCDEF Chart

Activating event	Consequences	Beliefs	Disputing statements	New effective outlook	Future plan

Cartoon template – Heaven and Hell

Flower

Forces for Change Exercise

Forces for change	Forces resisting change

Jelly Baby Tree

Consequences wheel

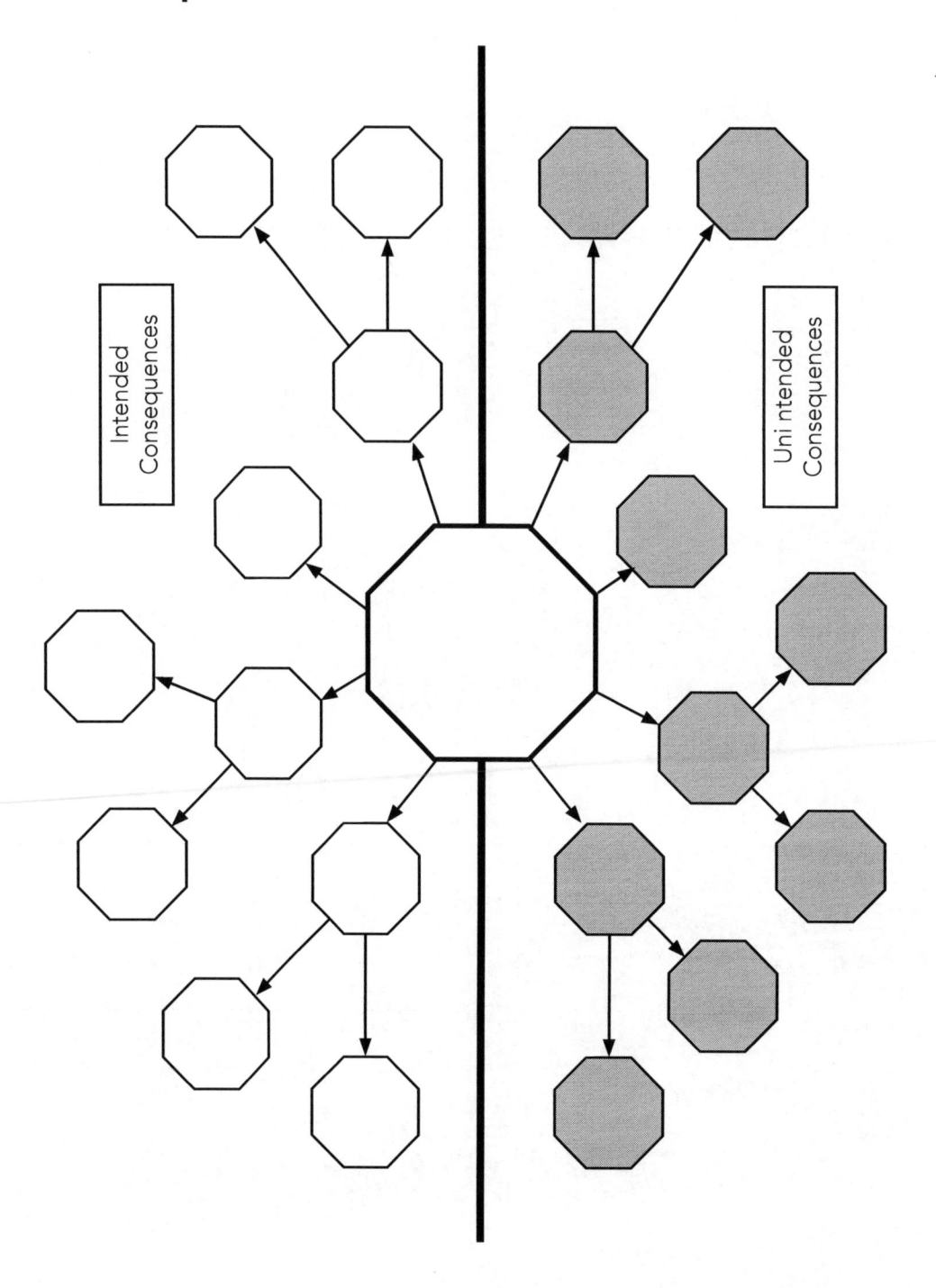

Intended Consequences

Unintended Consequences

Wheel of life

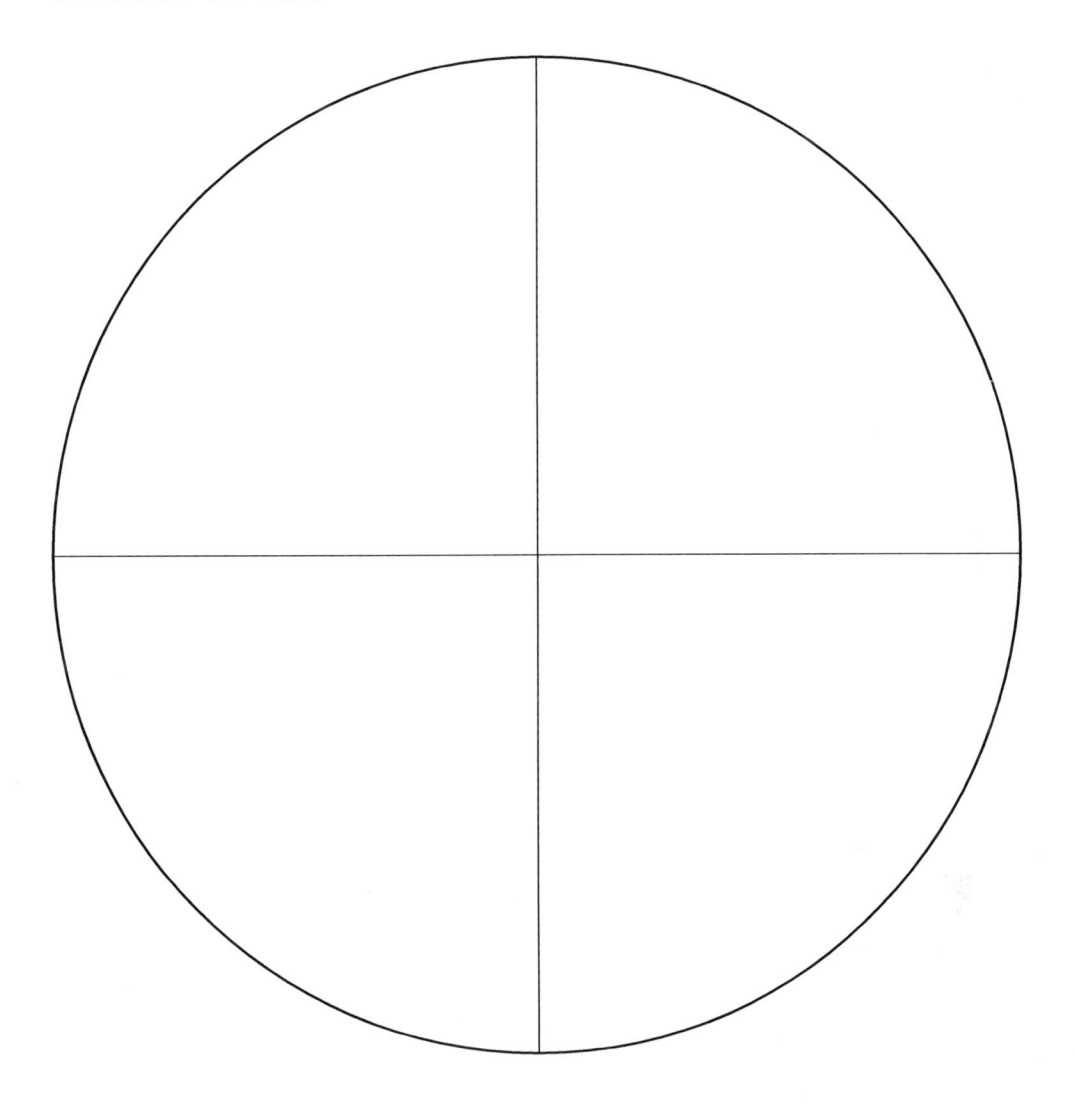

DOUSE Checklist (Closing)

Double-check
What progress have you made during the conversation towards the goal you set at the start?

_____
_____

Obstacles
What might stop you taking your next step?
What allies can you invite to help progress?
Who can you invite to hold you to account?

_____
_____

Uncovered
What have you uncovered?
What have you learnt about yourself?
What have you learnt about this situation that you can apply going forward?

_____
_____

Support
What support do you need from here?

_____
_____

Ending
Is this a good place to end?

_____
_____

Henley8

Notice
What did you notice?
_____
_____

Response
How did you respond? (think about what you felt, thought, and did)
_____
_____

Implications for you
What does this say about you?
_____
_____

Implications for coaching
What does this say about you as a coach?
_____
_____

Strengths
What benefits might this offer?
_____
_____

Risks
What risks might this bring?
_____
_____

Learning
What did you learn about yourself?
_____
_____

New approach
What would you do differently next time?
_____
_____

Self-Supervision template

See chapter 29 on supervision

1. What went really well? (Reflect upon 2-3 areas of strength, using the coaching competency framework I was trained in (e.g. ICF) which competencies really showed up in my coaching?
2. Which competencies were less evident, could have been evidenced more?
3. What else could I have done more or less of?
4. Were there any missed opportunities on my part?
5. Deepening my reflection – how do I notice this piece of work through the lens of 1 or 2 models that I am familiar with? (e.g. PAC, Drama Triangle, Life Positions, Hogan or other profile, Psychological distance, 7-eyed model, cycles of change, cycles of learning and others etc)
6. What are any ethical considerations within the piece of work?
7. How was my doing/being balance and my coaching presence with my client – how was I being? Where was I personally in this piece of work?
8. What conscious bias do I notice or what unconscious bias might be outside of my awareness?
9. What might have been the parallel process and what did that mean for the work?
10. More generally in my coaching work – do I notice any patterns?
11. What are my own takeaways from my work? What am I learning about myself as a person, as a coach, about my work?
12. What difference does that learning make? What and how will I integrate this into my work?

For more information, resources and offers please visit:

www.becomingacoachbook.com/book-resources

Password: readytofly

Chapter 36: Appendices

Appendix 1: Definition of Coaching

ICF defines coaching as partnering with clients in a thought-provoking and creative process that inspires them to maximise their personal and professional potential.

Appendix 2: ICF Values

Core Values

We are committed to reliability, openness, acceptance and congruence and consider all parts of the ICF community mutually accountable to uphold the following values:

1. Integrity: We uphold the highest standards both for the coaching profession and our organization.
2. Excellence: We set and demonstrate standards of excellence for professional coaching quality, qualification and competence.
3. Collaboration: We value the social connection and community building that occurs through collaborative partnership and co-created achievement.
4. Respect: We are inclusive and value the diversity and richness of our global stakeholders. We put people first, without compromising standards, policies and quality.

Appendix 3: ICF Core Competency Model

A. Foundation

1. Demonstrates Ethical Practice

Definition: Understands and consistently applies coaching ethics and standards of coaching

1. Demonstrates personal integrity and honesty in interactions with clients, sponsors and relevant stakeholders
2. 2. Is sensitive to clients' identity, environment, experiences, values and beliefs
3. 3. Uses language appropriate and respectful to clients, sponsors and relevant stakeholders
4. 4. Abides by the ICF Code of Ethics and upholds the Core Values
5. 5. Maintains confidentiality with client information per stakeholder agreements and pertinent laws
6. 6. Maintains the distinctions between coaching, consulting, psychotherapy and other support professions
7. 7. Refers clients to other support professionals, as appropriate

2. Embodies a Coaching Mindset

Definition: Develops and maintains a mindset that is open, curious, flexible and client-centred

1. Acknowledges that clients are responsible for their own choices
2. Engages in ongoing learning and development as a coach
3. Develops an ongoing reflective practice to enhance one's coaching
4. Remains aware of and open to the influence of context and culture on self and others
5. Uses awareness of self and one's intuition to benefit clients
6. Develops and maintains the ability to regulate one's emotions
7. Mentally and emotionally prepares for sessions
8. Seeks help from outside sources when necessary

B. Co-creating the relationship

3. Establishes and Maintains Agreements

Definition: Partners with the client and relevant stakeholders to create clear agreements about the coaching relationship, process, plans and goals. Establishes agreements for the overall coaching engagement as well as those for each coaching session.

1. Explains what coaching is and is not and describes the process to the client and relevant stakeholders
2. Reaches agreement about what is and is not appropriate in the relationship, what is and is not being offered, and the responsibilities of the client and relevant stakeholders
3. Reaches agreement about the guidelines and specific parameters of the coaching relationship such as logistics, fees, scheduling, duration, termination, confidentiality and inclusion of others
4. Partners with the client and relevant stakeholders to establish an overall coaching plan and goals
5. Partners with the client to determine client-coach compatibility
6. Partners with the client to identify or reconfirm what they want to accomplish in the session
7. Partners with the client to define what the client believes they need to address or resolve to achieve what they want to accomplish in the session
8. Partners with the client to define or reconfirm measures of success for what the client wants to accomplish in the coaching engagement or individual session
9. Partners with the client to manage the time and focus of the session
10. Continues coaching in the direction of the client's desired outcome unless the client indicates
11. Partners with the client to end the coaching relationship in a way that honours the experience

4. Cultivates Trust and Safety

Definition: Partners with the client to create a safe, supportive environment that allows the client to share freely. Maintains a relationship of mutual respect and trust.

1. Seeks to understand the client within their context which may include their identity, environment, experiences, values and beliefs
2. Demonstrates respect for the client's identity, perceptions, style and language and adapts one's coaching to the client
3. Acknowledges and respects the client's unique talents, insights and work in the coaching process
4. Shows support, empathy and concern for the client
5. Acknowledges and supports the client's expression of feelings, perceptions, concerns, beliefs and suggestions
6. Demonstrates openness and transparency as a way to display vulnerability and build trust with the client

5. Maintains Presence

Definition: Is fully conscious and present with the client, employing a style that is open, flexible, grounded and confident.

1. Remains focused, observant, empathetic and responsive to the client
2. Demonstrates curiosity during the coaching process
3. Manages one's emotions to stay present with the client
4. Demonstrates confidence in working with strong client emotions during the coaching process
5. Is comfortable working in a space of not knowing
6. Creates or allows space for silence, pause or reflection

C. Communication

6. Listens Actively

Definition: Focuses on what the client is and is not saying to fully understand what is being communicated in the context of the client systems and to support client self-expression

1. Considers the client's context, identity, environment, experiences, values and beliefs to enhance understanding of what the client is communicating
2. Reflects or summarises what the client communicated to ensure clarity and understanding
3. Recognises and inquires when there is more to what the client is communicating
4. Notices, acknowledges and explores the client's emotions, energy shifts, non-verbal cues or other behaviours
5. Integrates the client's words, tone of voice and body language to determine the full meaning of what is being communicated
6. Notices trends in the client's behaviours and emotions across sessions to discern themes and patterns

7. Evokes Awareness

Definition: Facilitates client insight and learning by using tools and techniques such as powerful questioning, silence, metaphor or analogy

1. Considers client experience when deciding what might be most useful
2. Challenges the client as a way to evoke awareness or insight
3. Asks questions about the client, such as their way of thinking, values, needs, wants and beliefs
4. Asks questions that help the client explore beyond current thinking
5. Invites the client to share more about their experience in the moment
6. Notices what is working to enhance client progress
7. Adjusts the coaching approach in response to the client's needs
8. Helps the client identify factors that influence current and future patterns of behaviour, thinking or emotion

9. Invites the client to generate ideas about how they can move forward and what they are willing or able to do
10. Supports the client in reframing perspectives
11. Shares observations, insights and feelings, without attachment, that have the potential to create new learning for the client

D. Cultivating Learning and growth

8. Facilitates Client Growth

Definition: Partners with the client to transform learning and insight into action. Promotes client autonomy in the coaching process.

1. Works with the client to integrate new awareness, insight or learning into their worldview and behaviours
2. Partners with the client to design goals, actions and accountability measures that integrate and expand new learning
3. Acknowledges and supports client autonomy in the design of goals, actions and methods of accountability
4. Supports the client in identifying potential results or learning from identified action steps
5. Invites the client to consider how to move forward, including resources, support and potential barriers
6. Partners with the client to summarise learning and insight within or between sessions
7. Celebrates the client's progress and successes
8. Partners with the client to close the session

Approve and adopted by the ICF Global Board of Directors September 2019

Appendix 4: ICF CODE OF ETHICS

The ICF Code of Ethics is composed of five Main Parts:

1. INTRODUCTION
2. KEY DEFINITIONS
3. ICF CORE VALUES AND ETHICAL PRINCIPLES
4. ETHICAL STANDARDS
5. PLEDGE

1. INTRODUCTION

The ICF Code of Ethics describes the core values of the International Coach Federation (ICF Core Values), and ethical principles and ethical standards of behaviour for all ICF Professionals (see definitions). Meeting these ICF ethical standards of behaviour is the first of the ICF core coaching competencies (ICF Core Competencies). That is *"Demonstrates ethical practice: understands and consistently applies coaching ethics and standards."*

The ICF Code of Ethics serves to uphold the integrity of ICF and the global coaching profession by:

- Setting standards of conduct consistent with ICF core values and ethical principles.
- Guiding ethical reflection, education, and decision-making
- Adjudicating and preserving ICF coach standards through the ICF Ethical Conduct Review (ECR) process
- Providing the basis for ICF ethics training in ICF-accredited programmes

The ICF Code of Ethics applies when ICF Professionals represent themselves as such, in any kind of coaching-related interaction. This is regardless of whether a coaching Relationship (see definitions) has been established. This Code articulates the ethical obligations of ICF Professionals who are acting in their different roles as coach, coach supervisor, mentor coach, trainer or student coach-in-training, or serving in an ICF Leadership role, as well as Support Personnel (see definitions).

Although the Ethical Conduct Review (ECR) process is only applicable to ICF Professionals, as is the Pledge, the ICF Staff are also committed to ethical conduct and the Core Values and Ethical Principles that underpin this ICF code of ethics.

The challenge of working ethically means that members will inevitably encounter situations that require responses to unexpected issues, resolution of dilemmas and solutions to problems. This Code of Ethics is intended to assist those persons subject to the Code by directing them to the variety of ethical factors that may need to be taken into consideration and helping to identify alternative ways of approaching ethical behaviour.

ICF Professionals who accept the Code of Ethics strive to be ethical, even when doing so involves making difficult decisions or acting courageously.

2. KEY DEFINITIONS

- "Client"—the individual or team/group being coached, the coach being mentored or supervised, or the coach or the student coach being trained.
- "Coaching"- partnering with Clients in a thought-provoking and creative process that inspires them to maximize their personal and professional potential.
- "Coaching Relationship"—a relationship that is established by the ICF Professional and the Client(s)/Sponsor(s) under an agreement or a contract that defines the responsibilities and expectations of each party.
- "Code"—ICF Code of Ethics
- "Confidentiality"—protection of any information obtained around the coaching engagement unless consent to release is given.
- "Conflict of Interest"—a situation in which an ICF Professional is involved in multiple interests where serving one interest could work against or be in conflict with another. This could be financial, personal or otherwise.
- "Equality"—a situation in which all people experience inclusion, access to resources and opportunity, regardless of their race, ethnicity, national origin, colour, gender, sexual orientation, gender identity, age, religion, immigration status, mental or physical disability, and other areas of human difference.
- "ICF Professional"—individuals who represent themselves as an ICF Member or ICF Credential-holder, in roles including but not limited to Coach, Coach Supervisor, Mentor Coach, Coach Trainer, and Student of Coaching
- "ICF Staff"— the ICF support personnel who are contracted by the managing company that provides professional management and administrative services on behalf of ICF.
- "Internal Coach"— an individual who is employed within an organization and coaches either part-time or full-time the employees of that organization.

- "Sponsor"—the entity (including its representatives) paying for and/or arranging or defining the coaching services to be provided.
- "Support Personnel"—the people who work for ICF Professionals in support of their Clients.
- "Systemic equality"—gender equality, race equality and other forms of equality that are institutionalized in the ethics, core values, policies, structures, and cultures of communities, organizations, nations and society.

3. ICF CORE VALUES AND ETHICAL PRINCIPLES

The ICF Code of Ethics is based on the ICF Core Values and the actions that flow from them. All values are equally important and support one another. These values are aspirational and should be used as a way to understand and interpret the standards. All ICF Professionals are expected to showcase and propagate these Values in all their interactions.

4. ETHICAL STANDARDS

The following ethical standards are applied to the professional activities of ICF Professionals:

Section I – Responsibility to clients

As an ICF Professional, I:

1. Explain and ensure that, prior to or at the initial meeting, my coaching Client(s) and Sponsor(s) understand the nature and potential value of coaching, the nature and limits of confidentiality, financial arrangements, and any other terms of the coaching agreement.
2. Create an agreement/contract regarding the roles, responsibilities and rights of all parties involved with my Client(s) and Sponsor(s) prior to the commencement of services.
3. Maintain the strictest levels of confidentiality with all parties as agreed upon. I am aware of and agree to comply with all applicable laws that pertain to personal data and communications.
4. Have a clear understanding about how information is exchanged among all parties involved during all coaching interactions.

5. Have a clear understanding with both Clients and Sponsors or interested parties about the conditions under which information will not be kept confidential (e.g., illegal activity, if required by law, pursuant to valid court order or subpoena; imminent or likely risk of danger to self or to others; etc.). Where I reasonably believe one of the above circumstances is applicable, I may need to inform appropriate authorities.

6. When working as an Internal Coach, manage conflicts of interest or potential conflicts of interest with my coaching Clients and Sponsor(s) through coaching agreement(s) and ongoing dialogue. This should include addressing organizational roles, responsibilities, relationships, records, confidentiality and other reporting requirements.

7. Maintain, store and dispose of any records, including electronic files and communications, created during my professional interactions in a manner that promotes confidentiality, security and privacy and complies with any applicable laws and agreements. Furthermore, I seek to make proper use of emerging and growing technological developments that are being used in coaching services (technology- assisted coaching services) and be aware how various ethical standards apply to them.

8. Remain alert to indications that there might be a shift in the value received from the coaching relationship. If so, make a change in the relationship or encourage the Client(s)/Sponsor(s) to seek another coach, seek another professional or use a different resource.

9. Respect all parties' right to terminate the coaching relationship at any point for any reason during the coaching process subject to the provisions of the agreement.

10. Am sensitive to the implications of having multiple contracts and relationships with the same Client(s) and Sponsor(s) at the same time in order to avoid conflict of interest situations.

11. Am aware of and actively manage any power or status difference between the Client and me that may be caused by cultural, relational, psychological or contextual issues.

12. Disclose to my Clients the potential receipt of compensation, and other benefits I may receive for referring my Clients to third parties.

13. Assure consistent quality of coaching regardless of the amount or form of agreed compensation in any relationship.

Section II – Responsibility to practice and performance

As an ICF Professional, I:

14. Adhere to the ICF Code of Ethics in all my interactions. When I become aware of a possible breach of the Code by myself or I recognize unethical behaviour in another ICF Professional, I respectfully raise the matter with those involved. If this does not resolve the matter, I refer it to a formal authority (e.g., ICF Global) for resolution.
15. Require adherence to the ICF Code of Ethics by all Support Personnel.
16. Commit to excellence through continued personal, professional and ethical development.
17. Recognize my personal limitations or circumstances that may impair, conflict with or interfere with my coaching performance or my professional coaching relationships. I will reach out for support to determine the action to be taken and, if necessary, promptly seek relevant professional guidance. This may include suspending or terminating my coaching relationship(s).
18. Resolve any conflict of interest or potential conflict of interest by working through the issue with relevant parties, seeking professional assistance, or suspending temporarily or ending the professional relationship.
19. Maintain the privacy of ICF Members and use the ICF Member contact information (email addresses, telephone numbers, and so on) only as authorized by ICF or the ICF Member.

Section III – Responsibility to professionalism

As an ICF Professional, I:

20. Identify accurately my coaching qualifications, my level of coaching competency, expertise, experience, training, certifications and ICF Credentials.
21. Make verbal and written statements that are true and accurate about what I offer as an ICF Professional, what is offered by ICF, the coaching profession, and the potential value of coaching.
22. Communicate and create awareness with those who need to be informed of the ethical responsibilities established by this Code.
23. Hold responsibility for being aware of and setting clear, appropriate and culturally sensitive boundaries that govern interactions, physical or otherwise.

24. Do not participate in any sexual or romantic engagement with Client(s) or Sponsor(s). I will be ever mindful of the level of intimacy appropriate for the relationship. I take the appropriate action to address the issue or cancel the engagement.

Section IV – Responsibility to society

As an ICF Professional, I:

25. Avoid discrimination by maintaining fairness and equality in all activities and operations, while respecting local rules and cultural practices. This includes, but is not limited to, discrimination on the basis of age, race, gender expression, ethnicity, sexual orientation, religion, national origin, disability or military status.
26. Recognize and honour the contributions and intellectual property of others, only claiming ownership of my own material. I understand that a breach of this standard may subject me to legal remedy by a third party.
27. Am honest and work within recognized scientific standards, applicable subject guidelines and boundaries of my competence when conducting and reporting research.
28. Am aware of my and my clients' impact on society. I adhere to the philosophy of "doing good," versus "avoiding bad."

5. THE PLEDGE OF ETHICS OF THE ICF PROFESSIONAL:

As an ICF Professional, in accordance with the Standards of the ICF Code of Ethics, I acknowledge and agree to fulfil my ethical and legal obligations to my coaching Client(s), Sponsor(s), colleagues and to the public at large.

If I breach any part of the ICF Code of Ethics, I agree that the ICF in its sole discretion may hold me accountable for so doing. I further agree that my accountability to the ICF for any breach may include sanctions, such as mandatory additional coach training or other education or loss of my ICF Membership and/or my ICF Credentials.

For more information on the Ethical Conduct Review Process including the links to file a complaint, please click the button below.

Approved and adopted by the ICF Global Board of Directors September 2019

Appendix 5: Typical questions in the Coach Knowledge Assessment

In this section we have included some examples of the types questions that might be asked in the online Coach Knowledge Assessment. We should make clear these are not the questions you will receive. Our purpose in providing examples is to give you a sense of what you can expect. The ICF CKA draws its questions from a bank of some 300 questions, from which you will randomly receive your 155 questions. You will need to score 70% to pass.

The aim of the Coach Knowledge Assessment is to ensure you understand the core competences and how they might be applied.

When taking the test, we suggest you plan a period of 3 hours when you won't be interrupted. Have some snacks and a drink close to hand.

From our experience the test takes around 150-170 minutes for most candidates, the additional time is there for rest breaks during the period. Just work methodically through the questions, reading each one carefully in turn.

While you might want to have the ICF competencies close to hand as a comfort blanket, but the Knowledge Assessment is more interested in how you apply the competences and the principles that underpin these competencies.

Sample Question
Domain: Co-Creating the Relationship
2. A client is explaining a situation to a coach, who senses that there is more that the client is not sharing. How should the coach approach the situation? a. Interrupt the client and ask for greater disclosure. b. Give the client the "bottom-line" read on the situation. c. Ask the client's permission to probe a little deeper. d. Give the client feedback on the importance of honesty in coaching.

> **Domain: Communicating Effectively**
>
> 3. When dealing with a client who brings many issues to the table, it is best for the coach to pick the option
>   a. where the coach has the most expertise.
>   b. of asking what the client would like to start with.
>   c. that looks most likely to be handled in the time available.
>   d. that the coach thinks can do the most good for the client.

We have put the answers in a separate table, as it may be helpful to complete your responses before you look at the answers. If you have got the correct answer, that's great. If you got one or more wrong, take a second look, and review the competences. Reflect on why the answer may be different from your own.

> **Answers**
>
> c. Ask the client's permission to probe a little deeper.
>
> The coach aims to view the client as an equal, and thus we would tend to avoid directing and telling, and favour an approach which seeks permission from the client even when we may sense there is something else which can be usefully explored.
>
> b. of asking what the client would like to start with.
>
> In a similar way the coach seeks to partner with the client and thus seeks there views on what's most important for them, not what 'works' for the coach.

References

Adler, A. (1925). *The practice and theory of individual psychology* (Translated by P. Radin, Revised ed. 1929 & Reprints). London: Routledge and Kegan Paul.

Alexander, G. (2016). Behavioural coaching – the GROW model, pp99–112. In J. Passmore (ed.) *Excellence in coaching – the industry guide* (3rd ed). London: Kogan Page.

Anstiss, T., & Blonna, R. (2014). Acceptance and commitment coaching, pp253–276. In J. Passmore (ed.) *Mastery in coaching: A complete psychological toolkit for advanced coaches*. London: Kogan Page.

Anstiss, T., & Gilbert, P. (2014). Compassionate mind coaching, pp225–248. In J. Passmore (ed.) *Mastery in coaching: a complete psychological toolkit for advanced coaches*. London: Kogan Page.

Anstiss, T., & Passmore, J. (2011). Motivational interview, pp33–52. In M. Neenan & S. Palmer (eds). *Cognitive behavioural coaching in practice*. London: Routledge.

Beck, A. T. (1976). *Cognitive therapy and emotional disorders*. New York: Penguin.

Bozer, G., & Jones, R. J. (2018). Understanding the factors that determine workplace coaching effectiveness: A systematic literature review. *European Journal of Work and Organizational Psychology*, **27**(3), 342–361.

Brewin, C. R. (2006). Understanding cognitive behaviour therapy: A retrieval competition account. *Behavioural Research Therapy*, **44**(6), 765–784.

Checkland, P., & Scholes, J. (2009). *Soft systems methodology in action*. Chichester: Wiley.

Clutterbuck, D. & Megginson, D. (undated) Retrieved on 24 April 2020 from: https://www.davidclutterbuckpartnership.com/wp-content/uploads/Coach-maturity.pdf

Bachkirova, T., Cox, E., & Clutterbuck, D. (2010). *The complete handbook of coaching*. London: Sage.

Bachkirova, T., Jackson, P., Hennig C., & Moral, M. (2020). Supervision in coaching: a systematic review. *International Coaching Psychology Review*, **15**(2)

Bain, J. D., Ballantyne, R., Packer, R., & Mills, C. (1999). Using journal writing to enhance student teachers' reflexivity during field experience placements. *Teachers and Teaching*, **5**(1), 51–73.

Berne, E. (1962). Classification of positions. *Transactional Analysis Bulletin*, **1**(3), 23.

Boyatzis, R. (2008). *Intentional change theory*. Washington DC: American Psychological Association.

Brdar, I., Anić P., & Rijavec, M. (2011). Character strengths and well-being: are there gender differences? *The Human Pursuit of Well-Being*. doi: 10.1007/978-94-007-1375-8_13

Brock, V. (2012). *The sourcebook of coaching history*. (2nd ed). Self-published.

Burn, A., & Watson, A. M. (2020). Eco-coaching. In J. Passmore (ed.) *The coaches handbook: The complete practical guide for professional coaches*. London: Routledge.

Caldwell, R. (2003). Models of change agency: a fourfold classification. *British Journal of Management*, **14**(2), 131–142.

Chaskalson, M & McMordie, M. (2017). *Mindfulness for Coaches*. Abingdon: Routledge.

Clarkson, P., & Cavicchia, S. (2013). *Gestalt counselling in action*. London: Sage.

CPD (2020). Definition of CPD. Retrieved on 20 April 2020 from https://cpduk.co.uk/explained

Csikszentmihalyi, M. (2002). *Flow: The classic work on how to achieve happiness*. London: Rider.

de Shazer, S. (1991). *Putting differences to work*. New York: Norton.

Deal, T., & Kennedy, A. (1988). *Corporate cultures: The rites and rituals of corporate life*. London: Penguin.

DiGirolamo, J.A., Rogers, G., & Heink, P. (2016). *How coaches spend their time*. Lexington: International Coach Federation. https://coachfederation.org/app/uploads/2018/06/HowCoachesSpendTheirTime.pdf

Dierolf, K (2013). *Solution focused team coaching*. Verlag: Solution Academy.

Dweck, C.S. (2017). *Mindset*. London: Little Brown Book Group.

Eby, L. T., Rhodes, J. E., & Allen, T. D. (2007). *Definition and evolution of mentoring*, pp7–20. In T. Allen & L.

Eby (eds.) *The Blackwell handbook of mentoring: A multiple perspectives approach*. Hoboken, New Jersey; Blackwell.

Ellis, A. (1962). *Reason and emotion in psychotherapy*. New Jersey: Carol Publishing Group.

Ernst, F.H. (1971). The OK corral: the grid for get-on-with. *Transactional Analysis Journal*, **1**(4), 231–240.

Foy, K. (2020). Coaching contracts. In J. Passmore (ed.) *The coaches handbook: The complete practical guide for professional coaches*. Hove: Routledge.

Gallwey, T. (1986). *The inner game of tennis*. London: Pan.

Gilbert, P. (2009). *The compassionate mind: A new approach to the challenges of life*. London: Constable and Robinson.

Gordon, T. (1970). *Parent effectiveness training*. New York: Wyden.

Grant, A. M. (2001). *Toward a psychology of coaching: The impact of coaching on metacognition, mental health and goal attainment*. Sydney: Coaching Psychology Unit, University of Sydney.

Grant, A. M. (2016). Solution-focused coaching, pp112–129. In J. Passmore (ed.) *Excellence in coaching – the industry guide* (3rd ed). London: Kogan Page.

Grant, A. & Gerrard, B. (2019). Comparing problem-focused, solution-focused and combined problem-focused/solution-focused coaching approach: solution-focused coaching questions mitigate the negative impact of dysfunctional attitudes. *Coaching: An International Journal of Theory, Research and Practice*. 1–17. Doi: 10.1080/17521882.2019.1599030.

Grinder, M. (2007). *The elusive obvious*. Battleground, WA: Michael Grinder & Associates.

Hall, L. (2014). Mindful coaching, pp191–220. In J. Passmore (ed.) *Mastery in coaching: a complete psychological toolkit for advanced coaches*. London: Kogan Page.

Hardingham, A. (2004). *The coach's coach*. London: CIPD.

Hardingham, A. (2006). The British eclectic model of coaching: towards professionalism without dogma. *International Journal of Mentoring and Coaching*, **4**(1).

Hawkins, P. (2017). *Leadership team coaching: Developing collective transformational leadership*. London: Kogan Page.

Hawkins, P. (2018). *Leadership team coaching in practice: Case studies on developing high-performing teams*. London: Kogan Page.

Hawkins, P. & Smith, N. (2006). *Coaching and mentoring and organisational consultancy: Supervision and development*. Maidenhead: Open University Press.

Hawkins, P. Turner, E. & Passmore, J. (2019). *The Manifesto for Supervision*. Henley-on-Thames: Henley Business School. ISBN: 978-1-912473-24-3

Hayes, S. C. (2004). Acceptance and commitment therapy, relational frame theory, and the third wave of behaviour therapy. *Behaviour Therapy*, **35**, 639–665. doi: 10.1016/S0005–7894(04)80013–3

Hullinger, A. M., DiGirilamo, J., & Tkach, T. (2019). Reflective practice for coaches and clients: An integrated model for learning. *Philosophy of Coaching*, **4**(2) 5–34.

Hullinger, A. M., DiGirolamo, J. A., & Tkach, J. T. (2020). A professional development study: The lifelong journeys of coaches. *International Coaching Psychology Review*, **15**(1), 7–18.

Hullinger, A. M., & DiGirolamo, J. A. (2018). *Referring a client to therapy: A set of guidelines*. Retrieved on 16 April 2020 from: https://coachfederation.org/app/uploads/2018/05/Whitepaper–Client–Referral.pdf

Hullinger, A. M., DiGirolamo, J. A., & Tkach, J. T. (2019). Reflective practice for coaches and clients: An integrated model for learning. *Philosophy of Coaching: An International Journal*, 4(2), 5–34. doi:http://dx.doi.org/10.22316/poc/04.2.02

International Coaching Federation. (2007). Definition of coaching. Retrieved on 19 April 2020 from https://coachfederation.org/about

International Coaching Federation. (2019a). ICF code of ethics. Retrieved on 19 April 2020 from https://coachfederation.org/code–of–ethics

International Coaching Federation. (2019b). ICF core competency model. Retrieved on 19 April 2020 from https://coachfederation.org/core–competencies

International Coaching Federation. (2019c). ICF credential. Retrieved on 19 April 2020 from https://coachfederation.org/icf–credential

International Coaching Federation. (2019d). ICF PCC markers. Retrieved on 19 April 2020 from https://coachfederation.org/pcc–markers.

International Coaching Federation. (2020a). Knowledge Assessment. Retrieved on 20 April 2020 from https://coachfederation.org/coach–knowledge–assessment

International Coaching Federation. (2020b). Professional development. Retrieved on 20 April 2020 from https://coachfederation.org/icf-credential/professional–development

International Coaching Federation. (2020). Guidelines for mentor coaching duties and competencies. Retrieved on 20 April 2020 from: https://coachfederation.org/mentor–coaching.

Jackson, P. & McKergow, M. (2007). *The solutions focus: The simple way to positive change*, 2nd ed. London: Nicholas Brealey Publishing.

Johansson, F. (2019). Conference Paper: Converge 2019. Prague, Czech Republic.

Jung, C. (1923) *Psychological types*. London: Kegan Paul.

Kabat-Zinn, J. (1991). *Full catastrophe living: Using the wisdom of your body and mind to face stress, pain, and illness.* New York: Delta Trade Paperbacks.

Kadushin, A. & Harknes, D. (2002). *Supervision in social work*, 4th edition. New York: Columbia University Press.

Kilburg, R. R. (1996). Toward a Conceptual understanding and definition of executive coaching. *Consulting Psychology Journal: Practice and Research*, 48(2), 134–144.

Kline, N. (1999). *Time to think*. London: Cassell Publishers.

Kline, N. (2015). *More time to think*. London: Cassell Publishers.

Kolb, D.A., (1984). *Experiential learning*. Englewood Cliffs: Prentice Hall.

Lai, Y. (2014). *Enhancing evidence-based coaching through the development of a coaching psychology competency framework: focus on the coaching relationship*. School of Psychology, University of Surrey: Guildford, UK.

Larkin, P. (1974). *High Windows*. London: Faber.

Lazarus, A. (1981) *The Practice of Multimodal Therapy*. New York, NY: McGraw-Hill.

Leary, J. J. (2010) *Gestalt coaching handbook*. St Albans: Academy of Executive Coaching.

Lewin, K., & Dorwin C. (1951). *Field theory in social science*. New York: Harper and Row.

Litcanu, M., Prostena, O., Oros, C., & Mnerie, A. (2015). Brain-writing vs. brainstorming case study for power engineering education. *Procedia – Social and Behavioural Sciences* **191**, 387–390.

Love, D. (2018). *How can I use the GROW model in my coaching? Insight Guide #7*. Henley Business School: Henley-on-Thames.

Luft, J. & Ingham, H. (1955). *The Johari window, a graphic model of interpersonal awareness*. Proceedings of the Western Training Laboratory in Group Development: University of California, Los Angeles.

Maslow, A. H. (1968). *Toward a psychology of being* (2nd ed.). New York: D. Van Nostrand.

Moon, J. (2004). *The handbook of reflective and experiential learning*. London: Routledge Falmer.

Newton, T., & Napper, R. (2007), The Bigger Picture: Supervision as an Educational Framework for all fields. *The Transactional Analysis Journal*, **37**(2), 150–158

Oshry, B. (2007). *Seeing systems: Unlocking mysteries of organisational life*. Oaklands, CA: Berrett-Koehler.

O'Connor, S., & Cavanagh, M. (2013). The coaching ripple effect: The effects of developmental coaching on wellbeing across organisational networks. *Psychology of Well-Being*, **3**(2), 25-28. https://doi.org/10.1186/2211-1522-3-2

McCrae, R. R., & Costa, P. T. (1987). Validation of the five–factor model of personality across instruments and observers. *Journal of Personality and Social Psychology*, **52**, 81–90.

Miller, W., & Rollnick, S. (2002). *Motivational interviewing: preparing people for change* (2nd ed.). New York: Guilford Press.

Neenan, M., & Palmer, S. (2001). Cognitive behavioural coaching. *Stress News*, **13**(3), 1.

Neubauer, A. C., & Fink, A. (2009). Intelligence and neural efficiency. *Neuroscience and Biobehavioural Reviews*, **33**, 1,004–1,023.

Ocasio, W. (2011) Attention to attention. *Organization Science*, **22**, 1,286–1,296.

Oshry, B. (2007). *Seeing systems: Unlocking the mysteries of organizational life* (2nd ed). San Francisco: Berrett-Koesher.

Palmer, S. (2002). Cognitive and organisational models of stress that are suitable for use within workplace stress management/prevention coaching, training and counselling settings. *The Rational Emotive Behaviour Therapist*, **10**(1), 15–21.

Palmer, S. (2007). PRACTICE: A model suitable for coaching, counselling, psychotherapy and stress management. *The Coaching Psychologist*, **3**(2), 71–77.

Palmer, S., & Szymanska, K. (2019). Cognitive behavioural coaching: An integrative approach, pp108–128. In S. Palmer & A. Whybrow (eds.) *Handbook of coaching psychology: a guide for practitioners* (2nd ed). Hove: Routledge.

Palmer, S., & Williams, H. (2016). Cognitive behavioural approaches, pp319–338. In J. Passmore, D Peterson & T Freire (eds.) *The Wiley Blackwell handbook of the psychology of coaching and mentoring*. Chichester: Wiley Blackwell.

Passmore, J. (2007). Integrative coaching: a model for executive coaching. *Consulting Psychology Journal: Practice and Research*, **59**(1), 68–78.

Passmore, J., & Marianetti, O. (2007). The role of mindfulness in coaching. *The Coaching Psychologist*. **3**(3), 131-138.

Passmore, J. (2012). MI techniques – typical day. *The Coaching Psychologist* **8**(1), 50–52.

Passmore, J. (2012). *Psychometrics in coaching: Using psychological and psychometric tools for development*. London: Kogan Page.

Passmore, J. (2014). *Mastery in coaching: a complete psychological toolkit for advanced coaching*. London: Kogan Page.

Passmore, J. (2016). Integrative Coaching, p188–204. In J Passmore (ed.) *Excellence in coaching: The industry guide to best practice* (3rd ed.) London: Kogan Page.

Passmore, J. (2017a). Mindfulness Coaching Techniques: STOP. *The Coaching Psychologist*. **13**(2), 86-87.

Passmore, J. (2017b). Mindfulness Coaching Techniques: Identifying mindfulness distractions. *The Coaching Psychologist*. **13**(1), 31-33.

Passmore, J. (2018). Mindfulness Coaching Techniques: Choosing our attitude. *The Coaching Psychologist* **14**(1), 48-49.

Passmore, J. (2019). Mindfulness in organisations: Mindfulness as a tool to enhance leadership development, workplace wellbeing and coaching (Part 2). *Industrial & Commercial Training*, **51**(3),165–173. https://doi.org/10.1108/ICT–07–2018–0064

Passmore, J. (2019). Mindfulness at organisations: A critical literature review (Part 1). *Industrial & Commercial Training* **51**(2), 104–113. https://doi.org/10.1108/ICT–07–2018–0063

Passmore, J. (2019). Leading with compassion. *IESE Business School Insights* **152**, 56–63. https://dx.doi.org/10.15581/002.ART–3244

Passmore, J., & Amit, S. (2017). *Mindfulness at work: The practice and science of mindfulness for leaders, coaches and facilitators*. New York: Nova Science.

Passmore, J., Brown, H., & Csigas, Z. (2017). *The state of play in coaching and mentoring*. Business School–EMCC: Henley-on-Thames.

Passmore, J., & Fillery-Travis, A. (2011). A critical review of executive coaching research: A decade of progress and what's to come. *Coaching: An International Journal of Theory, Practice & Research*, **4**(2), 70–88.

Passmore, J., & Lai, Y.L. (2019). Coaching psychology: Exploring definitions and research contribution to practice? *International Coaching Psychology Review*, **14**(2), 69–83.

Passmore, J., & McGoldrick, S. (2009) Super-vision, extra-vision or blind faith? A grounded theory study of the efficacy of coaching supervision. *International Coaching Psychology Review*, **4**(2). 143–159.

Passmore, J., Peterson, D., & Freire, T. (2013). The Psychology of Coaching and Mentoring, pp1–13. In J. Passmore, D. Peterson & T. Freire (eds) *The Wiley-Blackwell handbook of the psychology of coaching and mentoring*. Chichester: Wiley.

Passmore, J., & Rogers, K. (2018). Are you GDPR ready? *Coaching at Work* **13**(4), 30–33.

Passmore, J., & Theeboom, T. (2016). Coaching psychology: A journey of development in research. In L.E. Van Zyl, M.W. Stander & A. Oodendal (ed.). *Coaching psychology: Meta-theoretical perspectives and applications in multi-cultural contexts*. New York, NY: Springer.

Passmore, J., Rawle-Cope, M., Gibbes, C., & Holloway, M. (2006). MBTI types and executive coaching. *The Coaching Psychologist*, **2**(3), 6–16.

Passmore, J. & Turner, E. (2018). Reflections on integrity: The APPEAR Model. *Coaching at Work* **13**(2), 42–46.

Passmore, J., Turner, E., & Filipiak, M. (2018). The answer my friend is blowin' in the wind: Coaching ethics: Part 1, *Coaching at Work*, **13**(6), 36–40.

Passmore, J., Turner, E., & Filipiak, M. (2019). Still blowin' in the wind: Coaching ethics: Part 2, *Coaching at Work*, **14**(1), 38–42.

Parsloe, E. (1992). *Coaching, mentoring, and assessing: A practical guide to developing competence*. London: Nichols Publishing Company.

Peltier, B. (2006). *The psychology of executive coaching*. New York: Taylor Francis.

Peterson, C., & Seligman, M. E. (2004). *Character strengths and virtues: A handbook and classification*. Oxford: Oxford University Press.

Proctor, B. (2000). *Group supervision: a guide to creative practice*. London: Sage.

Prochaska, J. O., & DiClemente, C. C. (1983). Stages and processes of self-change of smoking: Toward an integrative model of change. *Journal of Consulting and Clinical Psychology*, **51**, 390–395.

Pugh, M. (2017). Chairwork in cognitive behavioural therapy: A narrative review. *Cognitive Therapy and Research*, **41**, 16–30.

Quality Assurance Agency for Higher Education (QAA). (2009). *Personal development planning: Guidance for institutional policy and practice in higher education*. London: QAA.

Rogers, C. (1957). The necessary and sufficient conditions of therapeutic personality change. *Journal of Consulting Psychology*, **21**(2), 95–103.

Rogers, C. R. (1980). *A way of being*. New York: Houghton Mifflin Company.

Rogers, J. (2017). *Coaching with personality type*. Maidenhead: McGraw-Hill Education.

Rohrbach, B. (1969). "Kreativ nach Regeln – Methode 635, eine neue Technik zum Lösen von Problemen". (Creative by rules – Method 635, a new technique for solving problems)". *Absatzwirtschaft* **12**(19), 73–75.

Rosen, S. (1982). *My voice will go with you: The teaching tales of Milton Erickson*. New York: Norton.

Sandler, C. (2016). *Executive coaching: A psychodynamic approach*. Maidenhead: Open University Press.

Schön, D. A. (1983). *The reflective practitioner: How professionals think in action*. London: Temple Smith.

Segal, Z., Teasdale, J., & Williams, M. (2002). *Mindfulness-based cognitive therapy for depression*. New York: Guilford Press.

Searles, H. (1955). The informational value of the supervisor's emotional experience. *Psychiatry*, **18**, 135–146.

Shedler, J. (2010). The efficacy of psychodynamic psychotherapy. *American Psychologist*, **65**, 98–109.

Smallwood, J., & Schooler, J. W. (2015). The science of mind wandering: Empirically navigating the stream of consciousness. *Annual Review of Psychology*, **66**, 487–518.

Taylor, F. (1911). *The principles of scientific management*. New York: Harper & Row.

Tkach, T. T., & DiGirolamo, J. A. (2017). The state and future of coaching supervision. *International Coaching Psychology Review*, **12**(1), 49–63.

Toman, S., Spoth, J., Leichtman, R., & Allen, J. (2013). Gestalt approach, pp385–405. In J. Passmore, D. Peterson, & T. Freire (eds). *The Wiley–Blackwell handbook of the psychology of coaching and mentoring*. Chichester: Wiley.

Turner, E., & Passmore, J. (2017). *The trusting kind. Coaching at Work*, **12**(6), 23–26.

Turner, E., & Passmore, J. (2018). Ethical dilemmas and tricky decisions: A global perspective of coaching supervisors' practice in coach ethical decision making. *International Journal of Evidence Based Coaching and Mentoring*, **16**(1), 126–142. doi: 10.24384/000473

Whitmore, J. (1992). *Coaching for performance*. London: Nicholas Brealey.

Whittington, J. (2012). *Systemic coaching and constellations: An introduction to the principles, practices and application*. London: Kogan Page.

Whitworth, L., Kinsey-House, H., & Sandahl, P. (1998). *Co-active coaching: New skills for coaching people towards success in work and life*. Mountain View: Davies Black.

Williams, H., & Palmer, S. (2013). The SPACE model in coaching practice: A case study. *The Coaching Psychologist*, **9**(1), 45–47.

Williams, H., Palmer, S., & Edgerton, N. (2018). Cognitive behavioural coaching, pp17–34. In E. Cox, T. Bachkirova, & D. Clutterbuck (eds.) *The complete handbook of coaching* (3rd ed). Sage: London.